BILINGUAL EDUCATION AND BILINGUALISM 14
Series Editors: Colin Baker and Nancy Hornberger

Bilingual Education and Social Change

Rebecca D. Freeman

MULTILINGUAL MATTERS LTD
Clevedon • Philadelphia • Toronto • Sydney • Johannesburg

In memory of my father

Library of Congress Cataloging in Publication Data

Freeman, Rebecca D. (Rebecca Diane)
Bilingual Education and Social Change/Rebecca D. Freeman
Bilingual Education and Bilingualism: 14
Includes bibliographical references and index
1. Education, Bilingual–Social aspects–United States–Case studies. 2. Linguistic
minorities–Education–Social aspects–United States–Case studies. 3. Discourse analysis–United
States–Case studies. I. Title. II. Series.
LC3731.F72   1998
370.117'5'0973–dc21   98-22410

British Library Cataloguing in Publication Data

A CIP catalogue record for this book is available from the British Library.

ISBN 1-85359-419-9 (hbk)
ISBN 1-85359-418-0 (pbk)

Multilingual Matters Ltd

UK: Frankfurt Lodge, Clevedon Hall, Victoria Road, Clevedon BS21 7HH.
USA: 325 Chestnut Street, Philadelphia, PA 19106, USA.
Canada: OISE, 712 Gordon Baker Road, Toronto, Ontario, Canada M2H 3R7.
Australia: P.O. Box 586, Artamon, NSW, Australia.
South Africa: PO Box 1080, Northcliffe 2115, Johannesburg, South Africa.

Typeset by Archetype Infomation Technology (http://archetype-it.com)
Printed and bound in Great Britain by WBC Book Manufacturers Ltd

Contents

Acknowledgements

Low-income Spanish-speaking students pose an enormous and rapidly increasing challenge to US public schools. For the past 12 years, my research has been dedicated to understanding how educators can organize their programs and practices so that these students can participate and achieve in school. To date, this work has involved ethnographic/discourse analytic research in two transitional bilingual programs, one in Brooklyn, NY(1985–1986) and the other in Perth Amboy, NJ (1986–1987), and in two dual-language programs, one in Washington, DC (1989–1991) and the other in Philadelphia, PA (1996–present). This book is the result of this research, and while I am indebted to all of the students and educators who taught me how to understand their experiences in these bilingual programs, I would like to acknowledge specific people and institutions who have supported my work throughout this time.

First, I want to express my gratitude to John Devine, the man who introduced me to the challenges of urban educational reform, and to the possibilities of ethnographic research as a means of understanding the complex processes of learning and teaching at school. In 1985, I was invited to join John Devine and a group of students from New York University (where I was studying for my MA in TESOL) to help design and implement a drop-out prevention program in a public high school in Brooklyn, New York. Located in a low-income neighborhood and serving a predominantly Puerto Rican, Dominican, and African American population, the school had a 75% drop-out rate. Part of my job was to tutor ESL to the Spanish-speaking students in the transitional bilingual program who were considered 'at-risk' of dropping out. When it became obvious that these students were participating and achieving in the program that we had organized, I developed questions about their 'at-risk' status. While I had no formal training in ethnography of education at the time, my natural instincts led me to observe the students I was working with in their regular classes and to talk to their teachers about what was going on with these students and why. John Devine encouraged my interest in ethnographic research, and I began to learn how schools can function to limit students' opportunities. I thank Miriam Eisenstein and the TESOL program at New York University for supporting my work in this transitional bilingual program with a Research Assistantship.

My awareness of dramatic differences in students' interactions and performance across learning contexts inspired the need to understand how schools could organize their programs and practices so that students like those I had worked with in Brooklyn could achieve. In 1986, I began ethnographic research in a transitional bilingual middle school program in Perth Amboy, NJ that the State of New Jersey had labeled 'exemplary'. My original goal was to investigate how this bilingual program was providing equal educational opportunities to its low-income Spanish-speaking (predominantly Puerto Rican and Dominican) students. What I found, however, was that 'exemplary' simply meant a drop-out rate that was lower than in most bilingual schools in that area at that time. While I was beginning to question if and how transitional bilingual education could provide educational opportunities to students labeled 'Limited English Proficient' (as the Bilingual Education Act mandates), my experience using ethnographic and sociolinguistic methods in school-based research was allowing me to see relationships between the Puerto Rican and Dominican students' positioning in the micro-level classroom interaction and macro-level educational and societal discourses that discriminate against low-income Spanish-speaking populations. I thank the Anthropology of Education Department of the Graduate School of Education at Rutgers University in New Brunswick, New Jersey for supporting my research, and I am extremely grateful for Susan Gal's mentoring at this stage in my career.

I realized that in order to challenge discriminatory practices at school, I needed to better understand how discrimination is socially constructed in the face-to-face interaction. In 1989, I enrolled in the PhD program in Linguistics at Georgetown University to learn how social identities are constituted through discourse, and to learn how to analyze discourse. At the same time, I began ethnographic/discourse analytic research at Oyster Bilingual School, a 'successful' dual-language elementary school in Washington, DC, to learn how it was providing educational opportunities to its low-income native Spanish-speaking (primarily Salvadoran) population. This book provides a case study of dual-language planning and implementation at Oyster Bilingual School, and I want to express my extreme gratitude to the teachers, administrators and parents for the access they gave me to study their program and practices. In particular I thank the sixth grade and Kindergarten teachers and students who taught me how to look at what was happening at Oyster, and to understand why .

I am grateful to Georgetown University for the fellowship support that enabled me to complete my research at Oyster Bilingual School. I especially want to thank my mentor Ralph Fasold, my dissertation committee members Heidi Hamilton and Jeff Connor-Linton, my teachers Rom Harré, Deborah Schiffrin, and Deborah Tannen, and especially my friends Helaine Berman, Minako Ishikawa, and Carolyn Straehle. All of these people, in many different ways, challenged my thinking about sociolinguistics and society as I conducted my research at Oyster.

Since 1996, I have been doing ethnographic/discourse analytic research at Julia de Burgos Bilingual Middle Magnet School in North Philadelphia in order to learn how a group of educators is developing a dual-language program that can meet the needs of their low-income, primarily Puerto Rican student population. The challenges that these educators face are reminiscent of those I saw in Brooklyn, NY and in Perth Amboy, NJ, and of what the Oyster educators said they struggled against in the early days of dual-language planning at their school. Although this book is not directly based on my research at Julia de Burgos, my conversations with the educators, parents, students, and community members there have really helped me appreciate the complexity involved in challenging language prejudice and transforming social relations in a low-income urban public school setting. I want to thank José Lebrón, Barbara Mitchell, Carmen Cotto, and Olivia Dreibelbis for giving me the opportunity to do my research at Julia de Burgos, and I am especially grateful to Marjorie Soto, Angela Garay, Michael Trautner, and Helda Ortiz for allowing me to be so closely involved in their thinking about dual-language planning and implementation at their school. I also want to thank graduate students Crissy Cáceres, Serafín Coronel-Molina, Susan O'Malley, Anne Pomerantz, Anne Roberti, Mary Springer, and Doris Warriner for sharing their insights on dual-language education at Julia de Burgos with me. My experience at Julia de Burgos has made an important impact on my thinking about bilingual education research and practice, and about how universities, public schools, and community-based organizations can work together to provide opportunities to low-income Latino students who are too often marginalized in US schools and society.

My colleagues Nancy Hornberger and Teresa Pica in the Educational Linguistics Program of the Graduate School of Education at the University of Pennsylvania have been incredibly supportive of my research for the last five years, and I feel privileged to have the opportunity to exchange ideas about issues related to the education of linguistically and culturally diverse students with them on a regular basis. Their influence is readily apparent in my work, and I cannot thank them enough. I also want to thank the rest of my colleagues at the Graduate School of Education, and especially my students in the Educational Linguistics program who have helped me think through many of the ideas that I have developed in this book. I am very grateful to Colin Baker, Nancy Hornberger, Marilyn Martin-Jones and Anne Pomerantz for their contributions to this manuscript in its various stages.

Finally, I want to thank my family and friends for their never-ending support throughout this twelve year process. I especially appreciate my partner, Charles Field, for his love and encouragement as I brought this project to completion.

ACKNOWLEDGEMENTS

CHAPTER 1

Bilingual Education and Social Change: 'It's Much More Than Language'

Linguistic and cultural diversity poses an enormous challenge to schools in many parts of the world. Educational policymakers and practitioners have choices in how they respond to this challenge, and the choices they make reflect ideological assumptions about students, learning and teaching, and the role of schools in society. This book describes how one group of educators in the United States rejected mainstream US educational practices because they believe those practices discriminate against minority students and the languages they speak. By minority students, they mean students whose first language is not Standard English (the majority language in the United States) and/or who do not come from Standard English-speaking middle class backgrounds (the majority or mainstream cultural background in the United States). These educators, in collaboration with parents and community members, created an alternative educational program that provides equitable and effective education for their linguistically and culturally diverse student population. Because a primary organizing structure for that educational alternative is the school's dual-language policy, this book is about bilingual education. And because the school's bilingual program challenges and attempts to transform mainstream US minority/majority relations on the local level, this book is also about social change.

Bilingual education in the United States, as in other countries, is a controversial and frequently misunderstood field. There is considerable confusion and conflict about what bilingual education means, who bilingual programs serve, what the goals of a bilingual program are for its target populations, and whether bilingual education is or can be effective. Because there is so much variation from one bilingual education context to another in the United States and around the world, it is

1

important for bilingual education researchers to go beyond general discussions of *what* bilingual education means to investigate *how* and *why* actual bilingual programs function the way that they do in specific social and historical locations (Martin-Jones, personal communication, November 1997). This book provides a detailed, ethnographically-informed analysis of how and why one 'successful' dual-language public elementary school functions the way that it does in contemporary Washington, DC. While I change the names of all the participants throughout the book, I use the real name of Oyster Bilingual School with the permission and encouragement of school administrators. Close analyses of actual bilingual programs and practices such as the one provided in this book can then be used as the basis for future comparative research, as well as for more grounded discussions about whether and how bilingual education can be effective.

This book is intended for multiple audiences. It is specifically written for researchers who want to investigate and document how other bilingual programs function in their particular historical and sociopolitical locations, and for practitioners who want to design and implement bilingual programs that meet the needs of the communities they serve. The concrete example of how one successful dual-language program functions will also appeal to researchers and practitioners who are more generally concerned with how schools can provide educational opportunities to language minority and language majority students in increasingly diverse schools and societies. Finally, the detailed analysis of how one group of educators has organized their educational program in opposition to mainstream US programs that subordinate minority students will contribute to our developing understanding of dynamic relationships among discourse, social identity, and power in situated practice.

I have divided this first chapter into three major parts. The chapter begins with a very general discussion of bilingual education that is intended to clear up some of the confusion about how this term is used and what it can mean. The second part of the chapter provides an overview of existing dual-language programs in the United States and a brief discussion of sociolinguistic, language-planning, and second-language acquisition research that helps us understand the thinking behind these bilingual programs. The third part of the chapter introduces Oyster Bilingual School, the site of my research, and describes the ethnographic/discourse analytic approach that I took to understand that Oyster's dual-language program is about, in the words of one teacher, 'much more than language'. Their educational program and practices are organized to legitimize minority students and their ways of speaking so that all of the children, regardless of background, can participate and achieve more or less equally at school. The chapter concludes with an overview of the contents of the book.

WHAT IS BILINGUAL EDUCATION?: A GENERAL DISCUSSION

Technically, **bilingual education** means using two languages for instructional purposes. This same term, however, is actually used to refer to a wide range of programs that may have different ideological orientations toward linguistic and

cultural diversity, different target populations, and different goals for those populations (Hornberger, 1991). As a result, what bilingual education means and whether
it is effective has been and continues to be a source of confusion and conflict on the
policy level, in educational practice, and in the popular press. This section aims to
clear up some of this confusion by providing a general discussion of the different
types of bilingual education that are discussed in the literature with attention to the
kinds of variation across bilingual programs that can be found in practice.

Hornberger's (1991) review of existing typologies of bilingual education provides an excellent place to begin. First, she distinguishes between bilingual education **models** and bilingual education **program types**: models are defined in terms
of their language-planning goals and ideological orientations toward linguistic and
cultural diversity in society, and program types are defined in terms of specific
contextual and structural characteristics. Models can be understood as broader, more
abstract categories than program types, and help us understand on a very general
level what bilingual education means. Hornberger (1991) offers the following
conceptual framework of the three major bilingual education model types discussed
in the literature.

Transitional model	Maintenance model	Enrichment model
Language shift	Language maintenance	Language development
Cultural assimilation	Strengthened cultural identity	Cultural pluralism
Social incorporation	Civil rights affirmation	Social autonomy

Figure 1 Bilingual education model types (Hornberger, 1991: 223)

The **transitional model** encompasses all of those bilingual education programs
that encourage language minority students to shift to the majority language, assimilate to mainstream cultural norms, and be incorporated into the national society. By
majority language, Hornberger (1991) means the official language of the national
society, and by language minority students, she means students whose native
language is not the official language of the national society. The **maintenance
model** encompasses all of those programs that encourage language minority students to maintain their native language, strengthen their cultural identity, and affirm
their civil rights in the national society. The **enrichment model** encompasses all of
those bilingual education programs that encourage the development of minority
languages on the individual and collective levels, cultural pluralism at school and
in the community, and an integrated national society based on the autonomy of
cultural groups (Hornberger, 1991: 222).

Program types are more concrete categorizations than model types. According to
Hornberger (1991), analysis of specific contextual and structural characteristics
allows us to differentiate one bilingual program type from another, and can help us

begin to understand how and why actual programs vary the way that they do on the local level. By contextual characteristics, she means the nature of the student populations (e.g. numbers, stability, voluntary or involuntary placement in the program, socioeconomic status, immigrant or involuntary minority status, first language background) and the background of the teachers (e.g. ethnicity, degree of bilingualism, training). By structural characteristics, she means the location of the bilingual program in the school (e.g. school-wide or targeted, one-way or two-way), and the allocation of languages for instruction (e.g. across the curriculum, patterns of language use in the classroom). As Hornberger (1991) points out, researchers and practitioners use the terms transitional and maintenance to refer not only to model types but also to program types.

Transitional bilingual education is the most common type of bilingual education currently found in the United States. These programs exclusively target students defined as 'Limited English Proficient' or 'LEP'. As I discuss in detail in Chapter 2, the Bilingual Education Act (first passed in 1968) provides federal funding for programs that provide educational opportunities to LEP students in US public schools. While I recognize and agree with the criticism of the LEP label because it defines students in terms of what they *lack*, I use this label when I refer to students in terms of their assignment to bilingual programs.

Transitional bilingual programs aim to facilitate LEP students' quick transition to the all-English academic mainstream. To accomplish this, they segregate LEP students from the mainstream all-English classes and provide content-area instruction in the students' native language as well as instruction in English as a Second-language (ESL). In this way, LEP students are ideally able to continue to develop academically while they acquire English. The transition from the bilingual program to the academic mainstream generally takes place in one to three years depending on the nature of the program and the exit criteria used (see Chapter 3 for further discussion).

In language-planning terms, transitional bilingual programs can be understood as examples of language-acquisition planning (Cooper, 1989), or the organized efforts to promote the learning of a language — in this case English. According to Ruiz (1984), transitional bilingual programs are characterized by a 'language-as-problem' orientation because the native language is only used until the student has acquired sufficient English to transition to the mainstream English-speaking class-room (i.e. the language 'problem' has been overcome). The combination of no continued support for the LEP students' native language at school and strong pressure to acquire English as quickly as possible tends to produce a situation described as 'subtractive bilingualism' (Lambert, 1987). That is, after a brief period of bilingualism in the native language and English, LEP students in transitional bilingual programs in the United States tend to assimilate to monolingualism in English.

Maintenance bilingual programs are less common than transitional bilingual programs in the United States. These programs have two language-planning goals for their target population of LEP students: English language acquisition and native language maintenance. While maintenance bilingual programs also segregate LEP students from the mainstream all-English program, they are generally of longer duration than transitional bilingual programs and they encourage LEP students to retain their native language while developing proficiency in English. According to Ruiz (1984), underlying these programs is a 'language-as-right' orientation as LEP students have the 'right' to maintain their native language. The desired outcome of maintenance bilingual programs for LEP students is a situation described as 'additive bilingualism' (Lambert, 1987). That is, because the school supports continued development of the native language and does not pressure LEP students to use only English, students in these programs ideally become and remain bilingual in their native language and English.

The enrichment model of bilingual education is increasingly common in Canada and in the United States. There are several different program types that fall into this category, all of which are characterized by a 'language-as-resource' orientation (Ruiz, 1984) because the minority language is seen as a resource to be developed not only for language minority students but also for language majority students and the communities in which they live. The **immersion programs** in Canada have received the most attention in the literature. These programs exclusively target native English speakers (the language majority speakers in Canada), they provide most or all of the students' instruction through French, and the native English-speaking students in these programs ideally become bilingual in French and English (see Genesee (1987) and Heller (1994) for further discussion of French immersion schools in Canada). **Heritage language progams** in Canada are another type of enrichment bilingual education discussed in the literature. Emphasizing that heritage languages are both an individual and national resource, these programs target language majority and/or language minority students. Heritage language programs that use Greek, Italian, Portuguese, Spanish, Ukranian, German, Hebrew, Yiddish, Chinese (Mandarin), Arabic, and/or Polish can be found in various parts of Canada (see Cummins, 1995, for further discussion). **Dual-language programs** are the most common type of enrichment bilingual education found in the United States. Also referred to as **two-way bilingual**, **bilingual immersion**, **two-way immersion**, or **developmental bilingual**, these programs target students from two language backgrounds (e.g. Spanish and English) who study the content-areas through both languages in integrated classes. The goal of these programs is additive bilingualism for language minority and language majority students, academic achievement through two languages, and cultural pluralism (Christian, 1994).

In language-planning terms, these enrichment-type bilingual programs can be understood not only as examples of language-acquisition and language-maintenance planning but also of status planning. According to Cooper (1989: 32), status planning means 'the allocation of languages or language varieties to given functions, e.g. medium of instruction, official language, vehicle of mass communication'. One could argue that because transitional and maintenance bilingual programs use the minority language as the medium of instruction *for language minority students*, that each of these types of programs is also an example of status planning. My restricted use of the term status planning in relation to enrichment-type programs is intended to emphasize that enrichment bilingual programs officially allocate the minority language as a legitimate language of instruction *for language majority students*. This move functions to elevate the status of the minority language not only for language minority students but also for language majority students at school. I return to this point in my explanation of how dual-language programs challenge language prejudice at school and in society later in the chapter.

The preceding discussion of bilingual education models and program types was intended to help those interested in bilingual education research and practice understand what bilingual education means in very general terms, and to provide a basis for understanding the variation that can be observed from one bilingual context to another (for a much more detailed treatment of these issues, see Baker, 1993). Because Oyster Bilingual School, the focus of my research, is a dual-language program in Washington, DC, I turn now to a more detailed discussion of dual-language programs in the United States.

DUAL-LANGUAGE PROGRAMS AND PRACTICES IN THE UNITED STATES: AN OVERVIEW

This second part of the chapter provides a general discussion of what we know and what we do not know about dual-language education in the United States today. I begin with a profile of dual-language programs that are in operation throughout the country, and describe some of the kinds of the variation that can be found across contexts. Then I offer a sociolinguistic perspective on dual-language programs, and explain how these programs theoretically can challenge language prejudice at school and in the local community. I conclude this part by reviewing arguments that describe how dual-language programs can provide language minority and language majority students the opportunity to become bilingual and biliterate, achieve academically through two languages, and develop improved intercultural understanding and relations. Together, this part of the chapter gives an overview of dual-language programs in the United States today, and suggests directions for future research.

A profile of dual-language programs in the United States

Dual-language programs are an innovative way of providing educational opportunities to language minority and language majority students in the United States. The first dual-language program in the country was established in 1963 at the Coral Way School in Dade County, Florida, as part of an organized community and federal effort to serve the large numbers of Cuban refugees that were resettling in Miami

(Pedraza-Bailey & Sullivan, 1979). The Coral Way dual-language program has been described as an effective means of integrating the Spanish-speaking Cuban students into the academic mainstream and of providing equitable educational opportunities to the native English-speaking and native Spanish-speaking students that the school serves. PS 84 in New York City is another example of an established (Spanish–English) dual-language program that encourages additive bilingualism for its language minority and language majority students as a means of promoting academic achievement for all of the students (Morison, 1990). Bilingual education advocates argue that *well-implemented* dual-language programs like the one at Coral Way or at PS 84 can offer an equitable and effective means of educating language minority and language majority students (Crawford, 1997; Lindholm, 1990). As a result, this type of bilingual program has been attracting increasing attention and funding in the United States since the early 1990s. In 1987 there were only 30 documented dual-language programs in the United States. By 1994–95 that number had grown to 182 programs in 10 states (Christian & Whitcher, 1995).

The most up-to-date information on dual-language programs in the United States can be found in the *Directory of Two-Way Immersion Programs in the US* that the Center for Applied Linguistics (CAL) posts on the world wide web. As Figure 2 illustrates, in September 1997 CAL identified 202 dual-language programs in 110 school districts across the country. The following paragraphs summarize the kinds of variation that can be found across dual-language programs in the United States.

Dual-language programs vary in terms of which languages are used for instruction. While the overwhelming majority of these programs (184) use Spanish and English as the media of instruction, CAL identified dual-language programs that use Korean and English (4), French and English (4), Cantonese and English (3), Navajo and English (2), Japanese and English (2), Arabic and English (1), Russian and English (1), and Portuguese and English (1). As Figure 3 documents, the majority of these programs serve the elementary school grades.

Dual-language programs vary in terms of the proportions of speakers from each language background. According to Lindholm (1990) and Christian (1994), dual-language programs are the most effective when there are balanced numbers of students from each language background. This ideal, however, may not be possible in every context. As Christian (1994) describes, some school districts require their dual-language program to be open to everyone, which does not guarantee balanced numbers of students from both backgrounds. Other school districts have a restricted number of spaces available in dual-language programs, so program administrators may consider language background and proficiency as they make their enrollment decisions. Another problem that affects the proportion of speakers from each language is attrition; more students from one language background may not continue in a dual-language program over time, leaving unbalanced numbers of students in

State	Number of Districts	Number of schools
Alaska	1	1
Arizona	5	9
California	32	62
Colorado	2	5
Connecticut	3	3
District of Columbia	1	1
Florida	2	6
Illinois	3	14
Maine	2	2
Maryland	1	1
Massachusetts	8	13
Michigan	2	2
Minnesota	1	1
New Jersey	1	1
New Mexico	3	3
New York	27	48
North Carolina	1	2
Oregon	3	5
Pennsylvania	1	2
Texas	7	14
Virginia	3	6
Wisconsin	1	1
Total	110	202

Figure 2 Directory of dual-language programs in the United States (1997) (Center for Applied Linguistics, 1997, http://www/cal.org). This table reflects only the number of programs that CAL was aware of and that the programmers were willing to fill out and return a questionnaire to CAL since 1994–95. CAL acknowledges that there exist more dual-language programs in the US than the 202 profiled in their directory — some that they do not yet know about and some for which the programmers have not had time to complete CAL's questionnaire. The numbers that are posted in the directory change as CAL becomes aware of new programs or of discontinued programs.

Grade levels served	Number of schools
Pre-k/k	8
Pre-k/k–5/6	159
3/4–5/6/7	3
Pre-k/k/1–7/8	11
6–9	17
K–10/12	2
9–12	2

Figure 3 Grade levels served in dual-language programs in 1997 (Center for Applied Linguistics, 1997, http://www/cal.org)

the upper grades. To counter this potential problem, some schools organize their programs so that there are more dual-language classes available in the lower grades.

Dual-language programs in the United States also vary considerably in how they allocate the two languages for instructional purposes. Some programs allocate languages to content-areas (e.g. science is taught in French and social studies is taught in English); some programs allocate languages to people (e.g. the Korean dominant teacher speaks and is spoken to only in Korean and the English-dominant teacher speaks and is only spoken to in English); some programs allocate languages to the time of day or week (e.g. Japanese is used in the mornings and English is used in the afternoons); and some programs use a combination of these approaches (e.g. the Cantonese dominant teacher teaches social studies in the morning in Cantonese and the English-dominant teacher teaches science in English in the afternoon). While the most common approach to dual-language instruction is to allocate 50% of the time to one language and 50% of the time to the other, some schools use a 90/10 approach. Under this latter approach, the minority language (e.g. Spanish) is used for almost all of the instructional time (up to 90%) in the lower grades and English is introduced slowly over time. By the time the students reach the upper elementary grades, students receive 50% of their content-area instruction in each language (see Christian, 1994, for further discussion of language allocation in dual-language programs).

Another way that dual-language programs vary in design is the degree of student integration. In some programs, students from the two language backgrounds are integrated for all of their instructional time. In other programs, students are integrated for the majority of their content-area instruction, but segregated to receive additional language instruction in their second-language. Other programs segregate students from the two language backgrounds for the majority of their instructional time (which may be through one or two languages), and then integrate students for a small portion of each day and/or week for dual-language instruction. As Christian

(1994) points out, this third option is not as likely to yield the full benefits of the dual-language approach because students from the two backgrounds spend so little time together.

As the previous discussion demonstrates, there is tremendous variation in how dual-language programs are designed and implemented across contexts in the United States. According to Christian (1996), this variation can influence students' development of proficiency in their second-language. The next two sections present a few basic principles from research in sociolinguistics, language-planning, and second-language acquisition that help explain how dual-language programs function on the local level. The first section describes how dual-language programs interact with the larger sociolinguistic context in the United States, and the second section describes how the micro-level classroom interaction can provide language minority and language majority students the opportunity to acquire their second-language and develop the necessary academic competence in both languages to achieve at school.

Challenging language prejudice through dual-language education

The fundamental sociolinguistic notion that languages are never neutral is key to understanding dual-language programs in the United States. I begin this section by discussing how Standard English has become the dominant language in mainstream US society, and how speakers of Standard English are attributed more prestige as a result of their proficiency in English. This 'language prejudice' (Urciuoli, 1996) means that other languages and speakers of those languages are marginalized in mainstream US institutions and society. I continue by emphasizing the role that transitional and maintenance bilingual programs play in legitimizing the dominance of Standard English in US schools and society. I conclude by explaining how dual-language programs, which reject the mainstream US assumption of monolingualism in Standard English, can be understood as organized efforts to challenge language prejudice in US schools and their local communities.

Bourdieu's (1977, 1993) work on language and political economy helps us understand how members of a particular society come to value specific languages and speakers of those languages. Bourdieu (1993) argues that language can be understood as a form of 'cultural capital' whose value is negotiated on the 'linguistic market'. He writes, 'there is a linguistic market whenever someone produces an utterance for receivers capable of assessing it, evaluating it, and setting a price on it' (Bourdieu, 1993: 79). Speakers use language, like other forms of cultural capital, to pursue their interests. The power relations which dominate a specific linguistic market mean that certain products (i.e. languages, utterances, written texts) and their producers (i.e. speakers, writers) are automatically assigned more value in the linguistic marketplace because they have become legitimized within that context. Proficiency in the dominant or majority language can thus be understand as a form of cultural capital which is unequally distributed throughout society.

In the linguistic market in the United States today, Standard English is the dominant language that is used to fulfill the official functions of government and education. This social fact, combined with widespread recognition of English as a language of international importance, affords Standard English considerable status in US society (Ruiz, 1994). Other languages (e.g. Spanish, Korean) and non-standard varieties of English (e.g. African American Vernacular English) are marginalized in official domains. In Bourdieu's (1993) terms, speakers of Standard English in the United States today have more cultural capital in the linguistic marketplace. Every situation in which Standard English speakers interact with language minority speakers (i.e. speakers of languages other than English and/or varieties other than Standard English) reflects and helps perpetuate the dominance of Standard English and of speakers of Standard English in mainstream US society.

Martin-Jones and Heller (1996) apply Bourdieu's economic metaphor to the study of education in multilingual settings. They review a wide range of research that has been done in specific social and historical locations to illustrate the fundamental role that education plays in the production and reproduction of unequal power relations in multilingual communities. They argue that 'the language practices of educational institutions are bound up in the legitimisation of relations of power among ethnolinguistic groups' (p. 4). Although Martin-Jones and Heller (1996) do not focus on education in multilingual settings in the United States, their argument helps us understand how different types of bilingual programs can reproduce power relations in contemporary US society that legitimize the dominance of Standard English and of Standard English speakers. The transitional model of bilingual education, for example, encourages language minority students to transition to monolingualism in English. While maintenance bilingual programs encourage additive bilingualism for language minority students, they do not target language majority students. Neither transitional nor maintenance bilingual programs question the mainstream US assumption of monolingualism in Standard English for the majority of the US population.

Recent sociolinguistic research, however, emphasizes the need to develop Bourdieu's (1977, 1993) concept of symbolic domination through language to allow for the possibility of contestation or resistance (see, for example, Gal, 1995; Heller, 1994; Martin-Jones & Heller, 1996; Woolard 1985). This growing body of research illustrates how particular social groups may organize themselves politically to challenge the legitimacy of the dominant language. The notion of organized resistance to dominant language use is key to understanding how dual-language programs function in the United States. Because dual-language programs in the United States ideally elevate the status of minority languages and speakers of those languages at school, and because these programs expect additive bilingualism for language minority and language majority students and the communities in which they live, dual-language programs can be understood as contesting the legitimacy of monolingualism in Standard English as the unquestioned norm in mainstream US schools.

The preceding discussion has provided a larger sociolinguistic perspective on how dual-language programs can challenge language prejudice in the United States. The next section reviews research that describes how language minority students and language majority students ideally develop proficiency in two languages and achieve academically through both languages. Together these sections are intended to provide a foundation for understanding how dual-language programs, in general, and how Oyster Bilingual School, in particular, can promote social change for language minority and language majority students in the United States on the local level.

Developing academic competence through two languages

Conversations about dual-language programs often lead to a number of questions about how these programs can meet their goals of bilingual proficiency, academic achievement through two languages, and cultural pluralism for their language majority and language minority students. Since Spanish is the minority language used most frequently in bilingual programs in the United States, I continue this discussion using Spanish to exemplify the minority language. A similar process would hold for other minority languages relative to English in the United States. Because Spanish-speaking and English-speaking students' needs are very different, my discussion addresses questions about goals for these populations separately.

Dual-language programs are the only type of bilingual program in the United States that targets native English-speaking students. A common concern is whether intensive instruction through Spanish threatens native English-speaking students' development of English language and literacy skills. Althought this concern at first may seem well-founded, there is no evidence to support it. The reason that intensive instruction through Spanish at school poses no threat to the native English-speaking students' continued development of English is that considerable support for English language development is available to the native English-speaking student at home and throughout the community (Lindholm, 1990).

The situation is quite different for native Spanish speakers in the United States. Since English has more cultural capital in society, there are strong pressures for native Spanish-speaking students to assimilate to monolingualism in English. Without support for Spanish at school, native Spanish-speaking students tend to lose proficiency in Spanish. As mentioned earlier, subtractive bilingualism is a typical outcome for Spanish-speaking students in transitional bilingual programs. Both maintenance and dual-language programs, however, provide native Spanish speakers with intensive instruction through Spanish, and they both expect additive bilingualism for native Spanish speakers.

Critics of bilingual education argue that it is not the school's responsibility to encourage native-language maintenance or development. In response to this criticism, Cummins (1987) argues that a certain 'threshold' level of proficiency in the native language (e.g. Spanish) is necessary for Spanish-speaking students' development of high levels of proficiency in English. Although Cummins' (1987) threshold hypothesis is problematic because it has never been demonstrated empirically, many bilingual education advocates argue that providing Spanish-speaking students with intensive instruction in Spanish is one way that schools can help Spanish-speaking students develop high levels of proficiency in English.

Well-implemented dual-language programs provide environments that are conducive for second-language acquisition for both native English speakers and native Spanish speakers. The large number of Spanish and English speakers studying together through both languages provides considerable second-language input for the native speakers of each language as well as tremendous opportunities for both groups to negotiate meaning through their second-language. These conditions, large quantitities of comprehensible input, opportunities to negotiate meaning to make incomprehensible input comprehensible, and opportunities to produce the second-language, are all theorized as being necessary for second-language acquistion (see Pica, 1991, for further discussion).

Dual-language programs, however, are about much more than language. In fact, academic achievement is the primary goal, and dual-language instruction is an important means to that end. How does bilingual instruction relate to academic achievement? Lindholm (1990) claims that subtractive bilingualism is associated with low levels of academic achievement. Cummins (1987) argues that knowledge acquired in the native language provides a basis for knowledge acquisition in the second-language. If Cummins (1987) is right, academic concepts and literacies learned through the native language do not need to be learned again in the second-language because these underlying proficiencies transfer to the second-language. What is learned in one language can be built on in the other language without needing to teach everything twice.

In addition to enhancing language minority and language majority students' development of academic competence in two languages, the ongoing interaction of these students ideally improves intercultural understanding and relations at school and in the community. Students learn about each other's language and culture as a regular part of the curriculum, which addresses dual-language program goals of greater multicultural understanding within a culturally pluralistic educational discourse.

According to Lindholm (1990), dual-language programs combine what bilingual education researchers consider the best features of maintenance bilingual programs for language minority students and immersion programs for language majority students. She identifies four 'critical' features of any dual-language program:

(a) The program essentially involves some form of dual language instruction, where the non-English language is used for a significant portion of the students' instructional day; (b) the program involves periods of instruction during which only one language is used; (c) both native English-speakers and non-native

English-speakers (preferably in balanced numbers) are participants; and (d) the students are integrated for most content instruction. (Lindholm, 1990: 96)

Her review of the literature that examines bilingual and immersion education led to 11 critieria that she argues form the core of successful dual-language education. I paraphrase and summarize her critieria as follows:

(1) In order for students to develop bilingual proficiency, dual-language programs must last at least four to six years;
(2) they must focus on academic achievement;
(3) there must be large quantities of comprehensible language input and opportunities for student output;
(4) separation of languages for instruction is required;
(5) the minority language must be used at least 50% of the time, or as much as 90–100 % of the time in the early grades;
(6) the program must foster an additive bilingual environment;
(7) a positive school environment is essential;
(8) while an equal number of students from each language is optimal, there must at least be a large number of students from each language background in the program;
(9) students should be actively involved with each other in their learning, with the teacher facilitating that process;
(10) high-quality instructional personnel is critical;
(11) home–school collaboration is required (Lindholm, 1990: 96–102).

This second part of the chapter has provided a profile of dual-language programs that are in operation today across the United States, and a review of the sociolinguistic, language-planning, and second-language-acquisition arguments that help explain how these programs can function. As we have seen, most discussions about dual-language education, like those about bilingual education in general, have tended to focus on language-related issues. Bilingual education research, policy, and practice have been concerned with understanding, for example, how long it takes for students to develop academic competence in a second-language, and how much time should be devoted to first and second-language instruction. Although research on dual-language programs is still in its infancy, questions about how the two languages are distributed throughout the program, how students from the two language backgrounds are grouped for instruction, and how dual-language programs can be organized so that they maximize the use of peer resources in language learning, dominate the conversation about how these programs achieve their goals (e.g. Christian, 1996).

While these areas are all important to further our understanding of bilingual education, they are only part of the story. Throughout this book, I argue that understanding how an actual bilingual program functions requires an understanding of how the program interacts with the multiple levels of context in which it is situated, including the larger society, the local community, the school, and the classroom. My earlier discussion of how language prejudice in the United States can be challenged through dual-language education provides a very general theoretical orientation to understanding relationships between dual-language programs and mainstream US societal discourse. Because there is so much variation from one bilingual context to another, careful ethnographic/discourse analytic studies that investigate and document processes of teaching and learning in specific dual-language programs are needed to deepen our understanding of how these programs are shaped by their particular historical and sociopolitical contexts. This book provides one such study. I turn now to a preliminary discussion of my research.

UNDERSTANDING OYSTER BILINGUAL SCHOOL: AN ETHNOGRAPHIC/DISCOURSE ANALYTIC APPROACH

The focus of the Oyster Bilingual School study is not on language in the traditional sense (e.g. Spanish or English), but on discourse practices. I assume that Oyster Bilingual School can be thought of as a 'community of practice', which Eckert and McConnell-Ginet (1992: 464) define as 'an aggregate of people who come together around mutual engagement in an endeavor'. The discourse practices that constitute a particular community of practice include both observable behaviors as well as the underlying sociocultural beliefs that give meaning to those behaviors. The ethnographic/discourse analytic approach that I took to understand Oyster Bilingual School's successful dual-language program mediates between the micro-level analysis of teaching and learning in the face-to-face classroom interaction and the macro-level analysis of social, political, and historical processes in which the school is situated.

This third part of the chapter argues that an ethnographic/discourse analytic approach provides a principled means of investigating how Oyster's dual-language plan functions on the local level. I begin this part by briefly describing what I mean by an ethnographic/discourse analytic approach. Then I introduce Oyster Bilingual School, the site of my research. I conclude this part of the chapter with a discussion of how I learned that the Oyster educators have organized their dual-language program and practices in opposition to mainstream US programs and practices in order to provide equitable and effective educational opportunities for their language minority and language majority students.

What is an ethnographic/discourse analytic approach?

This section provides a brief introduction to **ethnography** and **discourse analysis**. Because I describe my research design in detail in Chapter 4, the discussion that follows is very general. My purpose here is simply to define what I mean by ethnography and discourse analysis, explain what these research methods are used for, and argue that a combined ethnographic/discourse analytic approach such as the one that I take in this study helps address limitations of either ethnography or discourse analysis in isolation.

Ethnography is the art and science of describing a group or culture (Fetterman, 1989). According to Hammersley and Atkinson (1995: 1),

> in its most characteristic form it in involves the ethnographer participating, overtly or covertly, in people's daily lives for an extended period of time, watching what happens, listening to what is said, asking questions — in fact, collecting whatever data are available to throw light on the issues that are the focus of the research.

By studying the group or culture in question in its natural state over time, the ethnographer attempts to provide a holistic account of the social organization or patterned behavior of that group or culture.

Relevant to any discussion of ethnography is the distinction between **etic** and **emic** approaches to data collection and analysis, first pointed out by Pike (1954) with respect to the phon**etic**/phon**emic** distinction in linguistics. An etic approach bases definitions and categorizations of meanings on concepts, frameworks, and categories used in social science research. An emic approach, in contrast, sees the participants' definitions, their categories of meaning, and their idea systems as the most important explanations for observed behavior. The purpose of an emic approach is for the researcher to discover the ways that the insiders define and categorize meaning within their cultural context.

Although a primary goal of ethnographic research is to provide an emic analysis of social organization, an ethnographic study is not exclusively emic. Because most ethnographers begin their research as social scientists who are outsiders to the group or culture being studied, they necessarily begin the analysis with an etic understanding of the issues to be investigated. Then, through extended time doing participant-observation, ethnographers develop an emic understanding of the values, the social symbolism, and the norms of interaction that govern behavior (verbal and non-verbal) within the cultures they study. Finally, ethnographers translate their emic understanding of that social organization to an etic discussion that contributes in some way to more general social science theory development. According to Hymes (1990: 421), 'these three moments (the etic-1, emic, and etic-2 of Pike, 1954) are fundamental to linguistics and anthropology'.

While ethnography is a powerful tool for understanding how particular people in specific social and historical locations accomplish what they do in their everyday lives, as well as for understanding the cultural significance that those people attach to those doings, ethnography is not without criticism. For example, ethnography is an interpretive method and the primary research tool is the individual ethnographer. This has led to criticisms that ethnographic research is too subjective. Ethnographers respond that subjectivity is a characteristic of all research. Because researchers are part of the social world that they study, they are able to act in the world and reflect on those actions. Rather than dismiss ethnography as an approach to social science research, ethnographers should instead make explicit how the knowledge obtained about a particular cultural group was jointly constructed by the researcher and the participants in the study. One way to do this is to clearly describe the researcher's role throughout the research process (see Hammersley & Atkinson, 1995, for further discussion).

Another criticism of traditional ethnography is that it privileges certain perspectives and marginalizes others. In some cases, when the ethnography is written exclusively from the individual ethnographer's perspective, it may present a relatively uniform explanation for the patterns of behavior observed. This approach can obscure other perspectives that do not agree entirely with the ethnographer's, and gloss over contradictions or competing interpretations of phenomenon that are a regular part of all social life. In other cases, the ethnographer may have limited his/her research by interviewing and/or observing activities that are dominated by one social group, for example the powerful men in the cultural group, while excluding the perspectives of other social groups within the culture. In reponse to these criticisms, contemporary ethnographic research emphasizes the need to include a wide range of participants' perspectives and voices throughout both the research process and the writing of the actual ethnographic product (see Clifford & Marcus, 1986; Clifford, 1988, for further discussion).

The discourse analytic approach that I take in this study provides a means of addressing many of the limitations of traditional ethnography. Because the terms **discourse** and **discourse analysis** are used in different ways throughout the sociolinguistics and cultural studies literature, I provide the following discussion to review how these terms are used in the literature, and then describe what I mean by discourse and discourse analysis in my work.

On the one hand, American sociolinguists generally use the term discourse to refer to a continuous stretch of naturally occurring spoken or written language that is larger than a sentence and that, in some structural or functional way, hangs together as a unit for analysis. Following Fairclough (1989), I use the term **text** to refer to this notion. Discourse analysis in this sense refers to a description of how linguistic features function to make meaning. Taking research on language and gender as an example, researchers working in this tradition may analyze transcripts of audio- or video-taped recordings of naturally occurring face-to-face interaction to identify patterns in how men and women use questions or in how they sequence their conversational moves. Explanations for the gender-differentiated language use that is observed are often based on theoretical assumptions about cross-cultural differences between men and women and/or about patriarchal power structures in society (see Freeman & McElhinny, 1996, for extensive review of this literature).

Cultural or symbolic studies researchers, on the other hand, generally use the term discourse in a much broader sense to refer to ideologically structured assumptions and expectations about social groups that reflect and shape power relations in particular cultural contexts. Following Fairclough (1989), I retain the term **discourse** for this second, more abstract notion. The goal of this type of discourse analysis is to examine a wide range of social practices, including written documents and/or social activities, in order to make explicit the underlying cultural notions that link forms of writing and/or talk to social groups in a way that seems natural within that context. Again, taking language and gender research as an example, researchers working in this tradition may document and critique the way that women are represented (or not) and evaluated within and across public institutions in western society (see Freeman & McElhinny, 1996, for examples and further discussion).

Gal's (1995) discussion of research on language and gender argues that an integration of work in sociolinguistics and cultural studies is necessary to further our understanding of language, social identity, and power. Her notion of power as symbolic domination assumes that power rarely goes without resistance. She writes,

> The notions of domination and resistance alert us to the idea that the strongest form of power may well be the ability to define social reality, to impose visions of the world. And such visions are inscribed in language, and most important, enacted in interaction. (Gal, 1995, 178)

A primary goal of critical discourse analysis is to describe, interpret, and explain how macro-level sociopolitical struggles between social groups play out in micro-level spoken and written texts (Fairclough, 1989).

This study takes a critical discourse analytic approach and assumes that schools and other institutions in society are largely discursively constituted. That is, institutions are made up of people who talk and/or write about who they are and about what they say, do, believe, and value in patterned ways. Actual micro-level spoken and written texts produced by people in situated activities within the institution both reflect and shape the abstract macro-level discourses that constitute that institution. These abstract, underlying institutional discourses are never neutral; they are always structured by ideologies (see also Fairclough, 1989, 1992; Gee, 1991; Lemke, 1989, 1993).

An **intertextual** approach to discourse analysis allows the researcher to piece together actual spoken and written texts in order to make the underlying ideological discourses explicit. According to Fairclough (1993: 84):

> Intertextuality is basically the property texts have of being full of snatches of other texts, which may be explicitly demarcated or merged in, and which the text may assimilate, contradict, ironically echo, and so forth.

Actual texts can be understood as instantiations of underlying discourses, and each text provides traces of those underlying discourses. An intertextual analysis enables the researcher to identify, for example, relationships between different individual's or groups' ideological assumptions and expectations about certain issues or social groups, or the evolution of ideological stances toward a particular issue over time.

An ethnographically informed intertextual analysis of discourse allows the researcher to link spoken and written texts that are produced by a wide range of participants who interact with one another on a regular basis in actual communities of practice, and to make explicit the underlying discourses that structure their everyday interactions and interpretations. I have intentionally used the plural form of the term discourse here to emphasize that no institution is constituted by a static monolithic discourse to which all people orient themselves in the same way. Rather, there are always multiple discourses within any institutional context, or within any society. An intertextual analysis also enables the researcher to link one institutional discourse to another, and to explore relationships between these discourses. It is important to remember that discourses are dynamic, and they can, and do, shift over time.

This section has provided a very brief introduction to ethnography and discourse analysis, and has shown how these two research orientations can mutually inform each other. An ethnographic/discourse analytic approach provides a principled means of studying how a dual-language plan is interpeted and implemented in a specific social and historical location. By collecting and analyzing a wide range of spoken and written texts produced by policymakers, educators, students, and parents over time, and by investigating multiple persectives on those texts in isolation and then collectively, the researcher can piece together the underlying discourses that structure social relations at the school and throughout the local community, and relate those discourses to larger societal discourses about linguistic and cultural diversity. Because I provide a more detailed discussion of my research design in Chapter 4, the preceding discussion has been very general. I turn now to a discussion of Oyster Bilingual School, the site of my research.

Oyster Bilingual School: An overview

This section introduces Oyster Bilingual School, and is intended to give the reader an overall sense of the historical, social, and physical context of its dual-language program. First, I discuss the civil rights atmosphere in Washington, DC, in the late 1960s and early 1970s that gave rise to Oyster's dual-language program. Then I describe Oyster Bilingual School today on a very general level, with attention to its student population, physical conditions, and social organization. I conclude this section with a discussion of criteria that I used as evidence of Oyster's success. This section is intentionally brief, and simply serves as an introduction to the rich, ethnographic description of how Oyster's dual-language program functions that is presented throughout Chapters 5–10.

Consideration of the history of Oyster's dual-language program is crucial to understanding why and how the program was inititiated, and it provides an important foundation for understanding how Oyster's program functions today. The Civil Rights Movement of the 1960s in the United States meant that groups that had traditionally been denied access to public institutions were asserting their rights to full participation in US society. At the same time, changing immigration laws in the

1960s allowed more immigrants to enter the United States (see Chapter 2 for further discussion of civil rights and immigration movements in the United States during this period), and the District of Columbia became a port of entry for many Latin Americans. Unlike other Latino communities in the United States that are predominantly a single nationality (e.g. Cubans in Miami, Puerto Ricans in New York, Mexicans in the southwest), the Latino community in Washington, DC is made up of immigrants from many different Central and Latin American countries, and they represent a wide range of racial and socioeconomic backgrounds. According to a paper entitled 'The History and Politics of Oyster Bilingual School' that Oyster parents presented to the 1980 National Association for Bilingual Education (NABE) conference participants who were visiting the school, this context encouraged Latinos in Washington, DC to unify and fight for their rights as a community.

The rhetoric of the Civil Rights period stressed education, and a series of local collaborations intended to address the growing needs of the Latino community in Washington, DC led to the decision to develop an integrated bilingual school. First, a committee of Latino spokespersons was organized to discuss the educational plight of Latinos in the District, and they decided to recruit and train about 20 bilingual teachers to work in the DC public schools. The Spanish Educational Development Center (SED) became responsible for training these bilingual teachers, and also became a strong advocate for bilingual education for Latino children in Washington, DC. Early in 1971, the new Superintendent of Schools in the District pushed hard for funding for bilingual education, and the Director of SED emphasized the need for an integrated bilingual program that would involve English speakers and Spanish speakers. In June of 1971, a director of bilingual education was appointed. His first job was to find an appropriate location to develop the first dual-language program in Washington, DC.

Oyster Elementary School, located on 29th and Calvert in northwest Washington, DC, was targeted as the site for the development of an innovative bilingual education program. Although the majority of the students were white at that time, approximately 45% of the total student population was Latino, making Oyster the elementary school with the largest concentration of Latinos in Washington, DC. The idea of a dual-language program at Oyster Elementary School was originally met with considerable resistance, but the local Latino community members and politicians launched a public relations effort and won support for the opportunity to develop a bilingual program that would encourage bilingualism, academic achievement, and improved intergroup understanding and relations for the English-speaking and Spanish-speaking students who attended the school. Oyster's bilingual program began with one dual-language classroom in the fall of 1971, and spread throughout the school over the next several years. Details of the development of this program are provided in Chapter 6.

The student population at Oyster Bilingual School in the 1990s is linguistically, culturally, and socioeconomically diverse, reflecting the composition of the Washington, DC, area in which it is located. While it is difficult to gather exact statistics about student demographics, a synthesis of site documents that I collected at Oyster provides a relatively accurate approximation. According to Oyster's March 1993 Fact Sheet, the students are 58% Hispanic, 26% White, 12% Black, and 4% Asian, with the children representing over 25 countries; 74% of the student population is language minority; 24% are LEP; and 40% of Oyster's children are on the free and reduced lunch program available to low-income children in the DC Public Schools. *Oyster Bilingual School: Escuela Bilingüe*, a booklet compiled by Oyster administrators, teachers, students, and parents in 1991, provides the following description:

> Oyster Bilingual School is comprised of 311 students from multicultural, multilingual backgrounds and diverse socioeconomic groups. Students at Oyster represent over 30 nationalities. Some students are recent immigrants from nations facing internal conflict such as El Salvador, Lebanon, Vietnam and Afghanistan. Parents of other students seek out Oyster while on temporary assignment in the United States. These students might be from Japan, Germany, Iceland or Australia. Students are from countries as close as Nicaragua, or as far away as South Africa. (*Oyster Bilingual School: Escuola Bilingüe*, 1991)

According to the student profiles that I collected, over 65% of the Oyster students come to school speaking a language other than English as their first language. While the majority of these students are native Spanish speakers (primarily from El Salvador), 2% of students are neither native English-speaking nor native Spanish-speaking.

When one visits Oyster Bilingual School today, it is difficult to imagine that this was once a declining community, or that so many of the students are low-income Latino. The immediate neighborhood looks primarily middle- to upper-middle class, and the majority of the surrounding residences are relatively large, single-family homes. Down the street from the school is an Omni-Sheraton Hotel, and a few blocks away is Connecticut Avenue, a busy corridor with many thriving restaurants, shops, and the National Zoo. Oyster's proximity to Embassy Row (Massachusetts Avenue) means that there are many diplomats and their families in the area, and there tend to be a few students attending the school who speak neither Spanish nor English as their first language.

Differences in language background at Oyster closely parallel differences in socioeconomic class background. As mentioned earlier, approximately 40% of the Oyster School students are native English-speaking students. About half of the native English-speaking students are African American, and about half are white, and the vast majority of these native English-speaking students come from middle-class homes. Although some of the Latino children who attended Oyster are middle class, the majority of the Latino students are from low-income Salvadoran backgrounds, and they live across the bridge in the Adams Morgan and Mount Pleasant communities. The area of Columbia Road and 18th Street, for example, has a large number of Latino small businesses, restaurants, and local service agencies, and the

Latino community tends to live in tight quarters nearby. As I discuss and illustrate throughout Chapters 5–10, this difference in socioeconomic class between the native English speakers and the native Spanish speakers has important implications for the ways that the Oyster educators work with students and their families.

Although Oyster Bilingual School is filled beyond capacity, it is in relatively good physical condition. The school is a small, red-brick three-story building that sits on top of a grassy hill in which several poplar trees are growing. The trim around the windows is freshly painted, and the first floor windows are covered with protective grids, also freshly painted in white. The two flights of stairs that lead up to the main entrance in the front of the school have a large central landing where children often play or study together on sunny days. There is a sign on the lower landing that reads OYSTER BILINGUAL SCHOOL, and underneath of the sign is a plaque that is made up of a series of ceramic tiles made by students that represent things that kids do. To the left of the building is a small playground, and to the right is a much larger playground. Two trailers that house the pre-K and kindergarten classes are located close to the school at the top of this larger playground, and there is a grass playing field below where children often play soccer. Before school, during lunch, and at other times throughout the day, the playground is filled with children from a wide range of backgrounds playing together, adults supervising and playing with the children, and the sounds of Spanish and English mixed in the air.

Visitors, students, and teachers enter the lobby of the school after walking up the two flights of stairs and passing through brightly painted double doors. There is a sofa and two easy chairs which are almost always being used by children and/or visitors on the left, and a large bulletin board above the sofa that gives a message about the school in Spanish and in English. Sometimes the Spanish version is above the English, and sometimes the English version is above the Spanish, but both languages are represented equally on this bulletin board as in the majority of other official documents produced by the school. At the far end of the lobby through another set of double doors is the cafeteria/auditorium. This space is regularly used for celebrations, presentations, musical performances, and of course, lunch.

To the right of the lobby is a flight of stairs leading to classrooms on the second and third floors. To the left is a hallway with classrooms, and another flight of stairs leading to the upper floors. The lower grades are on the first floor, the middle grades are on the second floor, and the upper grades are on the third floor. The school always serves students from pre-k to sixth grade, but the number of classes in each grade level or the combinations of grades in one class change depending on the make-up of the total student population at any time. The lobby, the hallways, the classroom walls, and the ceilings are covered with children's art, schoolwork, and commercial posters, and there are books, learning centers, desks, tables, and chairs in every imaginable space. Spanish and English are represented more or less equally in this very print-rich environment.

While the physical structure of the school is quite traditional in US terms, the space is used in very untraditional ways. Because there are two teachers in each class, one Spanish-dominant who ideally speaks and is spoken to only in Spanish and one English-dominant who ideally speaks and is spoken to only in English, sometimes one classroom may be used for two separate classes at the same time, one conducted in Spanish and the other in English. At other times, the Spanish-dominant teacher may teach the entire class in Spanish, and later in the day the English-dominant teacher may teach the entire class in English. As I describe in more detail in Chapter 7, there is considerable variation in how the teachers work together to allocate content-area instruction through the two languages. Regardless of how the teachers divide up the classroom and the instructional time, the students are generally organized to work together in small groups in the classroom, or in the hallway, or wherever there is space. There is a tremendous amount of energy throughout the school as children learn together through Spanish and English.

As the next few paragraphs describe, Oyster's dual-language program is considered successful by several distinct bodies who use different assessment criteria. I begin with a discussion of Oyster's standardized test scores, the criteria that DC public schools use to measure achievement. Then I move to a review of evidence that suggests that insiders and outsiders alike also consider Oyster Bilingual School successful with its linguistically and culturally diverse student population.

First, Oyster Bilingual School is considered effective by DC public schools because its students are achieving at or above grade level on standardized tests. The principal at the time of my study (1991) showed me charts that a former principal had organized mapping the third graders' and sixth graders' performance in the years 1980, 1981, 1982, and 1983 on the Comprehensive Tests of Basic Skills (CTBS) in reading, math, language, reference skills, science, and social studies. These charts illustrated that the third-grade students performed between one and three grade levels above the national average on each of the skill areas, and the sixth-grade students performed between two and five grade levels above the national average.

The 1991 CTBS scores for third-grade and sixth-grade student performance are consistent with the scores reported from the years 1980–83. Figure 4 presents the 1991 scores and the national norm. As the figure shows, in 1991 the Oyster third-grade students performed between 1.6 and 1.8 grade levels above the national norm, and the Oyster sixth grade students performed between 4.4 and 6.2 grade levels above the national norm.

The increase in overall student achievement as measured by standardized test scores between third and sixth grades deserves mention. According to statistics on school performance, the gap in average achievement level between middle-class children and low-income and/or minority children increases as a function of grade level. These statistics have been interpreted as evidence of the negative effects of the US public school process on minority children (Gumperz, 1981; Oakes, 1985). I was unable to obtain a statistical breakdown of Oyster students' test scores according to socioeconomic class or cultural background. The Guidance Counselor told me that Oyster did not analyse their test scores that way because they believed that such groupings were discriminatory. However, given that the majority of the Oyster students are from minority backgrounds, the increase in overall test scores from third grade to sixth grade suggests minority student success.

Oyster Bilingual School also has a reputation among DC parents as being successful. The 1980 talk that the Oyster Bilingual School parents presented to NABE conference participants who were visiting the school provided the following description of how the school functioned in 1980:

> Since its founding as a bilingual school, Oyster has thrived. While once it was losing enrollment, and seen as a candidate for closing, today the school operates at full enrollment. Actually that underestimates the case. The school operates officially at something like 130% of the supposed maximum physical capacity. Pre-kindergarten and kindergarten classes meet in the so called 'temporary' metal buildings adjacent to the main brick building. Inside, every nook and cranny is put to double use. Sometimes instruction goes on in hallways, or even converted closets. The school is overcrowded, in a city where declining enroll-ments are such a problem that nearly half the classroom space is excess, and where schools are closed about every two years, to save money. Statistically, Oyster is by far, the most extensively used school in the city. And its waiting list is close to 300. (p. 3)

My ethnographic experience at the school from 1989–91 supports the Oyster parents' 1980 description. The pre-K and kindergarten classes were still held in the 'temporary' buildings outside on the playground, and the school still operated above capacity with a long waiting list. As I witnessed one spring morning, many parents (from a variety of backgrounds) had lined up and had been waiting outside of the school for several hours to enroll their children for the following school year. According to the 1991 *Oyster Bilingual School: Escuela Bilingüe* booklet, 305 students were on the waiting list, a number that is almost as high as the entire Oyster student population.

	Grade 3				Grade 6			
	GE		Percentile		GE		Percentile	
Reading	4.8	(3.0)	74	(50)	10.4	(6.0)	85	(50)
Mathematics	4.7	(3.0)	81	(50)	11.4	(6.0)	96	(50)
Language	4.6	(3.0)	75	(50)	12.2	(6.0)	90	(50)
Science	4.8	(3.0)	74	(50)	10.8	(6.0)	85	(50)

Figure 4 Comprehensive Test of Basic Skills (CTBS) median scores and percentiles from Oyster Bilingual School students' May 1991 exams (GE = grade equivalent; national norm given in parentheses)

Oyster's dual-language program is also considered a model by several external groups. For example, in 1991, the National Association of Bilingual Education (NABE) held a series of school visits at Oyster so that bilingual educators from around the country could learn about Oyster's successful dual-language program. In 1993, Oyster received the National Schools of Excellence Award from Hispanic Magazine and the Ryder Corporation. Given that Oyster Bilingual School is considered successful by several independent criteria, it provides an excellent site for investigating how a group of educators organize their program and practices to meet the needs of their linguistically, culturally, and socioeconomically diverse student population.

'You know, it's much more than language'

This section describes how I learned that Oyster Bilingual School's dual-language program is about, in the words of one teacher, 'much more than language'. I begin with a description of my original, unsuccessful approach to researching the program. This brief discussion is intended to demonstrate the need for researchers to gain an insider's understanding of what makes a dual-language function the way that it does in its particular social and historical location.

When I began my investigation of Oyster Bilingual School in 1989, I assumed that the dual-language policy was the reason for the program's success. The goal of my study was simply to provide a descriptive case study of how the children acquired and used Spanish and English in this successful dual-language program. My original approach to studying the Oyster program was to relate extended classroom observation of the sixth-grade Spanish and English Language Arts classes to analyses of the official Bilingual Education policy statement and to conversations with the principal of the school, teachers of the class, and students in the class. I began my study of how Oyster's dual-language policy was interpreted and implemented in practice by observing the use of Spanish and English in a sixth grade classroom. I took careful notes and audio-taped many classroom interactions to document who used what languages, to whom, when, where, and for what reasons in order to understand how the plan was implemented on the classroom level.

I compared my analysis of classroom interaction with Oyster's official policy statement, which provides the following description of the Bilingual Program:

Bilingual Program

Oyster's Bilingual Program has been in operation since 1971. It is considered unique in the city and the country. The teaming of English-dominant and Spanish-dominant teachers provides language models for students in both their first and second-languages.

Students hear and respond to both languages throughout the day. A final average of instruction is approximately half and half for each language, each day. Students read in both languages every day. Mathematics and content-area groups are developed by the teaching teams. Often key vocabulary may be introduced in both languages.

The end result of instruction at Oyster is the development of students who are biliterate and bicultural and who have learned all subject areas in both languages. (*Oyster Bilingual School Teachers' Handbook*: 1)

As is obvious from the Bilingual Program policy statement, the explicit goal of the dual-language plan is for all students to become bilingual in Spanish and English and to learn content-areas in both languages. This goal of additive bilingualism is the same for language minority and language majority students.

Using policy statements and my classroom observations as guidelines, I asked the principal and the teachers language-related questions about instruction, abilities of the students from the different backgrounds to use the languages, how they allocated Spanish and English in their classes during the day, different kinds of bilingual and ESL programs, etc. In sum, I was interested in documenting the Oyster educators' approach to Spanish and English language-acquisition planning and implementation.

Near the end of my first semester of study, however, my classroom observations suggested a need to question my original assumption that the school's language policy was the reason for the program's success. For example, there was a considerable amount of code-switching to English in Spanish-speaking content classes, but the reverse was not true in English-speaking content classes. Spanish was not evaluated in the same way as English; there was no District-wide standardized testing of Spanish as there was of English. The English-dominant students did not seem to be as conversationally competent in Spanish as their Spanish-dominant counterparts were in English. Although there was some Spanish used in the lunchroom and on the playground, English was the language most frequently heard in unofficial domains (see Chapter 8 for an explanation of these observations). It seemed to me that the explicit goal of bilingualism for all students, as described to me by both teachers and policy statements, was not being fully realized, and I wondered what made the program work. One day, a teacher told me in response to my language-related questioning, 'You know, it's *much more* than language' (italic indicates the teacher's emphasis).

In methodological terms, my original approach to studying Oyster's dual-language can be considered etic. The assumptions about bilingual education that I brought to my investigation of Oyster's program, which were based on my readings about bilingual education as well as on my practical experience in bilingual schools in other contexts, initially led me to focus exclusively on language, and they blocked my ability to gain a more holistic understanding of Oyster's bilingual program. As mentioned earlier in the chapter, a primary goal of an ethnographic study is to develop an emic understanding of the cultural context being studied. The teacher's statement —'You know, it's much more than language' — led me, first, to critically examine my own assumptions as a researcher and, second, to develop an understanding of Oyster's perspective on how their program functioned within this particular sociopolitical context.

Chapters 5–10 provide an emic analysis of Oyster's dual-language program, and argue that Oyster Bilingual School has organized itself to provide an alternative to mainstream US educational discourse with respect to language use, participation rights, and intergroup relations. As I describe in Chapters 2 and 3, within mainstream US schools and society there has been a prevailing assumption (in sociolinguistic research as well as in educational practice) that linguistic and cultural differences lead to communicative breakdown. Mainstream US public schools have tradition- ally addressed the 'problem' of linguistic and cultural diversity by pressuring language minority students to become monolingual in Standard English and to behave according to white middle-class norms of interaction and interpretation in order to participate and achieve in school and society.

While it is true that linguistic and cultural difference *can* lead to communicative breakdown, *this is certainly not a necessary outcome.* As my study of the Oyster Bilingual School illustrates, students' linguistic and cultural differences can be seen as 'resources' to be developed. Rather than requiring language minority students to assimilate to language majority ways of speaking and interacting, Oyster requires all students to become bilingual and biliterate in Spanish and English, and to expect, tolerate, and respect diverse ways of interacting. Dual-language-planning at the Oyster Bilingual School can be seen as dynamic, multi-level processes in which language minority and language majority members of the Oyster community collaborate in their efforts to define bilingualism as a resource to be developed within a culturally pluralistic school, and not as problems to be overcome (see Chapter 6 for discussion of this notion of community).

Oyster's language-as-resource orientation should be understood as in opposition to and struggling against the language-as-problem orientation that characterizes most bilingual and ESL programs in the United States. Limiting discussion of Oyster's success with its linguistically and culturally diverse student population to language alone, however, would allow only a superficial understanding of how the dual-language program functions. I argue that the Spanish–English language plan can be read as one part of a larger social identities project that aims to promote social change on the local level by socializing children differently from the way children are socialized in mainstream US educational discourse. Rather than pressuring language minority students to assimilate to the positively evaluated majority social identity (white middle-class native English-speaking) in order to participate and achieve at school, the Oyster educational discourse is organized to positively evaluate linguistic and cultural diversity. As I describe throughout the book, this socializing discourse makes possible the emergence of a wide range of positively evaluated social identities, and offers more choices to both language minority and language majority students than are traditionally available in mainstream US schools and society. The Oyster educators argue that students' socialization through this educational discourse is the reason that LEP, language minority, and language majority students are all participating and achieving more or less equally.

SUMMARY OF CHAPTER 1

Because there is so much confusion and conflict in the United States and around the world about what bilingual education means, who bilingual programs serve, and what the goals of a bilingual program are for the target populations, I began this chapter by briefly reviewing bilingual education model and program types. My discussion of transitional, maintenance, and enrichment models of bilingual education described the different ideological orientations toward linguistic and cultural diversity that characterize these models, and my discussion of transitional, maintenance, immersion, heritage and dual-language types of programs differentiated between these programs in terms of their structural and contextual characteristics. The sections in the first part of the chapter provided a very general background for understanding what dual-language education means in relation to other types of bilingual programs.

Because Oyster Bilingual School is a dual-language program in the United States, the second part of the chapter reviewed what we know and what we do not know about dual-language education. First, I profiled dual-language programs across the country today, and described some of the variation that is found across contexts. Then I presented a few basic principles from sociolinguistics, language-planning, and second-language acquisition research that help us understand how a dual-language program can function on the local level. The sociolinguistic perspective on dual-language education explained in very general terms how dual-language programs can challenge language prejudice in US schools, and the review of the language-planning and second-language acquisition research presented arguments about how dual-language programs can provide opportunities for language minority and language majority students to develop academic competence through two languages. Together, the sections in the second part of the chapter offered an overview of dual-language education in the United States today, and suggested directions for future research.

Because there is so much variation from one bilingual education context to another, a major thesis of this book is that we need to look closely at how and why actual bilingual programs function the way that they do in their particular sociopolitical locations before we can really address questions about the effectiveness of bilingual education. This book provides a detailed analysis of how and why Oyster Bilingual School, a 'successful' dual-language elementary school program, functions the way that it does in contemporary Washington, DC. The third part of the chapter described the ethnographic/discourse analytic approach that I take in my work, and introduced Oyster Bilingual School, the site of my research. Close analyses of actual bilingual programs and practices like the one presented in this book can provide the basis for future comparative research and for more grounded discussions about whether and how bilingual education can be effective.

OVERVIEW OF THE BOOK

This book provides a detailed analysis of how the Oyster educators have designed and implemented their dual-language program as an alternative to mainstream US educational and societal discourse for their linguistically and culturally diverse student population. Because the program is organized in opposition to US programs and practices that they believe discriminate against minority students, an understanding of mainstream US discourses surrounding bilingual education, linguistic and cultural diversity, and minority education is crucial to understanding Oyster's alternative educational discourse practices. Chapter 2 provides a historical perspective on the discourses surrounding bilingual education in the United States. This discussion situates dual-language programs in the larger context of important sociopolitical movements in the United States, ongoing bilingual education research, and major bilingual education, civil rights, and immigration policy decisions. Chapter 3 moves from the larger sociopolitical context of bilingual education in the United States to an investigation of mainstream US educational discourse practices. The chapter begins with a theoretical discussion of how schools can be understood as cultural communication systems. I then synthesize the literature about minority students in US schools and demonstrate how the organization of mainstream US programs and practices contributes to the subordination of minority students in school and society. As I discuss in the conclusion of Chapter 3 and illustrate throughout Chapters 5–10, however, schools do not have to be organized this way. Because educators have choices about how they organize their programs and practices, they can (1) recognize discriminatory discourse practices; (2) refuse those discourses; and (3) construct an alternative discourse that provides more equitable educational opportunities to language minority and language majority students.

Chapter 4 describes the ethnographic/discourse analytic approach that I used to understand how Oyster's dual-language program interacts with the larger sociopolitical context. In addition to addressing issues of validity and reliability of my research methods, this discussion is intended for researchers who are interested in taking a similar approach in other contexts. Chapter 5 links analyses of Oyster policy statements and the Oyster educators' stories about their program to each other and to mainstream US educational and societal discourses. My analyses illustrate the Oyster perspective on the problem for minority students in mainstream US discourse, and the Oyster solution to that problem. The chapter concludes by describing the underlying social identities project that I argue informs and explains Oyster's program and practices. I deliberately use the plural of the term 'identity' here to emphasize my understanding of identity as multiple (see Chapter 3 for discussion of social identity construction through language).

Chapters 6, 7 and 8 describe in ethnographic detail the parts of the Oyster Bilingual School cultural communication system. While it is artificial to take apart the parts of the system, it is useful for analytic purposes. Because of the Oyster focus on identity, Chapter 6 begins with the Oyster educators' definitions of students, teachers, and school. This analysis reveals that the Oyster educators have very different assumptions and expectations about students, teachers, and school than those commonly held in mainstream US educational discourse. Chapter 7 then illustrates how the Oyster educators' assumptions about students, teachers, and schools lead to very different ways of organizing learning and teaching at Oyster Bilingual School. Chapter 8 provides a more detailed discussion of the norms of interaction and interpretation that structure discourse practices at Oyster Bilingual School. This explicit statement of the underlying norms at Oyster allows an understanding of how the organization of classroom activities provides equitable and effective educational opportunities for all students. Because Oyster does not exist in a sociopolitical vacuum, we can expect discrepancies between the ideal plan and actual implementation. Chapter 8 concludes with a discussion of these discrepancies, and offers a sociopolitical explanation for them.

Chapters 9 and 10 present micro-level analyses of how the dual-language program is implemented on the classroom level. These micro-level interactions reflect the macro-level sociopolitical struggle between the Oyster educational discourse and mainstream US educational and societal discourses that Chapters 2 through 8 describe. Because the Oyster educators are attempting to socialize minority and majority students differently from mainstream US schools, these micro-level interactions also contribute to that larger sociopolitical struggle from the bottom up.

Chapter 11 moves beyond the case study of Oyster Bilingual School to suggest implications of the study for research and practice in other educational contexts. Whenever I describe how Oyster's dual-language program is organized to challenge mainstream US discourse practices, I am asked what happens when students leave Oyster Bilingual School. While this study was not designed to address this question, the first part of Chapter 11 provides a preliminary answer and suggests directions for future research on the local level. More importantly, it suggests directions for educational research and practice. The second part of Chapter 11 then expands on these suggestions by summarizing the main theoretical and methodological points of my ethnographic/ discourse analytic approach for researchers and educators who want to analyze how bilingual educational policies are interpreted and implemented in other school and community contexts.

My hope is that this book will stimulate bilingual education researchers, in particular, and educational researchers more generally to look at the complexity involved in transforming practice through educational interventions. I also hope this book will inspire educators who work with linguistically and culturally diverse student populations to critically examine their own assumptions about diversity and to consider how these assumptions shape the ways they organize their educational programs and practices. While I am not suggesting that the particulars of the Oyster School dual-language program be reproduced in another context, this case study provides empirical evidence for one alternative to mainstream US educational discourse that meets the needs of the students it serves. I encourage readers to consider how the underlying ideological discourses described in this book relate on a much more general level to the educational and societal contexts with which they are familiar.

CHAPTER 2

Societal Discourses Surrounding Bilingual Education in the United States: A Historical Perspective

As in other parts of the world, the field of bilingual education is highly politicized in the United States. The term bilingual education draws strong ideological reactions from those inside and outside the educational system. While it is not possible to depoliticize the field, I believe it is instructive to situate contemporary discussions of bilingual education within a larger historical and sociopolitical framework. This chapter presents a brief history of major events and ideological trends that have shaped and continue to shape the discourses surrounding bilingual education in US schools and society. The chapter thus provides an important foundation for understanding how Oyster Bilingual School functions in relation to contemporary US society.

Historically, the United States has been characterized by a 'tolerance-oriented' tradition of language rights (McGroarty, 1992). For the most part, the individual has been free to select whatever language best meets his or her needs. This ideological discourse is reflected in the Constitution which makes no reference to the choice of a national language, and in Constitutional protections of free speech that have included the freedom to choose the language one uses, as well as the content one discusses (Heath, 1981).

This dominant discourse of tolerance, however, has been challenged repeatedly throughout US history, and it is being directly confronted today. This chapter examines bilingual education in relation to changing demographics, sociopolitical movements, and trends in educational practice, policy, and research to illustrate that language policy decisions in the United States are often based on other than linguistic issues. Understanding how an actual bilingual program functions therefore requires analysis of the larger historical, sociocultural, political, and economic contexts in which that program is located.

The history of bilingual education in the United States is frequently divided into two periods, the first lasting until the beginning of World War I and the second beginning in the 1960s (Malakoff & Hakuta, 1990). Reflecting this division, I have organized Chapter 2 into two major parts. The first part briefly discusses the history of bilingualism and bilingual education in the United States until the 1920s, and provides a foundation for understanding the competing discourses about linguistic and cultural diversity that we hear in US schools and society today. This part illustrates how the United States moved from being a country of widespread bilingualism and bilingual education to being a nation that expected its citizenry to be (or become) monolingual in English in a very short period of time. The second part of the chapter provides a more detailed discussion of policy, research, and practice in the United States since the 1960s. It relates the different types of bilingual education that federal policy has supported to larger ideological debates about linguistic and cultural diversity in society. While the historical overview presented in this chapter is not intended to be detailed or exhaustive, it provides necessary background information for understanding how Oyster Bilingual School's dual-language program functions on the local level.

PRE-WORLD WAR I: FROM LINGUISTIC DIVERSITY TO MONOLINGUALISM IN ENGLISH

The current controversy in the United States about the status of English and about the effectiveness of bilingual education programs (discussed later in the chapter) may seem to suggest that bilingualism and bilingual education are recent phenomena. The first part of this chapter briefly reviews the history of bilingualism and bilingual education during the pre-World War I period, and comes to two important conclusions. First, contrary to common knowledge today, bilingualism and bilingual education were actually quite widespread in the United States until the early 1900s. Second, changing demographics and changing expectations about the role of schools in society radically transformed the discourses surrounding bilingualism and bilingual education in the United States at the turn of the century. While there was no uniform federal language policy throughout this period, a linguistically diverse United States became a largely monolingual country over the course of one generation.

Bilingualism, bilingual education, and language policy until the 1900s

This section describes the extensive bilingualism and bilingual education that was a natural part of life in many communities in the United States throughout the majority of the history of this nation. Although linguistic and cultural diversity was generally tolerated if not encouraged throughout the country until the early 1900s, this section also identifies some important exceptions to that tendency. These exceptions demonstrate that bilingual education policy in the United States has always been about much more than language or educational issues. Since early in US history, there have been competing discourses surrounding language policy in particular and linguistic and cultural diversity more generally that reflect and structure power relations between social groups at particular moments in time.

Bilingualism was commonplace in the early United States, and the US Constitution makes no mention of an official language. While English had become the dominant language throughout the 13 colonies by the late 17th century, it was still possible to hear, for example, German, Dutch, French, Swedish, or Polish spoken in different communities. When the US Constitution was drafted and ratified, bilingualism in these languages was widespread not only among the working classes but also among the elite, especially in New York, Pennsylvania, Delaware, and New Jersey. In addition, Spanish was a dominant language in some of the soon-to-be-acquired territories, for example, in Florida and in the Southwest. The fact that there is no mention of an official language in the Constitution suggests that a linguistically and culturally diverse United States was not considered terribly problematic at that time. In fact, Schiffman (1996) argues that the British perceived the articulation of a language policy to be something French, not English. Given the problems of the French Revolution and a desire not to be associated with France, no policy was stipulated in the US Constitution.

Although there is no mention of official language in the US Constitution, there is evidence that large numbers of speakers of one language concentrated in the same geographic location was cause for some concern. For example, Benjamin Franklin worried that Anglo supremacy would be threatened by the large German linguistic, cultural, and political presence in Pennsylvania, and Thomas Jefferson feared that French-speakers in the Louisiana territories might not be capable of governing themselves. These and other colonial leaders were concerned that immigrants from non-democratic countries, especially from non-Protestant religious backgrounds, might not easily embrace the ideals of the newly-formed constitutional democracy. It was further believed that the use of non-English languages would perpetuate foreign ideas and threaten civil society (see Ricento, 1995, for further discussion).

The lack of official language policy and the existence of bilingual education programs throughout the United States, however, suggests that linguistic pluralism was at least tolerated, if not encouraged, in many communities in the 18th and 19th centuries. German-speaking Americans, for example, were operating mother-tongue schools in Philadelphia as early as 1694, and in the mid-19th century a number of German–English parochial and public schools were established by the German communities in Baltimore, Cinncinnati, Cleveland, Indianapolis, Milwaukee, and St Louis. French-language public schools served the French-speaking communities in northern New England and in Louisiana, and Spanish-language schools served the Spanish-speaking communities in Florida, California, and New Mexico. Other languages (e.g. Norwegian, Lithuanian, Czech, Dutch) were part of the curriculum in areas with large numbers of immigrants from these linguistic communities. Most of these mother-tongue schools were established by recently arrived immigrant groups who were intent on preserving their native languages and cultures. Although there was no uniform language policy at that time, language loyalties were strong among the new European arrivals.

In some cases, bilingual school practices were authorized by state law. For instance, in 1847 Louisiana law authorized instruction in English, French, or both languages according to parental request. Spanish–English bilingual education was authorized in New Mexico in 1884 with the choice of language of instruction left to the school director. Reflecting a general tolerance for linguistic diversity in the United States at the time, Pennsylvania, Colorado, Illinois, Iowa, Kentucky, Minnesota, Missouri, Nebraska, and Oregon all passed laws sanctioning instruction in languages other than English (see Crawford, 1991; Malakoff & Hakuta, 1990, for further discussions).

The fact that these states passed laws sanctioning instruction in languages other than English, however, suggests that educational language policy had been an issue in some places for some groups during this time. In the 1880s, for example, laws restricting the use of German in public and parochial schools were passed in Wisconsin and Illinois (both laws were later repealed). And as the following discussion about the US government's attitude and action toward language use by the Cherokee clearly indicates, bilingual education policy is often not based on language or education issues at all. Bilingual education policy often reflects power struggles between particular social groups with competing political interests.

In 1828, the federal government recognized the language rights of the Cherokee tribe and agreed to subsidize the first newspaper published in an Indian language. In the 1830s, however, when the Cherokees used the printing press to advocate resistance to the forcible removal of Indians from the Eastern United States, the federal government confiscated and destroyed the printing press. After the Cherokee resettlement in Oklahoma, the tribe established an educational system of 21 schools that used the Sequoyah's Cherokee syllabary and achieved a 90% literacy rate in the native language. Although the Oklahoma Cherokees were using bilingual materials effectively, the US government soon mandated instruction only in English for Indians. This language policy coincided with a larger campaign to repress Indian culture. In 1879 the government began separating Indian children from their families and sending them to off-reservation boarding schools where students were punished for speaking their first language. The Cherokee's tribal printing press, which had been used to produce native-language teaching materials, again was confiscated. Cherokee educational attainment began to decline, and by 1969, only 40% of the tribe's adults were functionally literate (Crawford, 1991).

This section has illustrated that although there were competing discourses surrounding bilingual education in particular and linguistic and cultural diversity more generally, the dominant discourse in the United States emphasized tolerance until the end of the 19th century. Language of instruction was not an important or prominent issue in federal and state education policy throughout this early period. Because education policy was primarily left to the towns or districts to decide, the local government would levy the necessary taxes to support their school. In this way, schools were supported entirely by the community, teachers were often recruited from the community, and the language of instruction was frequently the language of the community (Malakoff & Hakuta, 1990).

Changing demographics and changing attitudes toward linguistic diversity

This section describes how changing immigration patterns to the United States in the 1900s challenged the discourse of tolerance that had characterized mainstream US schools and society until that time. Monolingualism in English came to be equated with political loyalty to the United States as public institutions and officials exerted strong pressure on new arrivals to abandon their native language and culture as quickly as possible. Linguistic and cultural diversity began to be negatively evaluated as un-American.

Waves of new immigrants from southern and eastern Europe who were predominantly Catholic, poorly educated, and lower class created a strong xenophobic reaction among the old immigrants who were primarly Anglo-Saxon, northern European and protestant. While the largest numbers of immigrants were European, other immigrant groups were increasingly represented and were therefore also the targets of discrimination. Chinese immigrants, for example, were attacked, barred from employment, disqualified from owning land, not allowed to vote due to English literacy requirements, and were not allowed to testify against whites in court (Crawford, 1992). Immigration restrictions at the turn of the century were directed toward the Chinese and Japanese. In 1882 Congress passed the Chinese Exclusion Act, and then in 1908 a 'Gentlemen's Agreement' restricted Japanese immigration. Although these policies were not the United States' first efforts to restrict immigration, they were the first policies to target immigrants of specific national origins (Lefcowitz, 1990).

The increase in numbers of immigrant children coincided with a national movement in the United States that advocated compulsory public school education for all children. City and town leaders, who largely controlled the local educational institutions, became increasingly worried about changes in their communities resulting from the large influx of 'foreigners'. The public school came to be seen as the primary institution for socializing immigrant children and for producing literate individuals who were assimilated into the democratic values of American society. This move raised the issue of a common measure of assimilation, and linguistic assimilation became a goal for immigrant children. State legislatures began to pass laws regulating the language of instruction in public and then in private schools, and by the end of the 19th century, California and New Mexico both had English-only instruction laws. In 1898 the US government banned the use of Spanish in newly acquired Puerto Rico, despite the fact that the entire population was Spanish-speaking (see Zentella, 1981, for a discussion of the history of US language policy in Puerto Rico).

An 'Americanization' campaign throughout the early 1900s increasingly equated proficiency in English with political loyalty. For example, the Nationality Act of 1906 required aliens seeking naturalization to speak English, a stipulation that was later codified in the Nationality Act of 1940. Mertz (1982) suggests that the ability to understand the ideas articulated in the US Constitution may have been a partial motivation for this campaign. Then, in 1915 the National Americanization Committee launched an 'English First' project in Detroit with the cooperation of the local Board of Commerce, and Henry Ford required that his immigrant employees take 'Americanization' classes. Boards of Education also became active in this effort; in 1918 the Superintendent of New York City schools said Americanization would cultivate 'an appreciation of the institutions of this country and absolute forgetfulness of all obligations or connections with other countries because of descent or birth' (cited by Crawford, 1991).

The expectation of linguistic and cultural assimilation was clearly expressed by Theodore Roosevelt in his 1919 address to the American Defense Society:

> for it is an outrage to discriminate against any such man because of creed or birthplace or origin. But this is predicated upon the man's becoming in very fact an American and nothing but an American. If he tried to keep segregated with men of his own origin and separated from the rest of America, then he isn't doing his part as an American...We have room for but one language here, and that is the English language, for we intend to see that the crucible turns our people out as Americans, of American nationality, and not as dwellers in a polyglot boarding-house. (cited by Crawford, 1992: 59)

Native-language maintenance began to be seen as un-American, and new arrivals attempted to assimilate to monolingualism in English as quickly as possible.

As World War I approached, attacks on language differences were aimed increasingly at Germans. The anti-foreign and, in particular, anti-German sentiment of this period speeded up the move towards linguistic and cultural assimilation, and essentially eliminated any talk of bilingual education. The remaining foreign language schools, most of which were German, were shut down either by laws mandating English-only instruction or by laws reserving public funds for English-only schools. In several states, laws were passed requiring compulsory education in

English in public schools. Numerous states attempted to ban teaching through the medium of a foreign language in both private and public schools under laws that carried criminal penalties. In 1919–20, the year following the war, 15 states legislated that English be the basic language of instruction, bringing the total to 34 states, and in 1923 Nebraska passed a constitutional amendment making English the official language of that state. At the federal level, a bill to designate English 'the language of instruction in all schools, public and private' was proposed to Congress but it failed to pass.

By the mid 1920s, major Americanization efforts were beginning to subside, and there were fewer attempts to legislate language loyalty. The 1923 Meyer *v.* Nebraska Supreme Court ruling marked an important move away from the linguistic xeno-phobia that had characterized the previous years. The court decided that the Nebraska state law prohibiting the teaching of a foreign language to elementary school students was unconstitutional and wrote,

> The protection of the Constitution extends to all, to those who speak other languages as well as to those born with English on the tongue. Perhaps it would be highly advantageous if all had a ready understanding of our ordinary speech, but this cannot be coerced by methods which conflict with the Constitution — a desirable end cannot be promoted by prohibited means. (Cited in Crawford, 1991: 24)

Major school systems were also beginning to lift bans on German studies throughout this period. Although English remained the language of the classroom, by 1934 the Bureau of Indian Affairs had retracted its official policy of repressing Indian vernaculars.

While English-only laws were largely repealed or ignored, the dominant dis-course about linguistic and cultural diversity had changed dramatically by the early 20th century. Learning in languages other than English was considered less than patriotic, and immigrant groups felt strong pressures to assimilate. English was increasingly seen as a means to attaining social power. The 'language-as-means' orientation that came to characterize mainstream US society assumed that without a high proficiency level in English, the non-native English-speaker should not expect a good education, a good job, or acceptance into middle- and upper-class society (Ruiz, 1994). As native languages became devalued by younger generations, there was less enthusiasm for preserving old-country customs. The Immigration Act of 1924, which legislated the strictest immigration quotas in the nation's history, drastically reduced the number of immigrants entering the United States. By the late 1930s, bilingual education was nearly eliminated from US schools, and interest in foreign languages fell dramatically. As Crawford (1991: 24) writes, 'within a generation, Americanization's goal of transforming a polyglot society into a mono-lingual one was largely achieved'.

The preceding discussion of the evolution of competing discourses about linguistic and cultural diversity in the United States provides an important historical foundation for understanding the currrent debate about bilingualism and bilingual education in the United States. Since very little attention was paid to the education of language minority children in the US between the 1920s and the 1960s, my discussion of the contemporary context of bilingual education policy, practice and research begins in the 1960s. The following discussion, in turn, provides an important foundation for understanding dual-language programs, in general, and Oyster Bilingual School, in particular.

BILINGUAL EDUCATION POLICY, PRACTICE AND RESEARCH SINCE THE 1960S

The Civil Rights Movement of the 1960s, with its emphasis on minority participation and ethnic pride, brought renewed interest in bilingual education. Since that time, questions about how schools can provide equitable and effective educational opportunities to an increasingly diverse student population have become a concern of the federal government. This part of the chapter discusses major sociopolitical movements, bilingual education research findings, and government policy decisions that have given rise to the increased interest in and funding for dual-language programs that we see in the United States in the 1990s. This overview is intended to make explicit some of the underlying ideologies that structure US discourses about how schools should organize themselves to educate a linguistically and culturally diverse student population.

This part of the chapter is divided into three parts, and illustrates the competing discourses that have surrounded bilingual education, in particular, and linguistic and cultural diversity more generally in the United States over the last four decades. The first section describes the discourse of tolerance that dominated the Civil Rights period of the 1960s and 1970s. The second section moves to the 1980s, and reviews the increasing English-only activity and growing opposition to bilingual education throughout US educational and societal discourse. The third section describes the heated debates that we currently hear in the 1990s about, for example, official language policy, immigration, bilingual education, and the role of schools in society. These contemporary debates reflect the larger ideological struggles between assimilation, on the one hand, and cultural pluralism, on the other, that the United States continues to grapple with as the nation moves into the 21st century. Together, this part of the chapter provides a foundation for understanding the historical and sociopolitical context of dual-language education today.

Dominant discourses of tolerance in the 1960s and 1970s

I begin this section with a discussion of the early civil rights legislation in the United States that reflected a concern for how schools could provide equal educational opportunities to all students regardless of their background. Changes in immigration law in the mid-1960s, however, led to unprecedented immigration from many parts of the world and bilingual education came to be seen as the solution to the problem of unequal educational opportunity for students defined as Limited English Proficient (LEP). The section continues with a description of the evolution of bilingual education and civil rights policy that sought to require schools to find ways to enable LEP students to acquire English and participate in school throughout this early period. I conclude this section with a discussion of the ideological discourses that surrounded bilingual education in educational practice, policy, and research at the end of the 1970s.

The Civil Rights Movement in the United States gave rise to the question: *How can schools provide equal educational opportunities to all students?* This question had its origin in the landmark Brown *v.* Board of Education case of 1954, in which the Supreme Court ruled that segregation according to race was unconstitutional and mandated 'education on equal terms'. Congress passed Title VI of the Civil Rights Act in 1964, which prohibited discrimination on the basis of race, color, or national origin in federally assisted programs and activities. To enforce Title VI compliance in federal education programs, the Office of Civil Rights (OCR) was established in the Department of Health, Education, and Welfare (HEW). HEW issued general Title VI guidelines in 1968 that held school systems 'responsible for assuring that students of a particular race, color, or national origin are not denied the opportunity to obtain the education generally obtained by other students in the system'.

The general climate of tolerance that pervaded this period was accompanied by major demographic changes due largely to changes in immigration law. The Immigration and Nationality Act Amendment of 1965 abolished the national origins quota system that had been established by the Immigration Act of 1924, and thereby eliminated national origin, race, or ancestry as a basis for immigration to the United States. Immigrants from all over the world came in unprecedented numbers. For the first time since the early 1900s the United States admitted large numbers of immigrants from Asian countries. Political and economic unrest throughout Latin America encouraged immigrants from many Latin American countries to move to the United States. The 1975 airlift of Vietnamese out of Saigon initiated an influx of Southeast Asian refugees that continues to this day. The former Soviet Union's brief opening to the West in the late 1970s led to an increased migration of Soviet Jews, and other changes in Eastern European political situations led to increased numbers of refugees from those countries (see Goode & Schneider, 1994, for further discussion of changing immigration trends at this time). Because the majority of these new immigrants did not speak English, those concerned with providing 'education on equal terms' needed to consider what this would mean for students from non-English-speaking backgrounds.

Bilingual education soon gained credence as a solution to the problem of how to provide equal educational opportunities to students who spoke languages other than

English. For example, in the late 1950s and early 1960s Dade County, Florida, saw a tremendous influx of Cuban refugees. In response, the Coral Way School in 1963 initiated an experimental dual-language program in the first three grades. The success of the program attracted local and national attention, and dual-language programs spread to other elementary and junior high schools in Dade County and to several other cities throughout the United States (García & Otheguy, 1995).

In 1968 Congress passed Title VII of the 1965 Elementary and Secondary Education Act, also known as the Bilingual Education Act. This legislation marked an important point in federal education policy because it defined bilingual education as falling within the domain of federal education policy. Title VII also undermined the English-only laws still on the books in many states (Malakoff & Hakuta, 1990).

Because research on bilingual education was in its infancy in the 1960s, no one could say with certainty whether bilingual education would be effective (Crawford, 1997). At that time, the prevailing assumption in research on bilingualism in the United States was that bilingualism was a disorder that could be corrected through instruction in a standard majority language (see Bialystok, 1994, for discussion; see also Peal & Lambert, 1962, for an important exception to this research trend). The Bilingual Education Act reflected this deficit-model thinking. Its focus was compensatory, and its programs were aimed at children who were both poor and 'educationally disadvantaged because of their inability to speak English'. As the label 'Limited English Proficient' (LEP) makes clear, these children were (and continue to be) defined by Title VII in terms of what they lack.

The first Bilingual Education Act was conceived of as an experiment, and it offered financial assistance to foster 'new and imaginative elementary and secondary school programs' to meet the special educational needs of LEP students. Title VII legitimized bilingual education programs, allocated funds to school districts that submitted voluntary proposals for special projects to address the needs of LEP students, and fostered research on bilingual education. The Bilingual Education Act of 1968, however, did not define bilingual education. As a result, the question of whether the goal of a bilingual program was to promote bilingualism or to speed transition to English was left unanswered. Ideally, educators were to develop special programs and instructional approaches that were appropriate for LEP students in their contexts, researchers would evaluate their effectiveness, and policymakers would respond accordingly (see Crawford, 1997, for further discussion).

Title VI of the Civil Rights Act became an important target of civil rights activism on behalf of language minority students across the United States in the 1970s. Mexican-American, Puerto Rican, and Chinese parents across the country began to file lawsuits challenging the schools' failure to address their children's language needs. These parents argued that equal treatment for LEP students meant unequal opportunity to succeed at school.

Of these civil rights cases, the 1974 Lau *v.* Nichols Supreme Court ruling had the most far-reaching consequences for language minority students in US public schools. Parents of nearly 3000 students in the San Francisco public school system (out of 16,500 students total) had filed a class-action suit complaining that only one-third of the Chinese students received supplemental English instruction. Both the Federal District Court and the Ninth Circuit Court of Appeals had found that because the Chinese students were receiving the same curriculum in the same classroom, they were being treated no differently than other students and therefore were not the victims of discrimination. Upon appeal, however, the Supreme Court unanimously found the San Francisco school system in violation of Title VI of the Civil Rights Act. Justice Douglas wrote in the preface to his opinion,

> No specific remedy is urged upon us. Teaching English to the students of Chinese ancestry who do not speak the language is one choice. Giving instruction to this group in Chinese is another. There may be others. Petitioners only ask that the Board of Education be directed to apply its expertise to the problem and rectify the situation.

In the end, San Francisco officials signed a consent decree agreeing to provide bilingual education for the city's Chinese, Philippino, and Hispanic children.

The Lau decision was extended to all public school districts that year with Congressional passage of the Equal Educational Opportunity Act (EEOA). The EEOA required school districts to 'take appropriate action to overcome language barriers that impede equal participation by its students in its instructional programs' (cited by Malakoff & Hakuta, 1990: 35). Because the EEOA did not specify what constituted 'appropriate action', the courts varied in their case-by-case interpretation of this act.

The Department of Health, Education, and Welfare (HEW) began to specify what 'appropriate action' would mean in 1975. J. Stanley Pottinger of the Office of Civil Rights (part of DHEW) issued a memorandum in May of that year demanding special language instruction for LEP students, prohibiting tracking of LEP students to special education classes, and mandating that school administrators communicate with parents in a language that the parents could understand. Later that year, HEW launched a major Title VI enforcement program known as the Lau Remedies. Recognizing that few school districts were providing any type of special instruction to LEP students, HEW began the effort by developing 'remedial' rather than 'compliance' guidelines for districts not in compliance with Title VI under Lau. These remedies specified proper approaches, methods, and procedures for (1) identifying and evaluating language minority students' English language skills; (2) determining appropriate instructional treatments; (3) deciding when LEP students were ready for mainstream classes; and (4) determining the professional standards to be met by teachers of language minority children. Elementary schools were required to provide LEP students special ESL instruction and subject-matter instruction through a student's dominant language until that student had mastered enough

English to learn in a monolingual English classroom. Three alternative instructional models were specified for elementary schools, all requiring schools 'to utilize the students' native language and culture factors in instruction'. From 1975 to 1980 HEW aggressively enforced Title VI compliance, with the Office of Civil Rights carrying out nearly 600 national-origin compliance reviews, leading to the negotiation of 359 Lau plans by July 1980 (Crawford, 1991).

Bilingual education legislation in the 1970s also began to clarify what a federally funded bilingual program would mean in practice. The 1974 amendments to the Bilingual Education Act encouraged transitional bilingual education and allowed maintenance bilingual education, but disallowed dual-language education (see Chapter 1 for discussion of these types of bilingual education). The 1974 Amendments to the Bilingual Education Act also marked the first time that schools receiving federal grants were required to include instruction in the child's native language. Native-language instruction was to be designed to allow children to progress in academic subjects while acquiring English. Title VII also authorized 'the voluntary enrollment to a limited degree of English-speaking children in bilingual education programs' accompanied by the prohibition that 'in no event shall the program be designed for the purpose of teaching a foreign language to English-speaking children'.

Like the 1974 amendments, the 1978 amendments to the Bilingual Education Act emphasized transitional bilingual education. The ban on programs designed to teach a foreign language to native English-speakers, however, was eliminated. These amendments stated that, 'the objective of the program shall be to assist children of Limited English Proficiency to improve their English language skills, and the participation of other children in the program must be for the principal purpose of contributing to the achievement of that objective'. Up to 40% of the children served by the bilingual education program could be native English-speakers 'in order to prevent the segregation of children on the basis of national origin'.

In sum, although the sociopolitical climate in the United States was generally relatively tolerant of linguistic and cultural diversity, most programs funded by the Bilingual Education Act over this time reflected an ideological assumption that the native language of the LEP student was a problem to be overcome. Because equal educational opportunity for these students was equated with English language proficiency, the majority of the federally funded bilingual programs were designed to help LEP students transition to English as quickly as possible. As a result, there was very little support for native-language maintenance throughout the period. Similarly, there was little interest in foreign language education. In 1979, the President's Commission on Foreign Langugage and International Studies released a report on American's 'scandalous' lack of foreign language ability, noting that not one state had foreign language requirements for high-school graduation, and many did not even require schools to offer foreign language instruction.

While federal education policy suggested a continued negative evaluation of LEP students' maintaining their native language, research efforts in the 1970s reflected a more positive ideological orientation toward bilingualism and bilingual education. Bilingualism came to be seen as a phenomenon worthy of scientific interest. Applied linguists focused on descriptions of the second-language acquisition process; sociolinguists documented and analyzed critical contextual features that distinguished one bilingual situation from another; and psycholinguists addressed questions about why some people learn languages more easily and thoroughly than others (see Bialystok, 1994, for further discussion of these research traditions). A number of studies conducted at this time were beginning to demonstrate cognitive benefits of bilingualism (Casanova, 1995). For example, the French immersion studies in Canada began to argue that there were cognitive benefits of bilingualism and bilingual education for language majority students (English-speakers) immersed in content-area instruction in French (see Genesee, 1987, for further discussion of French immersion studies).

As policymakers began to turn to research to determine whether bilingual education was an effective means of educating LEP students, research design and findings became the subject of heated ideological debate in the 1970s. For example, the 1977–78 American Institutes for Research (AIR) initial progress report on Title VII could find nothing conclusive to say about the overall effectiveness of bilingual education. Bilingual education researchers, however, were highly critical of this study's research design and worked to demonstrate the positive effects of bilingual education in the United States to counter the AIR report's claims. Troike (1978), for example, provided evidence that a well-designed bilingual program could be effective (see Crawford, 1991, for a discussion of the AIR report and the ensuing debate on research methods and findings). As the following section illustrates, questions about the effectiveness of bilingual education, in general, and about types of bilingual programs, in particular, became increasingly important throughout the 1980s.

Increasing English-only activity in the 1980s

This section describes the increasingly anti-bilingual education tone that came to dominate US public discourse in the 1980s. I begin with a discussion of demographics in the United States to explain the source and the nature of the unprecedented diversity in the country. I then move to a description of the increasing English-only movement in US governmental policy and public opinion, and relate it to the evolving discourses surrounding bilingual education research, policy, and practice throughout the decade.

As we saw in the first part of the chapter, dramatic changes in immigration have historically led to legislation that reflects the United States' efforts to deal with the changing face of America. The 1980s was no exception. The change to immigration law in 1965 resulted in a dramatic increase of immigrants from Latin America and

Asia (McGroarty, 1992). With the exception of the decade from 1901 to 1910, more immigrants arrived in the United States in the 1980s than in any other ten-year period since the census has been conducted (Ricento, 1995). This increase in the number of non-English-speaking immigrants was accompanied by an increase in number of native-born non-English-speakers.

These changes have resulted in a much more linguistically and culturally diverse US population. For example, while the overall population grew by 9.8% throughout the 1980s, US residents of Hispanic origin increased by 53% and those of Asian and Pacific Islander backgrounds by 108%. The minority language population grew by 38%; those who have difficulty with English by 37%; and the number of foreign-born residents, by 40% (see Crawford, 1997, for further discussion). Ricento (1995) provides the following description of how these changing demographics threatened 'many Americans' (who were presumably monolingual). He writes:

> many Americans, especially in large cities, felt their way of life was under assault. The sounds of Spanish, Korean, Chinese, Arabic, and many other languages were heard with increasing frequency in American towns and cities; the American border in the southwest was too porous; projections of demographic patterns showed that older immigrant populations were not replacing themselves as quickly as were the newer non-European groups. (Ricento: 1)

As in earlier times of major demographic change, the United States began to see increased English-only activity on a variety of fronts in the 1980s.

The Office of Civil Rights, for example, approved the first English-only Lau plan in 1980. Educators in Fairfax County, Virginia, had been fighting against federal pressure to establish a bilingual program since 1976. They argued that their LEP students represented more than 50 language groups, and therefore advocated an intensive ESL approach. ESL began to be popularized as a promising 'alternative method' to providing equal educational opportunities to LEP students.

English-only, however, came to mean much more than a promising alternative educational method. Conservative Republicans began to argue that linguistic diversity was a threat to national unity, and that English-only legislation was necessary to prevent national division along linguistic lines. In 1981, Senator Hayakawa (R-CA) proposed an English Language Amendment (ELA) to the Constitution that would make English the official language of the United States. This proposal, if approved by a two-thirds vote of the House and Senate, would have virtually banned all uses of languages other than English by federal, state, and local governments. When this ELA did not pass on the federal level, Senator Hayakawa joined forces with Dr John Tanton of the Federation for American Immigration Reform (FAIR), and founded US English in 1983. Because the initial strategy of amending the US constitution was unsuccessful, US English turned to the states. By 1984, Indiana, Kentucky, Tennessee, and Virginia had all passed English-only legislation. And as we see later, English-only activists targeted both the state and federal levels throughout the decade.

The Reagan Administration was also ideologically opposed to bilingual education. In 1981, President Reagan expressed his views on the relationship between bilingual education and participation in the US marketplace:

> It is absolutely wrong and against American concepts to have a bilingual program that is now openly, admittedly dedicated to preserving their native language and never getting them adequate in English so they can go out into the job market and participate. (Cited in Crawford, 1991: 43)

This official statement reflects the commonly-held (yet mistaken) assumption that time spent in a bilingual program studying content matter through the native language necessarily leads to reduced opportunity to acquire English (Crawford, 1997). It also overlooks the need for minority languages to serve the ethnic niches in local economies.

Social spending was cut drastically in the United States from 1980 to 1988 as the Reagan Revolution advocated smaller, more efficient government and less federal intervention in state and local affairs. According to Secada (1990), opponents of bilingual education had the advantage in this political battle because they could align their goal of less Congressional support for bilingual education with this political agenda. Bilingual education appropriations were hit particularly hard. Although the country had experienced a dramatic increase in the number of children eligible for Title VII programs and services, real spending under Title VII was reduced by 40%. Lau compliance reviews also plummeted during this period. Between 1981 and 1986, school districts were nine times less likely to be scheduled for a Title VI Lau review than in the period between 1976 and 1981 (Crawford, 1991).

Although funding for bilingual programs that would serve the large number of immigrant students during the Reagan era was drastically reduced during the 1980s, the judicial and legislative branches of the federal government recognized the country's responsibility to these children. For example, in the 1982 Plyer v. Doe case, the Supreme Court denied the state's right to exclude children of illegal immigrants from public schools. That same year, Congress passed the Emergency Immigration Act which acknowledged the impact of federal immigration policy on rising immigrant student enrollments and, hence, the federal government's financial responsibility to share in the cost of educating these students.

Interestingly, at the same time that strong voices in mainstream US public discourse criticized language minority groups' preservation and use of their native languages as a threat to national unity, foreign language education began to receive attention. The Education for Economic Security Act of 1982 authorized federal funding for the improvement of foreign language instruction. That same year, New York passed sweeping educational reforms that included foreign language requirements for all students. It is important to emphasize that foreign language instruction in the United States targets language majority students, not language minority students. These seemingly contradictory language policies suggest that bilingualism meant different things for language minority and language majority populations in the United States throughout this period.

A decade and a half after the Bilingual Education Act of 1968 was passed, the controversy surrounding bilingual education had grown rather than diminished (Lindholm, 1990). Bilingual education became the site of a heated ideological battle in the 1980s, and both sides turned to the results of evaluatory research to strengthen their positions. In 1980, the White House Regulatory Analysis and Review Group asked the Education Department to review the literature on the effectiveness of bilingual education. Baker and de Kanter's (1981) report, like the AIR report that the Education Department had released in 1978, found no consistent evidence supporting transitional bilingual education. Baker and de Kanter (1981) concluded their report advocating 'immersion in English' (note that here and later, this use of the term immersion does not mean immersing language majority students in the minority language as it does in Canada; it should perhaps more accurately be glossed as 'submersion in English'). Both the AIR study and the Baker and de Kanter (1981) report, however, were criticized for the researchers' lack of discrimination among various bilingual programs. The most ambitious of these critiques was Willig's (1985) sophisticated statistical meta-analysis of the same data that Baker and de Kanter (1981) had used. After adjusting for many variables that Baker and de Kanter (1981) had failed to take into account, such as student and teacher characteristics, instructional methods, and the language of achievement tests, Willig (1985) found that participation in bilingual programs consistently produced small to moderate differences favoring bilingual education (see Crawford, 1991; Casanova, 1995, for further discussion). While we still have no answer to the question about whether bilingual education is effective in general, the debates that arose in response to the bilingual education evaluation research in the 1980s have taught us that researchers must take into account the tremendous variation in how bilingual programs are implemented in practice because contextual variation matters (see Chapter 1 for further discussion).

The struggle to pass the 1984 Amendments to the Bilingual Education Act reflected the larger ideological debate about monolingual or bilingual instruction. Congress authorized both transitional bilingual education and developmental bilingul education (i.e. maintenance or dual-language), with 75% of the funding going to transitional bilingual programs. The stated goal of bilingual education was to enable LEP children 'to achieve competence in the English language...and to meet grade promotion and graduation standards'. Where possible, developmental bilingual programs were to enroll equal numbers of native English-speakers and English as a Second-language students. The Reagan Administration opposed the 1984 amendments because they did not authorize monolingual English instructional programs for LEP students. A compromise was reached by a bipartisan group of House members that authorized a third category of instructional grants for special alternative instructional programs (SAIP), a cover term for English-only approaches. Shortly thereafter, the then Secretary of Education, William J. Bennett, delivered a speech that questioned the effectiveness of bilingual education over other methods, including the 'sink or swim' approach. He called for eliminating the requirement that schools use native-language instruction to qualify for most grants under the Bilingual Education Act.

As the 1980s progressed, the official English debate became more intense. First, the English-only movement, characterized by a strong language-as-problem orientation, became increasingly active. In 1986, two more lobbies were organized to advocate declaring English the official language of the United States. English First, a project of the Committee to Protect the Family, was founded by Larry Pratt, a former Virginia state representative and president of Gun Owners of America. The American Ethnic Coalition, which was intended 'to prevent the division of America along language or ethnic lines', was organized by Lou Zaeske of Bryan, Texas. That same year, California passed Proposition 63, an extremely popular piece of legislation that made English the official state language (which the Ninth Circuit Court of Appeals later declared to be 'primarily symbolic'), and Georgia passed a non-binding resolution declaring English the official language of that state. In 1987, English-only attempted to ban the use of government funds in New York for the purposes of translation other than within the criminal justice system and in cases where emergency health care was needed. The organization also targeted bilingual education programs across the nation and the printing of ballots in languages other than English. Official English measures passed in Arkansas, Mississippi, North Carolina, North Dakota, and South Carolina in 1987, and in Arizona, Colorado, and Florida in 1988 (Arizona's English-only law was ruled unconstitutional in 1990; the measure's requirement that state officers and employees 'act in English and in no other language' was ruled to violate free speech guarantees under the First Amendment).

In response to the increasingly vocal English-only public discourse, the English-Plus Information Clearinghouse (EPIC) was established in 1986. EPIC was and continues to be a joint project of the National Immigration, Refugee, and Citizenship Forum and the Joint National Committee for Languages (a coalition of professional groups representing language teachers including the American Council on the Teaching of Foreign Languages [ACTFL], Teachers of English to Speakers of Other Languages [TESOL], and the National Council of Teachers of English [NCTE]). This project is characterized by a language-as-resource orientation, and promotes the concept of 'English-Plus' which

> holds that the national interest can be best served when all persons of our society have full access to effective opportunities to acquire strong English language proficiency plus mastery of a second or multiple languages.

That same year, Senator Breaux (D-LA) and Congressman Hayes (D-LA) proposed a Cultural Rights Amendment to the Constitution which would recognize 'the right of people to preserve, foster, and promote their respective historic, linguistic, and cultural origins'. Congress, however, took no action on this proposal. In 1988, the English-Plus Coalition was established. This group argued that since data show that immigrants are indeed learning English, it is counterproductive to require the officialization of English, particularly if it restricts freedom to draw on the resources, individual or social, of the native language. In the same spirit, English-plus resolutions were proposed in New Mexico, Oregon, and Washington in 1989.

The 1988 Amendments to the Bilingual Education Act, consistent with the dominant language-as-problem tone of public discourse throughout the 1980s, reflected an emphasis on the quick transition to English. The amendments allocated 75% of all grant monies to transitional bilingual education, and permitted the Secretary of Education to reserve up to 25% of Title VII appropriations for SAIPs. The remaining four bilingual education grant programs, including developmental bilingual programs, could either be funded or be set aside. Through these amendments, funding to state education agencies was increased, funding for SAIPs where only English was used was expanded, and participation in most Title VII programs was limited to three years.

At approximately the same time that federal policy was increasingly anti-bilingual, bilingual education research was becoming more methodologically rigorous, and was corroborating findings that well-implemented bilingual programs were effective. Between 1984 and 1988, the US Department of Education commisioned a team of researchers to conduct a major longitudinal study to compare the effectiveness of well-implemented examples of 'early-exit' bilingual education (TBE), 'late-exit' bilingual education (DBE), and English 'immersion (i.e. submersion) strategy' (SAIP). Over this four-year period, researchers charted the progress of 2000 Spanish-speaking students enrolled in well-implemented examples of these programs in California, Florida, New Jersey, New York, and Texas. They found that

(1) substantial amounts of native-language instruction do not slow down the acquisition of English language skills, including literacy;
(2) at the outset, early-exit students out-performed immersion students in English reading and mathematics, but there was little difference between the two groups after the third grade;
(3) early-exit and immersion students' rates of academic growth roughly paralleled those of English-proficient children in regular classrooms, but their achievement remained below national norms;
(4) in the late-exit model, growth curves became steeper the longer students remained in the program;
(5) late-exit students' achievement test scores in English reading, English language and mathematics approached (but did not quite reach) national norms by the sixth grade. (Ramirez *et al.*, 1991)

By the mid-1980s, there was a growing body of research demonstrating that well-designed bilingual programs can be an effective means of facilitating language minority students' academic achievement and English-language acquisition (see Crawford, 1997, for a review of this literature). These benefits are pronounced when the bilingualism is attained in an additive fashion (Hakuta, 1990).

The preceding section illustrated that although the dominant educational and societal discourses in mainstream US society throughout the 1980s increasingly emphasized monolingualism in English, researchers were beginning to positively evaluate bilingualism and bilingual education. I now move to the 1990s, and describe the competing discourses surrounding linguistic and cultural diversity that we hear in the United States today.

The 1990s: Diversity as problem or diversity as resource?

This section studies the question of how US schools can provide educational opportunities to all of their students into the 1990s. I begin this section with a brief discussion of the economic and demographic situation in the United States today. I then review the heated debates that we can hear about official language policy, immigration, bilingual education, and the role of schools in US society. This section provides the necessary background information for understanding how the increasing interest in and funding for dual-language programs in the 1990s relates to the competing educational and societal discourses about linguistic and cultural diversity more generally in the United States today.

The question of *how can US schools provide equitable and effective education to an increasingly diverse population* cannot be addressed without considering the economic situation of the country as we approach the 21st century. Concerns about how the US economy can compete effectively in a high-tech global marketplace and about how US citizens can be assured of an economically viable future dominate public discourse. Jobs increasingly require literacy and computer-based skills. At the same time, resources are limited, low educational achievement of language minority and language majority students is a national concern, and the gap between rich and poor is increasing. As we have seen in the past, linguistic xenophobia increases when the country perceives a national crisis, and 'foreigners' are often targeted for blame. Currently we hear strong voices on all sides of the issues. Underlying these debates is the question of whether the US population assumes that linguistic and cultural diversity is a problem to be overcome or a resource to be developed. The way this question is answered reflects an ideological orientation toward either linguistic and cultural assimilation, on the one hand, or toward multilingualism and cultural pluralism, on the other. As we saw in Chapter 1, these ideological orientations in turn underlie the different types of bilingual education found in US public schools today.

First, we need to understand the nature and source of the diversity that US schools and society are currently experiencing. The 1990 census counted 6.3 million youths aged 5–17 who speak languages other than English at home (a 38% increase over the previous decade), and 22% of school-aged children, or 9.9 million, reported living in a home where a non-English language was spoken. While it is difficult to know exactly how many of these language minority children are LEP, approximately 38% reported speaking English less than 'very well' on the 1990 census. In 1993–94, the State Education Agencies (SEAs) reported that 7% of the nation's elementary and secondary school population were LEP, with annual increases averaging nearly 10%. While Spanish is by far the most prevalent minority langauge, spoken by about three out of four LEP students, the range of languages spoken by the LEP population is increasing (Crawford, 1997).

As we have seen in times of economic and/or political uncertainty in the past, immigration becomes a target for reform. Congress passed the Immigration Act of 1990 which increased the level of employment-based immigration and allotted a higher proportion of visas to highly skilled immigrants. This Act revised the numerical limits and preference categories used to regulate immigration, and resulted in a rise in immigration from most European countries. The Immigration Accountability Act, the Immigration Moratorium Act, and the Immigrant Financial Responsibility and Sponsorshiop Act were introduced to Congress in 1995; these three bills attempted to limit both legal and illegal immigration to the United States and to limit immigrants' access to government services. On the state level, in 1994 California passed Proposition 187, which essentially withholds government services and benefits to 'illegal' immigrants (primarily Mexican) in the state, including support to families with dependent children, most health care, and all education to children of undocumented immigrant parents. Just as we saw in the pre-World War I period, immigration legislation is intended to attract 'desirable' immigrants (e.g. highly skilled, English-speaking, European) and exclude 'undesirables' (e.g. Mexican, low-income, non-English-speaking, unskilled).

While immigration accounts for the majority of the linguistic diversity in the United States, it is not the only source of this diversity. According to Crawford (1997), an estimated 41% of elementary school LEP children are native born. These are children of both recent immigrants and long-established ethnic groups such as Mexican Americans, Puerto Ricans, American Indians, Alaskan Natives, Chinese Americans and others. Because the average age of the ethnic minority population is about five years less than the national average, a large percentage of ethnic minorities are in their most active childbearing years; as a result, population growth is greater within these groups (Cortés, 1986; cited by Lindholm, 1990). Strict immigration legislation will not solve the problem of how to provide opportunities to these native-born LEP children.

Throughout this book, I argue that providing equitable and effective education to all students is about much more than language. Socioeconomic class has repeatedly been linked to educational outcomes, and language minority students tend disproportionately to be low-income in the United States. According to the 1990 census, the group of students who reported some difficulty with English was 12 times as likely as native English-speakers to have completed less than five years of schooling and half as likely to have graduated from high school; children from these households were 50% more likely to live in poverty. The segregation of low-income minority populations in low-performing inner-city schools has also been associated with minority students' underachievement. For example in 1991–92, 73% of Hispanic children attended elementary and secondary schools with predominantly minority enrollments, up from 55% in 1968–69. This pattern, however, is not consistent across ethnic groups. In 1991–2, about half of the LEP Hispanic first graders were in high poverty schools while only 8% of LEP Asian first graders were in such schools (see Crawford, 1997, for a review of this literature). It is obvious that in order to understand language minority achievement in US schools, we must take into account complex relationships among, for example, socioeconomic class, language background, and ethnicity.

Bilingual education researchers, like many researchers concerned with minority student participation and achievement in schools, increasingly recognize relationships between ideological orientations toward language minority students and their participation and achievement in school. Just as the language-as-problem orientation that characterizes transitional bilingual and ESL programs has been found to have negative implications for LEP students' educational opportunities, the deficit model of schooling that has dominated minority education in US schools has been found to limit minority students' opportunities to participate and achieve (see Chapter 3 for further discussion). Dual-language programs, characterized by a language-as-resource orientation, offer a potentially promising alternative to this deficit model thinking.

As I mentioned in Chapter 1, dual-language programs have been receiving increasing attention and funding in the United States because they are supposed to combine the best features of immersion education for language majority students and bilingual education for language minority students. In 1991, the Office of Educational Research and Improvement of the US Department of Education funded a long-term research project on dual-language education. The first phase of the project involved a nationwide survey of dual-language programs. Information from the survey was used to create a comprehensive directory of dual-language programs in order to facilitate the sharing and exchange of information among current and prospective programs (Christian & Whitcher, 1995). The survey also formed the basis for further research currently being conducted by the Center for Applied Linguistics in Washington, DC, on how language and cognitive development can be promoted in dual-language programs (see Chapter 1 for a discussion of the findings of this survey).

At the same time that researchers are criticizing the language-as-problem orientation that has characterized mainstream US educational discourse and conducting research on dual-language programs, English-only is making strides in the national debate about linguistic diversity. In 1991, English-only advocates changed their strategy. Recognizing the long odds against ratifying a constitutional amendment, they began to promote a statutory form of Official English. Such a bill would apply to the federal government alone and would require only a simple majority vote in Congress as well as the President's signature to become law. In 1993, the Languages for All People Initiative was introduced to Congress, which if passed would make English the official language of the government. While recognizing the cultural importance of many languages spoken in the United States, this initiative warned of the potential of language diversity to foment social discord and disintegration. Then, in 1995, the National Language Act was introduced to Congress by Congressman King (R-NY), which would make English the official language of the US Government, terminate federal support of bilingual education programs by repealing the Bilingual Education Act, repeal Section 4 of the Voting Rights Act (which allows for bilingual ballots), and amend the Immigration and Nationality Act.

This increasing English-only activity has not gone without response. The passage of the Native American Languages Act of 1992, for example, attempts to support the maintenance of native American languages, especially in communities in which language shift would result in the total extinction of the language. In 1995, an English-plus resolution was introduced to Congress by Congressman Serrano (D-NY). This resolution recognizes that English is the primary language of the United States, that many residents of the US speak native languages other than English, and that this linguistic diversity poses no threat to English. It argues that

> 'English-only' measures, or proposals to designate English as the sole official language of the United States, would violate traditions of cultural pluralism, divide communities along ethnic lines, jeopardize the provision of law enforcement, public health, education, and other vital services to those whose English is limited, impair government efficiency, and undercut the national interest by hindering the development of language, violate international human rights treaties to which the United States is a signatory, and contradict the spirit of the 1923 Supreme Court case Meyer v. Nebraska, wherein the Court declared that 'The protection of the Constitution extends to all; to those who speak other languages as well as to those born with English on the tongue'. (H.R. 83, 13 July, 1995)

The English-plus resolution advocated that the US government pursue policies that

(1) enable all residents to become fully proficient in English;
(2) conserve and develop the Nation's linguistic resources by encouraging all residents to learn or maintain skills in a language other than English;
(3) assist Native Americans, Native Alaskans, Native Hawaiians, and other peoples indigenous to the United States in their efforts to prevent extinction of their languages and cultures;
(4) continue to provide services in languages other than English as needed to facilitate access to essential functions of government, promote public health and safety, ensure due process, promote equal educational opportunity, and protect fundamental rights; and

(5) recognize the importance of multilingualism to vital American interests and individual rights, and oppose English-only measures and similar language restrictionist measures.

In 1996 the House of Representatives approved the English Language Empowerment Act declaring English the official language of government. Because the Senate did not approve this legislation, the measure failed to become law. Under this legislation (H.R. 123), any federal official or contractor who communicates in writing using a non-English language is subject to suit by any member of the public. The bill also prohibits all bilingual voting assistance by repealing key provisions of the Voting Rights Act. Much uncertainty remains about the practical impact of H.R. 123 on language services, including bilingual education, Social Security pamphlets, and sign-language interpreting. If passed, its interpretation would almost certainly be determined by the courts.

The English-only/English-plus debate has also been waged on the state level, resulting in considerable state legislation throughout the 1990s. On the English-only side, Alabama passed a constitutional amendment adopting English as the official state language in 1990 and Montana, New Hampshire, and South Dakota passed official English laws in 1995. At the time of this writing, Connecticut, Iowa, Kansas, Massachusetts, Michigan, Missouri, New Jersey, New York, Ohio, Utah, Washington, and Wisconsin were considering English-only legislation. On the English-plus side, Puerto Rico passed legislation making Spanish and English its offical languages in 1991. As this list makes clear, English-only is making inroads in not only federal but also state level legislation.

Despite attacks on funding for native-language maintenance, proficiency in foreign languages was positively evaluated by the National Security Education Act of 1993. In order to fulfill its goal of staffing American intelligence agencies and diplomatic posts with more multilingual personnel, the Act provided scholarships for undergraduates to study abroad, grants to colleges and universities to improve cultural and language training, and fellowships for graduate students to study in other countries.

The 1994 Amendments to the Bilingual Education Act stand in stark contrast to the language-as-problem orientation that characterized much of US societal discourse in the 1990s as well as previous versions of the Bilingual Education Act itself, and provide strong evidence that public discourses are mixed and at times contradictory. The change in the Bilingual Education Act came in response to developments in educational research over the past three decades about how children acquire languages and how they excel in other subjects. According to Crawford (1997: 1), the new law incorporated two important principles,

- Given access to challenging curriculum, language minority and limited English Proficient (LEP) students can achieve to the same high standards as other students.

- Proficient bilingualism is a desirable goal, which can bring cognitive, academic, cultural, and economic benefits to individuals and to the nation.

These amendments included new provisions to reinforce professional development programs, increase attention to language maintenance and foreign-language instruction, improve research and evaluation at the state and local levels, supply additional funds for immigrant education, and allow participation of some private school students. The amendments also included a provision which would require the secretary to 'give priority to applications which provide for the development of bilingual proficiency for all participating students'. This provision resulted in funding for a large number of new dual-language programs throughout the United States. For the first time in its history, the Bilingual Education Act explicitly recognized the value of bilingualism on the individual level for language minority and language majority students, and on the national level as a tool for cross-cultural understanding as well as a vital resource in the global economy.

Echoing familiar themes from the movement for school reform in the United States, the 1994 Amendments to the Bilingual Education Act placed new emphasis on high standards for LEP and language minority students. Efforts were made to address LEP students' concerns in the context of major innovations designed to improve schooling for all students (see Crawford, 1997 for details of these innovations). As Crawford (1997: 2) writes:

> These innovations also helped to frame the discussion of bilingual education in a larger policy context. No longer were LEP students viewed as a special case, defined primarily by a language 'deficit' and a need for compensatory programs. Now they were seen as children who share the same capabilities, face many of the same obstacles, and deserve all of the same opportunities as other American children. No longer was the policy focused narrowly on language of instruction — whether to favor bilingual or English-only approaches. Now a broad range of questions was considered, stressing the inclusion of language minority students in every step toward school reform.

Shortly after the reauthorization of Title VII, however, the policy it embodied came under fierce attack on Capitol Hill and in the press. Congress considered legislation to repeal the law and eliminate its funding. While this never happened, the political climate in the United States in the mid to late 1990s is heavily anti-bilingual. Title VII appropriations were reduced by 38% between 1994 and 1996, forcing deep cuts in grants for instructional programs, terminating aid for teacher training, and reducing the budgets for research, evaluation, and other support services.

The preceding section has provided a brief review of immigration, language, and education policy and practice in the United States throughout the 1990s. This discussion illustrates the complexity involved in understanding what bilingual education means in the United States today and how and why actual bilingual programs function the way that they do in their specific historical and social locations. Contemporary bilingual education programs are embedded in competing discourses about linguistic and cultural diversity in the United States. These discourses together reflect a larger ideological struggle between pluralism, on the one hand, and assimilation, on the other, that suggests a United States grappling with what kind of a nation it imagines itself to be as it moves into the 21st century. An individual bilingual program like Oyster Bilingual School must be understood in relation to these larger complex and contradictory discourses.

CONCLUSION

This chapter provided a historical discussion of the societal discourses surrounding bilingual education in the United States today. We saw in the first part of the chapter that, contrary to popular opinion, bilingualism and bilingual education were widespread in many communities in the United States throughout the majority of the nation's history. I also identified important exceptions to the dominant discourse of tolerance to argue that bilingual education policy in the United States has always been about much more than language or educational issues. Since early in US history, we have heard competing discourses surrounding language policy in particular and linguistic and cultural diversity more generally that reflect and structure power relations between social groups at particular moments in time.

Changing immigration patterns to the United States in the early 1900s, and the US response to this demographic movement, highlights the sociopolitical nature of bilingual education. The unprecedented linguistic and cultural diversity that the country experienced at that time challenged the discourse of tolerance that had characterized mainstream US schools and society. Monolingualism in English came to be equated with political loyalty to the United States, and new immigrants felt strong pressure to assimilate. In about one generation, the dominant discourse about linguistic and cultural diversity in the United States had been radically transformed.

The second part of the chapter looked more closely at policy, research, and practice in the United States since the 1960s, and illustrated the competing discourses that have surrounded bilingual education in particular and linguistic and cultural diversity more generally in the United States over the last four decades. The 1960s and 1970s were dominated by a discourse of tolerance, which gave rise to federal legislation that requires schools to provide equal educational opportunities to all of their students. In contrast, the 1980s saw increasing English-only activity and growing opposition to bilingual education throughout US educational and societal discourse. Throughout the 1990s, we hear heated ideological debates about official language policy, immigration, bilingual education, and the role of schools in society. These debates reflect a United States struggling with linguistic and cultural diversity as it moves into the 21st century, and they provide a context for understanding dual-language programs today.

As we have seen throughout this historical overview, our ideological beliefs about linguistic and cultural diversity reflect and shape the kinds of institutions we create in society. How we see linguistic and cultural diversity, for example, as a problem to be solved through assimilation to monolingualism in English or as a resource to be developed through bilingualism and cultural pluralism, has major implications for the ways that we organize our schools and other institutions in society. These ideological orientations have important consequences for language minority students, language majority students, and the nation as a whole.

Whatever our ideological beliefs, several facts are clear. There is tremendous linguistic and cultural diversity in the United States, and this diversity will almost certainly increase over time. It is important to emphasize, however, that bilingualism is not new in the United States and there is no evidence that English is losing ground to other languages in the United States. Although more world languages are spoken in the US today than ever before, this is a quantitative rather than a qualitative difference. Immigrants to the United States learned English in the past without any official English laws on the federal level, and there was no threat to English. While there is an assumption that newcomers to the United States are learning English more slowly now than in previous generations, today's immigrants in fact appear to be acquiring English more rapidly than ever before (Crawford, 1997). As the number of minority language speakers is projected to grow into the next century, the number of bilinguals is growing even faster.

The purpose of this book is to describe how one successful dual-language program provides equitable and effective educational opportunities to its linguistically and culturally diverse student population. This chapter has illustrated that the tolerance for linguistic diversity and cultural pluralism that characterizes well-implemented dual-language programs like the one at Oyster Bilingual School has a long-standing history in the United States. If implemented properly, dual-language programs do not restrict language minority students' opportunities to learn English nor do they threaten English-speaking students' opportunities to achieve academically. Instead, well-implemented dual-language programs provide all students the opportunity to become bilingual and biliterate, achieve academically through two languages, and develop improved intergroup understanding and relations.

It is important to emphasize, however, that we still know very little about how actual dual-language programs function on the local level. I suggest that researchers direct their efforts toward understanding how actual educators work with their local communities to design and implement bilingual programs that meet the needs of their target populations. Such detailed understanding across specific bilingual programs can then provide the basis for more grounded, less politicized discussions of whether and how bilingual programs provide equitable and effective means of educating the language minority and language majority students they serve.

CHAPTER 3

Schools as Cultural Communication Systems:The Example of Mainstream US Educational Discourse

Chapter 2 provided an overview of the history of bilingual education in the United States to illustrate the societal discourses surrounding dual-language education in the country. The Oyster Bilingual School educators believe that mainstream US schools discriminate against minority students, and they have organized their bilingual program to provide an alternative to those schools for their students. This chapter provides a detailed description of mainstream US educational discourse practices that the Oyster educators oppose, as well as a theoretical framework for understanding the significance of Oyster Bilingual School's alternative educational discourse.

The chapter begins with a brief theoretical discussion of schools as cultural communication systems. I then review and synthesize the literature on mainstream US educational discourse practices, and I emphasize implications of these practices for minority students. Conceptualizing schools as cultural communication systems provides an integrated means of understanding how minority students are positioned relative to majority students in mainstream US schools. Language minority students' negative positioning as LEP; as students who do not behave appropriately in classroom interaction; whose histories, arts, literatures, contributions, and perspectives are marginalized, stereotyped, or not included in the curriculum content; and whose performance is not validly assessed, can together contribute to the subordinate minority social role, first in school and later in mainstream US society. From the perspective of the mainstream US school, the language minority student has two options: assimilate to the positively evaluated majority social identity and succeed, or maintain the negatively evaluated minority social identity and fail.

Social reproduction, however, is not the only choice. The third part of this chapter provides a theoretical discussion that explains how social identities are jointly constructed through discourse. Recognizing the constitutive nature of discourse means that we have choices in how we define ourselves, each other, and the communities in which we live. This theoretical orientation prepares us for understanding how the Oyster Bilingual School has constituted itself by an alternative educational discourse that provides more opportunities to its language minority and language majority students than are generally available to either group in mainstream US schools and society.

SCHOOLS AS CULTURAL COMMUNICATION SYSTEMS

My work assumes that schools can be understood as cultural communication systems. I borrow Carbaugh's (1990) framework for modeling cultural communication systems to illustrate how the interrelated parts of the school fit together and mutually influence each other. Figure 5 shows what Carbaugh (1990) identifies as the main elements of any cultural communication system.

I use this framework to model how the cultural identities of minority students are negotiated and displayed through educational discourse systems, first in mainstream

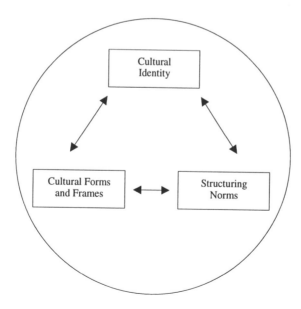

Figure 5 The circularity of a cultural communication system (Carbaugh 1990: 166)

US schools and then in the Oyster Bilingual School (I use the terms 'cultural communication system' and 'discourse system' interchangeably).

My discussion of the mainstream US educational system is based on a review and synthesis of the literature and is presented later in this chapter. There I argue that the cultural identities of minority students are produced and reproduced as subordinate through the organization of teaching and learning in mainstream US schools. My discussion of the Oyster Bilingual School system is based on a two-year ethnographic/discourse analytic study of how their dual-language program functions on the local level. Throughout Chapters 5–10, I argue that the Oyster educators have rejected mainstream US definitions of minority students as subordinate, and illustrate how they have organized teaching and learning in a way that defines minority and majority students more or less equally.

Before I discuss Carbaugh's (1990) framework, I want to emphasize that I do not assume that every educator or student in either the mainstream US educational discourse system or in the Oyster educational discourse system believes, thinks, and behaves in the same way. As I mentioned in Chapter 1, there are always competing discourses in any cultural context. The identification of more general cultural patterns in each of these discourse systems, however, can provide considerable insight into how the overall systems function. A comparative discussion of the general cultural patterns throughout mainstream US schools, on the one hand, and throughout Oyster Bilingual School, on the other, also highlights major differences in how these systems are organized, as well as the implications of those differences for minority students.

I begin my discussion of Carbaugh's (1990) heuristic with 'cultural identity'. Carbaugh (1990) stresses that cultural identity is encoded everywhere in communication, but that it is not coded exactly the same way in all contexts. His review of cultural identity display through cultural communication patterns in distinct cultural contexts illustrates considerable cross-cultural variation in the notion of cultural identity (see Carbaugh, 1990, for examples and discussion). He suggests that one way to unravel the variation is to ask: *What cultural model(s) for the person is being coded in a situation?* and *How is this coding accomplished interactionally?* My concern in this study is to understand the cultural identities of students and teachers and their relation to each other, first within the mainstream US educational discourse system, and then within Oyster's alternative educational discourse system.

The second part of Carbaugh's (1990) framework is 'cultural frames and forms for performance'. Carbaugh (1990) claims that every group has some sequences for communicating that it can and does identify. To understand such culturally coded sequences of communication, Carbaugh (1990) suggests asking the following questions: *What means of expression does the frame make available? What goals are being targeted? What is the relationship between this kind of talk and the cultural identity under study? Is this talk aligned with it? Valued? Why or why not?* This study compares local definitions of teaching, learning, and bilingual education within the mainstream US educational discourse system and within the Oyster alternative educational discourse system. In each case, I pay close attention to how minority students are defined relative to majority students through these cultural forms and frames at school.

Carbaugh (1990) argues that a detailed analysis of the 'structuring norms' within the cultural communication system allows for an understanding of how cultural identities and cultural frames and forms for performance are interactionally accomplished. He suggests that we consider structuring norms as made up of three parts: (1) the structuring of interaction, (2) the structuring of information, and (3) the structuring of content. Questions such as the following guide the analysis of this component of the cultural system: *Who should talk? How much should one say? How are turns exchanged? What constitutes appropriate participation? What topics are discussed?* and *How are those topics organized and developed?* To investigate structuring norms within the mainstream US and Oyster educational discourse systems, I analyze the curriculum content and the patterns of interaction within the classroom and throughout the school.

Carbaugh (1990) emphasizes several important characteristics of cultural communication systems. He writes:

> The model is *circular* because each element contributes to the others while itself being influenced by the others. Put another way, each element is both a medium, and outcome, of the communication process. It is this dynamic that makes cultural communication systems more or less stable, and more or less resistant to change, because any element (or subpart) is being continually reinforced by others within the system (cf. Scollon & Scollon, 1981: 192). (Carbaugh, 1990: 166–7, emphasis in original)

Because each discourse system is historically grounded, learned, and locally managed through the face-to-face interaction, there is likely to be considerable variation in how the parts of the system are actually realized within and across cultural contexts. As I discuss in more detail later in the chapter, there is also room for some individual choice in how actual individuals participate in specific language-mediated activities and in the cultural identities they take on. The degree of individual choice is, of course, constrained by the political, economic, and social context in which the discourse system is embedded.

The preceding discussion provides a framework for understanding how minority and majority students are defined through the mainstream US educational discourse system. I turn now to a discussion of that system.

THE MAINSTREAM US EDUCATIONAL DISCOURSE SYSTEM

Consistent with a well-established tradition of sociolinguistically-informed research on education of minority students in US schools (e.g. Scollon & Scollon, 1981; Erickson & Shultz, 1982; Heath, 1983; Philips, 1983), I assume that mainstream US public schools are generally guided by Standard English-speaking, white middle-class norms of interaction and interpretation. This part of the chapter provides a discussion of the basic components of the mainstream US educational discourse system and how they fit together in order to illustrate how this system functions. I begin with the mainstream US definition of students and teachers, continue with the mainstream US notions of teaching and learning, and conclude with the norms that structure mainstream US classroom interaction. This discussion offers a basis for understanding the cultural identities that are generally available to minority students in mainstream US educational discourse.

The following synthesis of research in mainstream US schools is not intended to suggest that all mainstream US classrooms and programs are constituted by identical norms of interaction and interpretation. Rather, I present this theoretical discussion (which is based on empirical evidence) to provide a more concrete understanding of the underlying assumption of homogeneity that the Oyster educators oppose.

What is a student? What is a teacher?

The meanings of student and teacher are relevant to a discussion of cultural identity in classroom discourse systems. The fact that mainstream US educational discourse requires students to speak Standard English and to behave according to white middle-class norms in order for them to participate effectively in classroom activities and to achieve in school (e.g. Heath, 1983; Philips, 1983) suggests an underlying assumption of (or at least a preference for) a homogeneous Standard English-speaking white middle-class student population. Since students in mainstream US schools are all assumed to be the same, there is no need for teachers to be concerned about who students are relative to each other, or with the diverse backgrounds that students bring with them to the classroom. Historically, the assumption of a homogeneous Standard English-speaking white middle-class student population was not problematic since the overwhelming majority were Standard English-speaking white middle class students. The assumption that all of the students are the same (sometimes described as 'color blind') reflects the mainstream US ideal of equality.

Within the mainstream US educational model, teachers are also assumed and expected to behave and to interpret student behavior according to Standard English-speaking, white middle-class norms. If the teacher comes from a different sociocultural background, he or she is expected to have assimilated to mainstream US norms of interaction and interpretation. Since the students and teachers are assumed to share the same underlying norms of interaction and interpretation, cross-cultural miscommunication between teachers and students theoretically is not an issue.

The role relationship between the teacher and students in the mainstream US educational model is very clearly defined: there is an asymmetrical power relationship with the teacher being older and more knowledgeable than the students (Holmes, 1978). Reciprocally, the students are defined as unknowing (at least with respect to the curriculum content being presented), and in need of the teacher's knowledge.

What is teaching? What is learning?

The meanings of teaching and learning structure my description of cultural frames and forms for performance within mainstream US educational discourse. The transmission model of teaching and learning characterizes the mainstream US classroom (Cummins, 1989). According to this model, the teacher transmits the curriculum content to the recipient student population. The sentence *The teacher teaches math to the students* grammatically reflects the transmission model. *The teacher* is represented as the grammatical subject of the sentence and as the agent in the process, or the one who is doing the action, and therefore central to the process. *Math* is represented as the grammatical object, which functions as the goal of the process *teach. The students* are represented as recipients of the object/goal *math*. In other words, the students are represented as circumstances in, not central to, the teaching process. Since the students are assumed to be homogeneous and to share the same background knowledge, the content can be received and learned by all of the students in approximately the same way.

Figure 6 illustrates the social space of the traditional classroom, which is often characterized by a competitive atmosphere (Kessler, 1992).

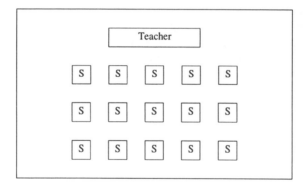

Figure 6 The social space of the mainstream US classroom

Symbolically reflecting the role relationships of the teacher as more powerful, more knowledgeable, and central to the transmission of knowledge process, and the students as a homogeneous group receiving the transmitted curriculum content, all of the desks face the teacher. The students are generally discouraged from talking with one another during the official classroom floor because such talk is viewed as potentially disruptive and not as part of the teaching and learning process. The students are encouraged to compete with each other for the teacher's attention and for the opportunity to demonstrate their mastery of content. The competitive classroom atmosphere, with its emphasis on individual achievement, can be understood as a reflection and perpetuation of mainstream US societal values of individualism and competition because in mainstream US society, competition among individuals is assumed to yield the best results (Scollon & Scollon, 1995).

The transmission model of teaching and learning can be seen to underlie many teacher preparation programs, and is reflected in the curriculum offerings. Pre-service teachers are required to take courses such as 'Teaching Social Studies', 'Teaching Math', and 'Teaching Science', and are certified in these content-areas. Again, the focus is on the content that is to be transmitted, and not on the students. Because the students are assumed to be homogeneous in the mainstream US educational model, this assumption should not be problematic.

Mainstream US curriculum content and assessment practices also reflect the assumption of a homogeneous (white) student population. Sleeter and Grant's (1991) extensive study of the treatment of various groups across the major subject areas used in grades 1 through 8 found the following:

- Whites still consistently dominate textbooks, although their margin of dominance varies.
- Whites receive the most attention and dominate the story line and lists of accomplishments in most textbooks.
- Women and people of color are shown in a much more limited range of roles than are White males.
- Textbooks contain very little about contemporary race relations or the issues that concern most people of color and women.
- Textbooks continue to convey an image of harmony among different groups and contentment with the status quo (cited by Nieto, 1992: 75).

Standardized national curriculum is the norm, and standardized tests are assumed to be an appropriate measure for all students. Academic achievement is often measured solely by standardized tests.

What are the norms that structure the classroom discourse?

To explore structuring norms within the mainstream US educational system, I synthesize research findings by Holmes (1978), Chaudron (1988), Cazden (1988), Lemke (1991), and Kessler (1992) in both first- and second-language classrooms. Because the teacher is defined as more knowledgeable than the students, he/she (generally she) is attributed the dominant role in the teaching–learning process. Teachers do the majority of the talking in the classroom and have the right to hold the floor at all times. Cazden (1988) considers teacher-talk to be its own register, characterized by the frequency of the known-answer question and the immediate evaluation of the student's response. Students have the obligation to listen, or at least not to interrupt. Students compete with each other for the teacher's recognition, as reflected in their bidding to be nominated by the teacher in the Initiation–Response–Evaluation (IRE) structure described below. Similarly, students compete with each other for grades. This competition for grades is reflected in the mainstream US assumption that grades should follow the normal bell curve, and that a teacher should not award too many A's.

The IRE structure, which has been identified as the primary interactional routine in the mainstream US classroom, contributes to the teacher's control/dominance. Although other participation frameworks are possible (e.g. lecture or teacher monologue, individual desk work, small group work, and one-to-one teacher–student interaction), the IRE is the participation framework most frequently found. I therefore limit my discussion to the parts of this triad.

Initiation

The teacher generally initiates the exchange because the teacher and not the student has the right to question at any time (students may question the teacher, but only at the appropriate time and in an appropriate manner). In general, teachers do not ask questions because they want to know the information; rather teachers ask questions because they want to know whether students know the information. The teacher then has the right to nominate a student to answer.

Response

The student who has been nominated by the teacher is obligated to respond to the question at the appropriate moment and in the appropriate manner. Students who do not respond when nominated by the teacher are viewed as unknowing, uncooperative or, at times, deliberately disruptive. If the teacher asks a question and does not nominate a particular student, all of the students are expected to bid to be nominated. Bidding is also appropriate if the student whom the teacher has nominated has failed to respond or has responded incorrectly, or if the student wants to give information that has not been specifically requested. According to Holmes (1978: 141), 'Bidding is the way pupils request the right to contribute to the discourse, nominating is one way in which they are given that right'.

Evaluation

In addition to having the right to question the students, the teacher has the right to evaluate student responses. By sequencing the response between the teacher's turns, the teacher 'retains the conversational initiative' (Burton & Stubbs, 1975; cited by Holmes, 1978), as well as the right to be the director of the discourse. Unsolicited contributions from students are usually ignored; the teacher alone has the right to decide whose utterances may contribute to the discourse by deeming them relevant or irrelevant. When the teacher does accept an unsolicited contribution from a student, he or she will evaluate it in the same way a response given within the IRE structure would be evaluated.

In order to participate effectively in the IRE structure, the student is required to know (1) what to respond, (2) when to respond, and (3) how to respond. As I discuss in the following section, research on minority students in mainstream US schools demonstrates that this participation structure tends to favor Standard English-speaking white middle-class students (see, for example, Lemke, 1993).

IMPLICATIONS OF MAINSTREAM US EDUCATIONAL DISCOURSE FOR MINORITY STUDENTS

Demographic changes in the United States have resulted in increasingly linguistically and culturally diverse student populations in US schools (see Chapter 2 for further discussion). This fact makes the assumption of a homogeneous native English-speaking white middle-class student population problematic. This section presents a discussion of implications of this mainstream US educational system for minority students. I begin with programs designed for LEP students and then move to discussion of research findings that illustrates how the organization of classroom interaction, curriculum content, and assessment practices position minority students relative to majority students at school. Together, this part of the chapter illustrates how minority cultural identities are negatively evaluated in mainstream US educational discourse.

Programs for LEP students

As discussed in Chapter 2, until the Civil Rights movement in the 1960s, schools were under no obligation to provide institutional support to students who did not fit the description of Standard English-speaking, white middle-class. It was assumed that the students would assimilate to the mainstream US model; in other words, immerse themselves into it and essentially sink or swim. The Civil Rights movement, however, brought discriminatory practices to public attention, and the Bilingual Education Act (first passed in 1968) mandates that public school programs:

> shall be designed to enable students to achieve full competence in English and to meet school grade-promotion and graduation requirements. (Public Law 100-297-April 28, 1988[1]).

The most common programs in the United States for LEP students are transitional bilingual programs or pull-out ESL classes. Because students are assumed to be linguistically and culturally homogeneous in the mainstream US educational system, the transitional bilingual model attempts to assimilate those students who speak other than Standard English to Standard English. In this way, the transitional model ideally enables LEP students to fit in.

Because policymakers have traditionally assumed that language is the problem preventing LEP students from equal educational opportunity and that English language instruction is the solution to that problem, LEP students are removed from the mainstream academic program which uses only English. Segregated in the transitional bilingual program, LEP students are given ESL instruction in order to facilitate their rapid acquisition of English while they are taught content-areas in their native language. Once the LEP students pass the exit criteria, they are 'exited' to the mainstream academic program. As we saw in Chapter 2, there was increasing emphasis on single exit criteria and quick transition to English in the 1980s, which meant that LEP students generally spend a maximum of three years in these programs. Whatever the exit criteria or duration of the transitional program, LEP students are expected to shift to monolingualism in Standard English, and to conform to mainstream US societal norms in order to have access to equal educational opportunities in the all-English program (see Chapter 1 for further discussion of transitional bilingual programs).

In school districts where there is not a sufficient population of students who speak the same language or a sufficient number of trained bilingual educators, LEP students have the right to receive instruction in English as a Second-language (ESL), and public schools are under legal obligation to provide that instruction. In this case, students are generally pulled out of their content courses (which are taught in English) so that they will have the opportunity to acquire English in order to participate equally in the mainstream US classroom. In both the transitional and the pull-out ESL models, the native language of the LEP student is implicitly defined as a problem that needs to be overcome in order for the student to participate equally in the classroom. By extension, the LEP student is implicitly defined as a problem that needs to be corrected.

Before moving to a discussion of what the Bilingual Education Act's goal of 'full competence in English' means, I want to draw attention to an unintended product of transitional bilingual and pull-out ESL programs. Segregating LEP students in special classes and implicitly defining them as problems to be solved often leads the student to see him/herself very negatively relative to that system. Problems like this suggest the need for educational planners to anticipate how an educational innovation like a bilingual education program will interact with the larger educational discourse system at the school. Without consideration of the overall system, we can predict an ineffective plan or, worse, outcomes which may be other than originally intended.

Another problem that has drawn increasing attention of researchers and practioners concerns the Bilingual Education Act's stated goal 'full competence in English'. Cummins (1992), for example, argues that the notion of language proficiency needs to be critically analyzed. He proposes the framework given in Figure 7 that allows language proficiency to be conceptualized along two continua: context embedded to context reduced and cognitively undemanding to cognitively demanding.

Cummins (1992) claims that the language most typically taught in ESL classrooms can be characterized as context-embedded and cognitively undemanding (e.g. telling a story about a personal experience: Quadrant A), while the academic English LEP students are required to use in schools can be characterized as context-reduced

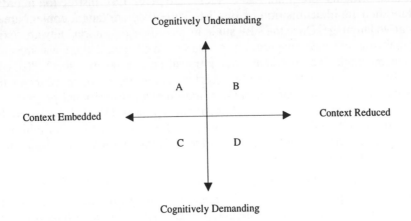

Cognitively Undemanding

A   B

Context Embedded   Context Reduced

C   D

Cognitively Demanding

Figure 7 Range of contextual support and degree of cognitive involvement in communicative activities (Cummins, 1992: 9)

and cognitively demanding (e.g. writing an essay in one of the content-areas of instruction: Quadrant D). He concludes that ESL programs need to facilitate LEP students' proficiency in academic English in order for the students to be able to participate equally in the mainstream academic discourse. ESL programs should therefore be designed to encourage a transition from proficiency in context-embedded, cognitively undemanding activities of Quadrant A through increasingly less context-embedded, more cognitively demanding activities of Quadrants B and C to proficiency in context-reduced, cognitively demanding activities in Quadrant D.

In addition to distinguishing between kinds of English language proficiency, Cummins (1992) argues that developing academic English language proficiency requires more than two to three years, the amount of time normally dedicated to bilingual education and ESL instruction in transitional bilingual programs. A similar concern was raised by the bilingual teachers and program administrators that I interviewed in PS 22 in Perth Amboy, NJ in 1986 (PS 22 is a pseudonym). PS 22 at that time was considered an 'exemplary' transitional bilingual middle school program by the State of New Jersey because of its low drop-out rate (1%). The PS 22 educators distinguished between 'survival English' and 'academic English', and regularly expressed their opposition to New Jersey's increasing emphasis on early exit criteria from the bilingual program. These bilingual teachers argued, like Cummins (1992), that their LEP students in two to three years did not have enough time to develop the necessary academic English to meet grade level and promotion requirements, and therefore were at a disadvantage from the moment they entered the all-English general program (Freeman, 1986). LEP students in transitional bilingual programs like the one at PS 22 were clearly not getting equal educational opportunities as the Bilingual Education Act mandates.

Minority students in mainstream US classroom interaction

The issue of what kind of English language proficiency is prerequisite to equal educational opportunities in mainstream US classrooms becomes further complicated when we consider that not only LEP students, but also native-speakers of non-standard varieties of English, are often blocked from equal participation opportunities. There is a body of ethnography of communication studies in schools (e.g. Scollon & Scollon, 1981; Michaels, 1986; Mohatt & Erickson, 1981; Heath, 1983; Philips, 1983) that finds that children who speak non-standard varieties of English learn to use language in ways that are appropriate within their home speech community but often misunderstood in the school's speech community. The structuring of mainstream US classroom interaction can be problematic for language minority students because they may not understand the norms of interaction that govern when and how to participate appropriately. Since the school and the teachers are in the more powerful positions, the cross-cultural miscommunication that arises due to different discourse strategies can contribute to the minority students' inability to perform certain academic tasks, which can in turn contribute to minority students' disproportionately low performance at school.

For example, Philips' (1983) investigation of Warm Springs Indian students and Mohatt and Erickson's study of Odawa Indians (1981) illustrate that Native American students tend to pause longer than Standard English-speaking white middle-class students before responding. The teacher, however, may interpret the longer pause as the child not knowing the answer or being intentionally uncooperative. Michaels (1986) and Heath (1983) both illustrate cross-cultural differences in the appropriate way to tell a story, a typical response to a question in the mainstream US elementary school classroom. If the teacher expects the story to be told according to white middle-class norms, he/she may not be able to interpret the language minority student's way of telling a story. The mainstream preference for demonstrating active involvement in the classroom through bidding and speaking publicly can also present problems for language minority students who may prefer a different way of participating, for example, silently, or in a one-to-one or small group participation framework (Philips, 1983). As these brief examples from ethnographies of communication in schools demonstrate, if the language minority student does not know and use English according to white middle-class Standard English-speaking norms, he/she can be denied equal participation opportunities and negatively defined relative to majority students.

It is important to remember that the goal of the Civil Rights legislation is to provide equal educational opportunities to students regardless of their background. Proficiency in English is to be instrumental in reaching this goal, but must not be equated with the goal of providing equal educational opportunities, especially given the difficulties in understanding exactly what kind of English is necessary for equal participation opportunities. I return to this point later in the chapter.

A focus on standardized curriculum and assessment

While analysis of how language minority students are positioned relative to majority students in classroom interaction and in overall program structure demonstrates negative implications for the language minority students, we must not overlook the norms that structure the curriculum content and assessment practices. According to Nieto (1992), if we define curriculum as the organized environment for learning in a classroom and school, we see that it is never neutral but represents what is thought to be important and necessary knowledge by those who are dominant in a society. Given the vast knowledge available, only a tiny fraction of it finds its way into textbooks and teachers' guides (Nieto, 1992: 74). What is included and what is omitted in the curriculum is evaluative.

My earlier discussion of mainstream US curriculum content identified an emphasis on white people, reflecting a European bias in mainstream US educational discourse. Marginalizing or not including minority students' histories, literatures, arts, etc. suggests that these contributions are not considered important subject matter for school study. Not talking about tensions between groups and conveying an image of contentment with the status quo can be understood as denying that such tensions exist, or at least denying these topics legitimacy within the mainstream US classroom. Although the Sleeter and Grant (1991) study finds more representation of women and people of color in school textbooks than earlier studies did, they found that minority groups are often portrayed in stereotypical ways, which can perpetuate those stereotypes. Taken together, the exclusion, marginalization, and stereotyping of minority populations also contributes to a negative definition of minority student relative to majority student at school. Evaluation can further aggravate the situation because standardized tests often exhibit a cultural bias in favor of Standard English-speaking white middle-class students, with the result that language minority students' achievement is often not accurately assessed (Mohan, 1992).

Implications of mainstream US schools for minority students: A synthesis

According to Civil Rights legislation, US public schools are required to provide equal educational opportunities to all students, regardless of background. Minority students, however, are presently blocked from equal educational opportunities, and minority populations are underrepresented in higher-paying, higher-status jobs. Schools, which function as one of society's primary socializing instruments, have been implicated in perpetuating the unequal distribution of rights.

The preceding discussion of minority students in mainstream US schools illustrates how this could occur on the classroom level in terms of program structure, classroom interaction, curriculum content, and assessment practices. As Carbaugh (1990) stresses, one part of the cultural communication system influences and reinforces the others. Within the mainstream US educational discourse system, students who come from other than white middle-class native English-speaking homes and communities are often seen as problems at school. Their differences are labeled deficits, and they are segregated in special classes (ESL, special education, transitional bilingual programs) for remediation. These segregated programs and classes place strong pressure on minority students to assimilate; the student, and not the educational system, has been required to change. If the individual student does not assimilate, that student (and not the system) is labeled a failure.

The social reproduction of subordinate minority students through mainstream US educational discourse discussed throughout the preceding section, however, is not the only choice available to educators. I turn now to a theoretical discussion of how social identities are jointly constructed through discourse. The next part of the chapter provides a foundation for understanding how the Oyster Bilingual School challenges US educational and societal discourses about language minority and language majority students at school.

CO-CONSTRUCTING SOCIAL IDENTITIES THROUGH DISCOURSE

Carbaugh's (1990) notion of **cultural identity**, which I understand to refer to cultural dispositions or preferences that govern an individual's way of believing, thinking, and behaving, was central to my earlier discussion of cultural communi-cation systems. A particular cultural identity can be understood as a kind of product or outcome of a specific cultural communication system that is displayed by an individual member of a culture in interaction, and that is recognized by other members of that culture. While I retain the term cultural identity when I refer to Carbaugh's (1990) framework, I use the term **social identity** throughout my own work. This part of the chapter provides a theoretical orientation for understanding what I mean by social identity, and for how social identities are jointly constructed through discourse. I begin by arguing that communication should be understood not as a transfer of information, but as a complex process that is jointly negotiated. Then I describe how people develop their understandings of themselves and their roles relative to others in the social world through their participation in language-mediated activities. Together, this section provides a basis for understanding how the Oyster Bilingual School educators organize their dual-language program and practices so that minority students and majority students alike have more options available to them than are traditionally available in mainstream US schools.

Communication as a joint construction

As we have seen, until very recently the Bilingual Education Act implicitly equated equal educational opportunity with the ability to speak English. As a result, the majority of the bilingual and ESL programs funded by Bilingual Education Act appropriations have emphasized English-language instruction, and have failed to prepare students with the academic competence necessary to participate and achieve in the academic mainstream. Rather than assume *a priori* that this is the case, especially given the inconclusive findings about the effectiveness of bilingual education, the difficulty in understanding what kind of English is necessary for academic achievement, and the disproportionately high dropout rate of language minority students, my focus in the study is on participation. In order to understand how educators can provide participation opportunities to all of their students, we need to understand what is involved in the process of communication. This section provides a discussion of two alternative models of communication: the **transmission model** and the **joint construction of meaning model**.

The transmission model of communication assumes that communication is a simple transfer of information, and underlies folk models of communication in English, traditional linguistic theory and, as we saw earlier, mainstream US educational discourse practices. For example, Reddy's (1979) analysis of stories told by English-speakers reflects what he calls a 'conduit metaphor'. He presents evidence

> which constitute[s] the 'major framework' of the conduit metaphor. The core expressions in these categories imply, respectively, that: (1) language functions like a conduit, transferring thoughts bodily from one person to another; (2) in writing and in speaking, people insert their thoughts or feelings in the words: (3) words accomplish the transfer of thoughts or feelings in the words; and (4) in listening or reading, people extract the thoughts and feelings once again from the words. (Reddy, 1979: 210)

Reddy provides the following examples from his data: (1) *try to get your thoughts across better*; (2) *you have to put each concept into words*; (3) *the sentence was filled with emotion*; and (4) *let me know if you find any good ideas in the essay* (emphasis in original). According to Reddy (1979), this linguistic representation of communication as a simple process in which a speaker packs up his or her ideas into words and sends them to the listener who unpacks them and understands the speaker's intent influences the way English speakers perceive the communication process.

The notion of communication as information transfer is also evident in linguistics and in education. In early work on speech act theory (e.g. Searle, 1975, 1969; Austin, 1975) and in pragmatics (e.g. Grice, 1975), for example, philosophers of language focused their discussion on speaker intent in their efforts to understand how actions are accomplished through language. Little consideration was given to the listener's active role in the communication process. And as discussed earlier in this chapter, the transmission model can be seen to structure mainstream US definitions of teaching and learning.

Interactional sociolinguistic research stands in opposition to this model, and sees communication as the joint construction of meaning by participants in interaction (see, for example, Gumperz, 1982; Erickson & Schultz, 1982; Tannen, 1986, 1992). According to Tannen (1992: 11),

> A central concern of IS (interactional sociolinguistics) is the interactive nature of conversation. The model of language as produced by a speaker alone is questioned; rather, listening and speaking are seen as inextricably intertwined.

Thus any utterance by any participant in a conversation is a joint production influenced by speaker, listener, and audience (including the investigators or their equipment).

In contrast to the philosophy of language orientation referred to above, interactional sociolinguists base their claims about the nature of the communication process on close analysis of audio- and/or video-taped and transcribed naturally occurring face-to-face interaction.

This study assumes that communication is a joint production that is locally produced in the face-to-face interaction. The negotiation of meaning is a complex process in any situation that becomes more complex in intercultural communication. Education, which is accomplished largely through communication, is a also a joint construction actively negotiated by teachers and students. It is important to remember, however, that people do not come to interactions as blank slates (Tannen, 1993). As I describe in the next few paragraphs, they bring expectations based on their prior experiences in similar situations which makes their interpretation of the ongoing situation possible.

Tannen and Wallat (1993) distinguish two types of structures of expectations — **interactive frames** and **knowledge schemas** — that people draw on in efforts to make sense of and construct events. The notion of interactive frame,

> refers to a definition of what is going on in interaction, without which no utterance (or movement or gesture) could be interpreted. (Tannen & Wallat, 1993: 59–60)

Participants in an interaction use 'contextualization cues' (Gumperz, 1982) to help them determine which interactive frame(s) to draw on in order to know how to interpret a situation and then how to interpret an utterance in that situation. For example, intonation provides a cue to assist participants in understanding a situation as playful or serious, and accordingly an utterance as a joke or an insult. The notion of an interactive frame is very dynamic, and subject to rapid change in face-to-face interaction, for example, as participants change their alignments relative to each other.

Knowledge schemas are less dynamic structures of expectations than interactive frames, but they are not entirely static. According to Tannen and Wallat (1993; 60), knowledge schema

> refers to participants' expectations about people, objects, events and settings in the world, as distinguished from alignments being negotiated in a particular interaction.

Since people develop their expectations of people, objects, events, and settings in the world over time through their participation in a variety of interactions, these ideologically structured notions are more resistant to change. Because of the naturalizing effect of ideology (Fairclough, 1989), people may have a difficult time imagining alternatives to their assumptions and expectations, for example, about language minority students at school. Their ongoing experience of believing that language is a problem that LEP students must overcome before they can participate equally in school can lead to seeing this ideological belief not as ideological, but as natural or simply the way it is.

Language socialization

Although the terms interactive frame and knowledge schema are not used in Soviet cognitive psychology, Vygotsky and his students' work on Activity Theory (see Wertsch, 1985, for discussion) has been very influential in providing (1) a means of understanding the relationship between individual's participation in the face-to-face interaction (i.e. interactive frame) and their development of an understanding of the social world and how to participate in it (i.e. knowledge schema), as well as (2) an understanding of the role of language in this developmental process. In this work, activity is the basic unit of analysis. Activity Theory assumes that in order for an individual to know how to participate appropriately in an activity, that individual must participate appropriately in similar activities. The only way that an individual can initially participate appropriately in activities is to engage in social interaction with more experienced members of the culture. Sign systems (semiotics) are assumed to play an important mediational role in this developmental process.

In other words, people are socialized through language (verbal and non-verbal) in activities in which their participation is guided by more experienced members of the culture to use language appropriately and independently in similar activities. Taking these theoretical notions and applying them to schools, my work assumes that people develop their assumptions and expectations about people (i.e. teachers, students, minority populations), objects (i.e. curriculum content), settings (i.e. schools, classrooms) and events (i.e. classroom interaction) in the world through their cumulative experience language-mediated activities. As Schieffelin and Ochs (1990: 3) write:

> Language in use is then a major if not the major tool for conveying sociocultural knowledge and a powerful medium of socialization. In this sense, we invoke Sapir (Mandelbaum 1949) and Whorf (1941) and suggest that children acquire a world view as they acquire a language.

As Schieffelin and Ochs's (1990) collection of case studies demonstrates, the way that children acquire knowledge of the social order and of local belief systems, as well as the nature of that knowledge, vary cross-culturally.

My concern in this study is also with language socialization, but specifically the socialization of language minority students relative to language majority students in school and society. Schools are one of society's primary socializing instruments. Teachers provide students with instruction in what to say and how to participate. As Philips (1983: 94) writes, the teacher socializes students in skills for regulating interaction that prepare them for the occupational world they will enter as adults, and for the organization of interaction through which they maintain working relations with others in that world.

Philips (1983) links the students' participation in the classroom discourse with their later participation in the occupational discourse. Her work has important implications for understanding how students are socialized through classroom discourse in other settings.

This section has provided a basis for understanding how students and teachers develop their understanding of the social world and their role in it through their participation in language-mediated interactions. My discussion in the next section focuses more directly on social identity construction.

The dynamic nature of social identity construction

Earlier in this chapter, I described cultural identity as a product or outcome of a relatively stable cultural communication system. My understanding of social identity includes but is not limited to this notion. According to Harré (1984), social identity refers to the attributes that an individual shares with others that make up some relevant reference class. Social identities are not fixed. Because culture is dynamic, negotiated, and negotiable, cultural communication systems and the social identities that they produce are continually evolving in response to changing circumstances. A broader, more flexible understanding of social identity is necessary to understand how the educational discourse that the Oyster educators have organized makes it possible for students and teachers to creatively co-construct minority social identities that are positively evaluated at school.

A parallel to my use of the terms 'social' and 'cultural' can be found in Ochs (1988) discussion of society, culture, and socialization. She writes:

> One of the distinctive characteristics of the human species is that it transmits both social skills and cultural knowledge to its young. The transmission of cultural knowledge has been referred to as *enculturation* (Mead, 1963), but a term that covers transmission of both procedures ('knowing how') and premises ('knowing that') is *socialization* (Cicourel, 1973). For purposes of the discussion here, socialization will be considered as a more general term referring to the process by which one becomes a competent member of society (Ochs & Schiefflin, 1984; Schieffelin & Ochs, 1983, 1986a). ... children's speech behavior over developmental time will be socially and culturally organized. To understand the form and content of children's language, it is necessary to incorporate a sociocultural level of interpretation. (Ochs, 1988: 5, emphasis in original)

Consistent with the work referred to here, my analysis of social identity construction displayed at Oyster Bilingual School is informed by a sociocultural understanding of local discourse practices.

Recent work by Harré (1990) in social psychology provides a theoretical basis for understanding how participation rights in the macro-level social order are structured by political and moral considerations which are learned in the micro-level face-to-face interaction. Like Schieffelin and Ochs's (1990) research into language socialization discussed earlier, Harré's (1984, 1990) work is also heavily influenced by Vygotsky's Activity Theory. According to Harré (1984: 65), 'people and their modes of talk are made by and for social orders, and social orders are people in conversation'. He argues that we can understand peoples' roles in the (macro-level) social order by analyzing their positions in (micro-level) conversation, or in what he calls the moral order of speaking.

Harré (1990) claims that a particular social identity within the moral order of speaking is made up of two interrelated notions: (1) position, a dynamic aspect of the moral order of speaking that relates to face-to-face interaction, and (2) role, the participant's associated rights and obligations in the social order. Davies and Harré (1990: 6) define positioning as

> the discursive process whereby selves are located in conversations as observably and subjectively coherent participants in jointly produced storylines. There can be interactive positioning in which what one person says positions another. And there can be reflexive positioning in which one positions oneself. However it would be a mistake to assume that, in either case, positioning is necessarily intentional. One lives one's life in terms of one's ongoingly produced self, whoever might be responsible for its production.

Davies and Harré emphasize the constitutive force of language. If an individual is repeatedly positioned in face-to-face interaction as a particular kind of social being, over time the individual assumes that role with its associated rights and obligations in the macro-level social order. An individual's role in the social order is thus considered to be generated through the learning and use of particular discursive practices in interaction.

Although Davies and Harré's (1990) study does not provide empirical evidence to support their claims, the ethnography of communication literature discussed earlier in the chapter provides concrete examples of the relationship between position in the face-to-face interaction and role in the social order. Philips (1983), for instance, concludes (although she does not use the term 'positioning') that the teacher's ongoing failure to incorporate the Warm Springs Indians' contributions into the official floor positions them first as non-participants in the interaction. Their positioning leads to the Warm Springs Indian students' understanding of their collective social role as non-participants in the mainstream institutional discourse.

Davies and Harré's (1990) notion of the very dynamic position in face-to-face interaction and the less dynamic although not static role in the social order can be integrated very easily with Tannen and Wallat's (1993) notions of the very dynamic interactive frame and the less dynamic although not static knowledge schema. Recall from our earlier discussion that interactive frame refers to expectations concerning an activity that allow the participants to understand the meaning of utterances, and that knowledge schema refers to expectations concerning participants, objects, events, or settings. Position can be understood as one specific aspect of the more general interactive frame, and role as one specific aspect of the more general knowledge schema, both referring to participation. Participants in inter-action draw on their frames and their schemas in order to understand their position in the interaction and their role in the social order respectively. Social identities are thus negotiated and displayed through people's ongoing participation in language-mediated activities. The ways that particular activities are organized, and the way that social identities are constructed through discourse, varies tremendously across contexts (see Hall & Bucholz, 1995, for further discussion and examples).

In any cultural system, the dominant language (in this case, Standard English) and the dominant social identity (in this case, white middle-class native English-speaking) are attributed more prestige by majority and minority groups. Minority languages/varieties of languages (Spanish, AAVE) and minority social identities tend to be stigmatized by all members of the discourse community (see Chapter 1 for further discussion). This stigmatization based on language use can negatively affect language minority students in mainstream US discourse in two interrelated ways. First, language majority speakers can discriminate against language mi-nority speakers as a result of cross-cultural differences in discourse strategies. As discussed earlier, in the mainstream US educational discourse system, the language minority students are less powerful than the language majority teachers. The teachers' failure to recognize (intentionally or inadvertently) cross-cultural differences in discourse strategies can lead to the teachers' misjudging the students' academic potential. The teachers' misunderstanding of the lan-guage minority students' academic potential can result in the language minority students' unequal educational opportunity at school. Second, because the lan-guage minority students are discriminated against for not speaking Standard English and continue to be denied equal access, these students can come to see themselves as not being equal participants in the mainstream educational and occupational discourse. Language minority students' assumptions and expecta-tions about their own inequality at school can also perpetuate the minority subordinate status.

A major thesis of this book is that we have choices in how we define ourselves, each other, and the communities in which we live. This means, at least theoretically, that the social order in US schools does not have to reflect and perpetuate dominant US discourses that discriminate against minority languages and speakers of those languages. The next part of the chapter provides a framework for understanding how Oyster's educational discourse challenges mainstream US educational and societal discourses about minority participation rights.

RECOGNIZING AND REFUSING DISCRIMINATORY DISCOURSES

Recognizing that social identities are constructed through discourse means that it is possible for an individual to first, recognize a discourse that positions him/her negatively and second, refuse that discourse. It then becomes possible for the individual to attempt to reposition him/herself favorably in a newly constructed discourse (Davies & Harré, 1990). This theoretical orientation provides considerable explanatory power on two levels. First, it explains how the Oyster educators have collectively recognized discriminatory practices against language minority students in mainstream US educational discourse, refused that discourse, and have collectively constructed the Oyster alternative educational discourse with its goal of socializing its students differently. The students, however, do not spend all of their lives at Oyster Bilingual School. Therefore, a second part of the Oyster agenda attempts to teach the students how to recognize discriminatory discourse practices themselves, to refuse the negative positioning of minorities, and to reposition those individuals more favorably (see Chapters 5–10 for illustration).

The theoretical notion of 'agency' is the key to understanding this agenda. Davies (1990) describes an agentive individual as one who speaks for him/herself, accepts responsibilities for his/her thoughts, speech and actions, and is recognizably separate from any particular collective. Drawing on feminist theory, Davies argues that agency, like any speaking position and role, is contingent upon discursive practices made available to the individual, and not automatically attributed to all human beings in the way that more traditional sociological theory assumes (e.g. Parsons, 1937; cited by Davies, 1990: 4). In other words, individuals and groups in society do not have equal rights to all speaking positions and social roles. While Davies (1990) focuses on how the educational discourse socializes discriminatorily based on gender, her discussion is relevant to minority students and populations more generally because they are rarely positioned as agentive. As we saw earlier in the chapter, for example, within the mainstream US educational discourse system, minority students have little choice in how they are defined through the norms that structure teaching and learning at school.

Davies (1990) discusses the tension in educational theory and practice. On the one hand lies the belief that children must be socialized into known and acceptable ways of being. On the other hand, there is the belief that the individual does and should stand outside and above the collective, make choices, and accept moral responsibility for his/her own actions.[2] There is always a tension, she argues, between being an individual and a member of various collectives, especially when being a member of one collective contradicts being a member of another.

As Kramsch (1991) points out, a focus on choice, or in the terms Davies (1990) uses, on agency, could alleviate such tension for the individual as he/she develops a new positively evaluated minority social identity. Kramsch (1991: 6) describes the challenge of the learner as follows:

The challenge of the learner, then, is not only to perform these roles which are relevant and appropriate in a given society, but to forge an identity that is not yet established, to realize a cross-cultural potential that is latent in any learner of a foreign language.

In order for the learner to 'forge an identity that is not yet established', Kramsch (1991: 13) argues for a language curriculum that focuses on choice. The language learner can choose to (1) assimilate to mainstream social practices, (2) reject existing social practices, or (3) create an alternative personal and national identity.

One of Oyster Bilingual School's goals can be understood as providing the minority student with opportunities to create alternative social identities that are not readily available in mainstream US schools and society. They have organized their discourse practices to make possible the emergence of positively evaluated minority social identities whose differences are expected, tolerated, and respected at school. The minority students gain the right to participate in the institutional discourse (first educational and later occupational) by acquiring an interactional history through their socializing experience at Oyster Bilingual School in which they are positioned as having that right, and by learning to refuse discourses in which they are positioned as not having the right to participate.

Oyster's agenda has different implications for minority and majority students. The minority student ideally learns to recognize discriminatory practices in which *he or she as an individual* is positioned negatively, and strategies to reposition him/herself more favorably. The majority student ideally learns to recognize discriminatory practices against *other individuals*, and strategies to refuse contributing to the perpetuation of such practices. If we assume that discrimination is jointly constructed through communication (Chick, 1990), then changing discriminatory practices requires minority and majority individuals and groups to recognize and refuse those practices. When both groups agree through their actions to challenge discourse practices that marginalize, exclude, or stereotype minority individuals and groups, then positively evaluated minority social identities whose differences are expected, tolerated, and respected can emerge within the discourse community.

To this point, I have concentrated on what the individual can do to change his or her negative positioning and social role. In order for discourse communities to change so that minority and majority individuals and groups have more or less equal participation opportunites, collective action is required. Tajfel's theory of social change (1974, cited by Coates, 1986) provides a framework for understanding options available to stigmatized groups in society. This discussion allows us to contextualize the strategy that Oyster has selected to support their efforts to provide equal participation opportunities to all of their students and to promote social change from the bottom up.

Figure 8 illustrates how members of an inferior social group can either accept or reject their inferior position in society.

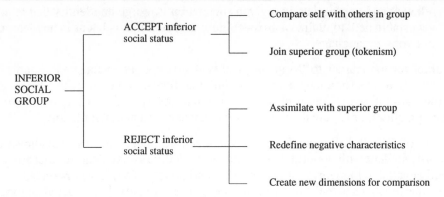

Figure 8 Tajfel's theory of inter-group relations and social change (Coates, 1986: 9)

If the inferior social group accepts their inferior social status, members of the social group will try to achieve self-esteem and a positive self-image by operating as individuals, not as a group. In this case, there are two strategies available to the individual. One option is to measure individual success solely against others within the stigmatized social group and not in comparison to members of the superior status group. This is the case, for example, when minority groups remain segregated from the dominant group and compare themselves only to those within that segregated group. A problem with this strategy is that although the minority group members may have high self-esteem and a positive self-image within that limited group, they are not afforded equal opportunities within the larger political and economic structure of mainstream society. A second option is for the individual to attempt to join the superior group, and possibly be accepted as a token. This strategy, however, can present the individual with a very difficult situation, because the individual may never be completely accepted by the dominant group, and having abandoned the minority group, may never be completely part of that group either.

If, on the other hand, the members of the inferior social group refuse to accept their inferior social status as fair, they can, as a group, attempt to change things. According to Tajfel (1974, cited by Coates, 1986), there are three ways to accomplish this, and these strategies usually occur historically in the order presented. The first strategy is to try to demand equality with the dominant group by assimilating to that group's norms. This is clearly the strategy that mainstream US educational and societal discourse encourages. As we saw earlier, in order for students defined as 'Limited English Proficient' to obtain equal educational opportunities in US public schools, they need to acquire Standard English and white middle-class norms of interaction and interpretation. Under this strategy, the characteristics associated with the inferior social group are considered handicaps to full participation. Members of, for example, Spanish-speaking groups abandon the Spanish language and norms of interaction and interpretation associated with their particular Spanish-speaking group because they learn that Standard English and white middle-class norms are the keys to success in mainstream US institutions. If the individual Spanish speaker, for example, does not assimilate, he or she as an individual is labeled a failure by the institution.

As discussed in Chapter 2, however, there is an increasing number of students who come from other than Standard English-speaking white middle-class backgrounds, and these individuals/(groups?) drop out of US public schools at a disproportionate rate. It is arguable that this assimilation strategy, as currently practiced, is not accomplishing its goal of providing equal educational opportunities to all students.

The second option available to minority social groups is to redefine negative characteristics. This is, however, a very slow process that is often met with resistance by minority and majority groups alike. As will be illustrated throughout the subsequent chapters, the goal of the Oyster status plan, as one part of the dual-language plan, is to redefine Spanish as equal to English within the Oyster educational discourse. Efforts to redefine bilingualism and cultural pluralism as positive qualities are present in every aspect of the curriculum design and implementation.

The third strategy is to create new dimensions for comparison. Because there is a collective belief at Oyster that minority students are discriminated against in mainstream US schools and society, a primary goal of the Oyster dual-language program is to make space for the co-construction of positively evaluated minority social identities. Oyster, therefore, makes a collective effort to socialize the minority and majority children alike into recognizing the existence of positive minority social identities whose differences are expected, tolerated, and respected. This required what were 25 years ago when the Oyster plan was first developed, very new dimensions of comparison. Chapters 5–10 illustrate how the Oyster educators use dual-language education, cooperative learning, and team-teaching as the means to reach their goals for their target populations. While these educational practices are not entirely new to educational researchers or practioners today, when the Oyster dual-language program began 25 years ago such practices were quite radical.

It seems reasonable to believe that if people from minority groups collectively and continually refuse negative positioning in the micro-level face-to-face interaction, and if people from majority groups become aware of the discriminatory practices that prevail in mainstream US institutional and societal discourse, that eventually people's knowledge schemas (minority and majority alike) will slowly change to expect more or less equal participation of people, regardless of background. Given the powerful role that schools have in socializing students into understanding what social identities exist in society, what the attributes associated with these identities are, and what activities these identities can and should participate in, schools can be considered a rich ground for social change. If educators recognize the discriminatory practices that are prevalent in mainstream US schools and society, and if they work together to construct alternative educational discourses, schools can help students find opportunities to define who they are relative to each other in a way that all students, regardless of background, have more options available to them. This is the goal of what I refer to as the Oyster social identities project.

The preceding section has provided a theoretical foundation for understanding how social identities are jointly constructed through discourse. People develop their understanding of who they are relative to each other in the macro-level social order through their ongoing positioning in the micro-level face-to-face interaction. Because there is an unequal distribution of speaking rights in the social order at schools and in society, not all individuals have the right to all speaking roles. In mainstream US schools, for example, the social order is organized in such a way that the subordinate minority role is reflected and perpetuated in the micro-level classroom interaction.

Recognizing that social identities are jointly negotiated by people in interaction means that it is possible for an individual and/or group to recognize discriminatory positioning, refuse those discourse practices, and construct alternative discourses which are less discriminatory. I argue throughout this study that the dual-language plan at Oyster Bilingual School should be understood as one part of a larger social identities project that refuses the negative positioning of minority students at school. The way that the Oyster educators have organized their dual language-program, curriculum content, classroom activities, and assessment practices reflects an integrated effort to elevate the status of minority students and the languages they speak so that all students, regardless of background, can participate more or less equally.

CONCLUSION

As this chapter has demonstrated, conceptualizing schools as cultural communication systems provides an integrated means of understanding how language minority students develop an understanding of their subordinate role in schools and society through their ongoing negative position in mainstream US educational discourse. Language minority students' negative positioning as Limited English Proficient in segregated bilingual or ESL programs; as students who do not interact appropriately in the academic discourse; whose histories, arts, literatures, contributions, and perspectives are marginalized, stereotyped, or not included in the curriculum content; and whose performance is not validly assessed, can together contribute to the subordinate minority role, first in school and later in mainstream US society. From the perspective of the mainstream US school, the language minority student can either assimilate to the positively evaluated majority social identity and succeed, or maintain the negatively evaluated minority social identity and fail.

The assumption underlying this study, however, is that the macro-level social order at school and in society is reflected in, and EITHER perpetuated OR challenged and potentially transformed by, the micro-level interaction (Fairclough, 1989). This critical discourse orientation provides a foundation for understanding Oyster's agenda. The Oyster Bilingual School has organized itself in opposition to mainstream US educational discourse. As opposed to expecting language minority students to either assimilate to monolingualism in English and to white middle-class norms in order to participate and achieve at school, or maintain their native language, culture, and minority social identity and fail, Oyster attempts to provide a third option to its minority students: maintain the native language and culture, acquire Standard English and the associated norms of interaction and interpretation, and achieve at school. As Chapters 5–10 illustrate, the Oyster educators have organized their discourse practices so that their language minority and language majority students are positioned more or less equally to each other. The students' ongoing participation in this socializing discourse provides language majority and language minority students with the opportunity to become bilingual and biliterate, and to see language minority students as legitimate participants in US institutions and society.

Notes

1. Because I conducted my research at Oyster from 1989 to 1991, the 1988 Bilingual Education Act is most relevant to my discussion.

2. I am not prepared to agree with Davies' (1990) statement universally because I do not know if all societies believe that the individual does and should stand outside the collective, make choices, and accept more responsibility for their own actions. I am, however, willing to agree with her in the case of societies that positively evaluate individualism. This is certainly the case in mainstream US discourse.

CHAPTER 4

The Discursive Construction of Oyster Bilingual School: A Framework for Analysis

Consistent with recent work in sociolinguistics and literacy studies, I see language and literacy as discourse practices that reflect cultural ideologies and that are implicated in power relations (e.g. Fairclough, 1989, 1992; Gee, 1990; Gal, 1995; Lemke, 1989, 1993; Street, 1995). A sociocultural perspective on how languages are used, taught, and learned at school demands an understanding of the cultural beliefs that underlie those practices as well as the historical and sociopolitical relations that gave rise to those beliefs and practices. This chapter describes my ethnographically oriented discourse analytic approach to understanding how Oyster's dual-language program functions on the local level, and it is divided into two parts. The first part situates my work within critical discourse analysis and language-plannning research and describes in general terms how I relate the dual-language plan to its sociopolitical context. The second part provides a detailed discussion of my data collection and analysis methods. This chapter is intended specifically for researchers who want to investigate how dual-language plans function in other contexts. The approach will also be of interest to researchers who investigate how social identity is constructed in situated practice in any institutitional context.

RELATING THE DUAL-LANGUAGE PLAN TO ITS SOCIOPOLITICAL CONTEXT

My analysis of how Oyster's dual-language program functions within its sociopolitical context draws heavily on work from critical discourse analysis. Following Fairclough (1989: 25), I begin by assuming different levels of social organization including, the level of the social situation or the immediate social environment in which the discourse occurs; the level of the social institution which constitutes a wider matrix for the discourse; and the level of society as a whole.

For the purposes of this study, sociopolitical context can be understood as dynamic interrelationships among the classroom (situational), Oyster Bilingual School (institutional), mainstream US school (institutional) and mainstream US society (societal) levels of context which mutually influence each other in important ways.

The assumptions that institutions in society are largely constituted through discourse, and that schools can be understood as discourse systems (discussed in Chapters 1 and 3 respectively) offers an important theoretical basis for progress in language-planning research. First, as Fishman (1973) argues, language-planning is primarily problem-oriented. Language-planning researchers need to understand how people in the institution under study define what the problem is for whom (Cooper, 1989). However, the researcher cannot assume *a priori* that a particular institution is constituted by one coherent ideological discourse that is reflected in official policy statements and that all participants embrace and act on in the same way. The possibility for competing discourses around the official policy within the institution always exists. Prator's description of language-planning and implementation reflects this possibility:

> The entire process of formulating and implementing language policy is best regarded as a spiral process beginning at the highest level of authority and ideally descending in widening circles through the ranks of practicioners who can support or resist putting the policy into effect. (Cited as personal communication by Cooper 1989: 160)

Recent work in language-planning is beginning to regard language teachers as language planners (e.g. Hornberger, 1997); a move which I strongly endorse. In an educational language plan, teachers have considerable autonomy in their implementation of high-level decisions which leaves room for significant variation in the way that the plan is actually implemented on the classroom level.

Implicit in Prator's description of the language-planning process is the notion of language-planning as a top-down activity in which high-level policymakers design policy that lower-level practitioners implement. Bamgbose (1989), however, stresses the importance of understanding the nature of the relationship between policy decisions and implementation. Bamgbose (1989: 25) writes:

> Since policy decisions can be taken at any stage in the planning process, there is a need to reconsider the unidirectional movement from policy formulation to implementation which is usually presented in models of language-planning (Fishman *et al.*, 1971, Jernudd, 1973). This account of the relationship obscures the fact that policy formulation is a dynamic process.

Considering teachers and administrators as planners allows an understanding of how practitioners potentially shape the language plan from the bottom up (see Hornberger, 1997, for further discussion).

Conceptualizing language-planning as dynamic, ideological processes that are shaped by multiple levels of institutional authority provides a principled basis for investigating how the dual-language plan is interpreted within the Oyster Bilingual School. After identifying the levels of authority at the school (i.e. the organizational or decision-making structure), I analyze power relations within and across these levels. The analysis of open-ended interviews with people who represent various levels of institutional authority enables me to investigate two important issues identified by language-planning researchers — the political interests of policymakers (Cooper, 1989), and the implicit and explict goals of the language plan for the various target populations (Skutnabb-Kangas, 1984). Moreover, triangulating the analyses of policymaker interests and goals with the analyses of official policy statements reveals important sociopolitical concerns that shape how Oyster's dual-language educational plan is interpreted and implemented in practice (details of my approach are provided later in the chapter).

Because no institution exists in a vacuum, my analysis of Oyster Bilingual School's dual-language-planning and implementation incorporates an understanding of the larger sociopolitical context into the analysis. Chapter 2 gave a brief history of the sociopolitical context of bilingual education in the United States, and Chapter 3 offered an analysis of the mainstream US school context that the Oyster educators oppose. These societal level discourses provide a basis of comparison for my analysis of the implicit and explicit goals of Oyster's dual-language program for the various target populations at the Oyster Bilingual School.

Analysis of policy statements and of interviews with language planners about their goals in relation to the sociolinguistics of society and in relation to mainstream US educational programs and practices yields an understanding of the school's ideal language-planning and implementation. However, as Bourdieu (1977: 18–19) warns:

> the informant's discourse, in which he strives to give himself the appearance of symbolic mastery of his practice, tends to draw attention to the most remarkable 'moves', i.e., those most esteemed or reprehended in the different social games rather than to the principle from which these moves and all equally possible moves can be generated, and which, belonging to the universe of the undisputed, most often remain in their implicit state.

To understand the implicit or underlying principles that inform the actual implementation of Oyster's dual-language program, I triangulate analyses of the language-planners' oral and written texts about practice with observation of actual practice. This takes us to a discussion of the situation level of context.

An ethnography of communication approach provides a means of investigating how ideal language-planning goals are realized in actual practice (see also Hornberger, 1988). As Saville-Troike (1989: 2) notes, this approach 'does not involve a list of facts to be learned so much as questions to be asked, and means for finding out answers'. The focus of a traditional ethnography of communication is the **speech community**. My study, in contrast, focuses on the **institution** (Oyster Bilingual School). The dynamic notion of institution that I assume in this study addresses problems associated with the static, isolated, relatively homogeneous concept of speech community that an ethnograpy of communication study assumes (see Gal, 1989, for further critique of 'speech community').

The ethnographer of communication then identifies what **speech situations** and **speech activities** constitute the community through an analysis of who, says what, to whom, when, where, how, and with what effects. The research questions that guide the analysis emerge through investigation of communicative behavior within that speech community (see Hymes, 1974; and Saville-Troike, 1989, for detailed discussion of this approach). Likewise, the research questions that guide my study emerge through my analysis of the school's explicit and implicit goals in relation to my observation of how those goals are realized in actual face-to-face interaction. My understanding of the larger sociopolitical context in which Oyster's dual-language program is situated then provides explanations for the discrepancies that I identify between the ideal plan and actual implementation.

The discussion of my ethnographic/discourse analytic approach has been general to this point. I now present more specific description of my data collection and analysis that is intended to address issues of validity and reliability of the Oyster School case study, and to facilitate replication of this approach in other contexts. Before I proceed to a discussion of my actual data collection and analysis methods, I describe how I gained access to the Oyster Bilingual School.

GAINING ACCESS TO OYSTER BILINGUAL SCHOOL

Experience in the mid-1980s as a participant-observer in two transitional bilingual programs, one in Brooklyn, New York, and the other in Perth Amboy, New Jersey, led me to question if and how bilingual programs could provide educational opportunities to the low-income Latino (predominantly Puerto Rican and Dominican) student populations that these programs were intended to serve. In 1989 I learned of a public elementary school in Washington, DC, that was 'successful' with its low-income Latino student population. I decided to volunteer my services as an ESL tutor at the Oyster Bilingual School in exchange for the opportunity to observe how the dual-language program functioned. Because access to study in US public schools is often problematic and involves going through a number of channels in order to obtain permission from all the necessary parties, I provide the following discussion of how I gained access to do research in Oyster Bilingual School in the hope that it will stimulate ideas for others who are interested in doing research in US public schools.

In the Fall of 1989 when I began my doctoral work in sociolinguistics at Georgetown University, I decided to volunteer my services to Oyster Bilingual School in exchange for the opportunity to learn about their successful bilingual program. I want to emphasize this point. I feel very strongly that researchers should look for ways to give something back to the people and places they research. I believe that the relationship between researcher and researched, whenever possible, should be mutually beneficial. This is especially true in the United States where relationships between university-based researchers and public schools are often characterized by mistrust and even hostility. While I believe that researchers need to be aware of how their presence in the school is interpreted by the people they are studying in any kind of research, it is essential in an ethnographic study. Since the ethnographer is the primary research tool, the relationships he/she develops shape the research process and product. I return to this point in a variety of ways throughout this chapter.

When I began my work at Oyster Bilingual School, I was not expecting it to become the site for my dissertation research. When I called the school to volunteer, I was referred to one of the guidance counselors who was responsible for coordinating volunteers. I explained that I had considerable experience teaching English as a Second-language (ESL) and would help in any way they needed. I also expressed my interest in learning about their bilingual program. I positioned myself not as an outside expert who was going to evaluate their program, but as a student who wanted to learn how they were able to provide educational opportunities to their low-income Latino population. I was genuinely interested in learning how these educators could accomplish what other educators throughout the country did not seem to be able to accomplish (for example, in the two transitional bilingual schools where I had previously done research). I return to this point in the next section.

The guidance counselor introduced me to one of the sixth grade teachers, Mrs Washington, who told me, 'I can use all the help I can get!' I learned at that time that each class has one English-dominant teacher, in this case Mrs Washington, and one Spanish-dominant teacher, Señor Xoci. In the Fall semester of 1989, I spent at least two mornings a week, from 9–12, tutoring writing and reading in the English Language Arts class, observing the Spanish Language Arts class, and tutoring math in Spanish to a girl who had just arrived from Spain with no English skills. In sum, the Fall 1989 semester provided me the opportunity to study the last year (sixth grade) of the implementation of the dual-language plan by working as a participant-observer in both the Spanish and English Language Arts classes, as well as the opportunity to work very closely with all of the sixth grade students and the two teachers in the class.

As I discussed in Chapter 1, through my work as a participant-observer, by the end of the Fall 1989 semester I had begun to understand that the Oyster Bilingual School program can be better understood as a dual-language plan within a larger social identities project. In order to investigate the multiple levels of educational planning and implementation at Oyster, I requested permission from the principal to do my dissertation research at the school. After receiving her permission, written permission from all of the teachers in the school, and written permission of the parents of the students, I began to expand the scope of my study.

As I discuss in more detail in the next section, in order to investigate the short-term outcomes of the program, I needed to follow the students to PS 33, the public junior high school that the majority of the students attend after graduating from Oyster Bilingual School (PS 33 is a pseudonym). In the Spring of 1990, I wrote to Mr Wilson, the principal of PS 33, describing my Oyster Bilingual School study. I had learned from Señora Ortega, a director of OBEMLA (Office of Bilingual Education and Minority Language Affairs in Washington, DC) and the principal of Oyster Bilingual School during the first year of my study, that Mr Wilson had collaborated with a particularly active Oyster Bilingual School (Anglo) parent the year before to initiate an 'extension class' of the Oyster Bilingual School model in PS 33 for the Oyster Bilingual School graduates so that they would have the opportunity to maintain their Spanish beyond their Oyster Bilingual School experience. Because Mr Wilson was enthusiastic about the new extension class, he granted me access to PS 33. After meeting with the teacher who had taught the extension class in 1989–90, the guidance counselor at PS 33, and the teacher who would teach the extension class for the year 1990–91 (during which time I would observe), and after receiving written permission again from the students' parents, I was granted permission to observe and tape the interaction of the students in that class. After pursuing all the necessary channels to gain access, I was able to follow the students who I had worked with in the sixth grade at Oyster Bilingual School to the 'same class' in the seventh grade at PS 33.

As the preceding discussion suggests, gaining access to conduct research in US public schools is a time-consuming and challenging process. I have found that when the educators are not threatened by the presence of the researcher, and when the educators and the students' parents believe that either the research and/or the researcher will in some way benefit the students and/or the school, that the school and the people in it open themselves to a dynamic, continually evolving, mutually beneficial research relationship. I turn now to a discussion of my data collection and analysis.

DATA COLLECTION AND ANALYSIS

This section describes how I related interviews with policymakers, teachers, parents, and students to official policy statements and other site documents that I collected at Oyster and to my observations and discourse analyses of actual face-to-face interaction in the classes and throughout the school over the course of my study. I begin by describing the open-ended interviews that I conducted, and then move to a discussion of how I analysed classroom discourse. I conclude this section with a diagram of my research design that locates the situational level of the classroom interaction within the institutional level of Oyster Bilingual School within the societal level of mainstream US discouse. This diagram illustrates my understanding of the dynamic interrelationships among problem identification, planning, and implementation on the different planning levels that I identified at Oyster, as well as how these processes interact with the larger sociopolitical context.

Collecting and analysing interview data

I collected a considerable amount of data through what I refer to as relatively **open-ended interviews**. Since the type of interview that I conduct is different from the standard social science interview, I want to clarify what I mean by interview. To do this, I need to first briefly describe the standard social science interview.

I understand the standard interview in social science research to be a series of pre-determined questions that the interviewer asks in the same way to numerous respondents, and their answers, although open-ended in the sense that they are not multiple choice questions, are not in-depth accounts. In fact, lengthy answers to standard interview questions are often considered off-topic. Additionally, in the standard interview, the interviewer is not considered to play an important role in the process, but is regarded as an objective recorder of information (see Mishler, 1986, for a discussion of the standard interview and alternative approaches).

The interview technique that I adopt, in contrast, combines qualities of **life-history** and **focused interviews**, and can be characterized more as a conversation than as a standard interview. Although I do enter the interview situation with questions I would like to have answered, I do not necessarily follow the questions in any set order. This is because the answers that the interviewee provides continually inform our evolving conversation. By the end of the interview/conversation, I find that most, if not all, of my questions have been explored. In addition, because I try to follow the topics that the interviewee raises, I inevitably collect data that I would not have thought to ask about, and often these data turn out to be the most instructive. This was the case that I referred to in Chapter 1 when the teacher I was talking with told me, 'You know, it's much more than language'. This response, which I might have dismissed as off-topic in a more standard interview approach, ultimately led me to understand the underlying social identities project that I argue informs and explains Oyster's dual-language program.

With respect to my role in the interview process, I assume that I am an active participant, jointly constructing meaning with the interviewee. I do not pretend to be a neutral interviewer who is simply collecting information. Rather, in talking with teachers and administrators and parents, I made explicit my personal interest as a teacher and as a researcher in understanding how the Oyster dual-language program works because of my concern for the disproportionate minority drop-out rate in this country. My interests were therefore aligned with the interviewee's. My emphasis on the role of the teacher was reflected in the questions I asked, for example, about their personal histories, why they entered the field, what their training was, what their personal goals were. When I interviewed students, I explained that I was also a student trying to learn about bilingual education, and that I wanted to understand their perspective as student because I assume that students know a lot about what is going on in schools. In all of the cases I tried to adopt the role of learner, and they all seemed to adopt the role of my teachers.

I do not pretend that the data I collected contain 'objective' accounts of the Oyster Bilingual School program. My goal was rather to understand as many individual subjective accounts of the Oyster Bilingual School program, and to look for coherence in those accounts. In order to understand a variety of perspectives on the same situation, my questions were often similar to those described by Mishler (1986) as characteristic of focused interviews. For example, I would regularly ask a variety of individuals who had all participated or witnessed the same situation, e.g. in the classroom, or in a meeting, or in the city, to tell me what happened in that event. In this way, I could compare multiple representations and evaluations of the same thing.

Perhaps because of the open-ended nature of the interviews I conducted, narratives regularly emerged in the texts; for example, by any of the participants in interviews or in casual conversation to me, by students to teachers, by students to other students, by teachers to other teachers, by teachers to students as part of the official classroom interaction, by teachers to students more informally as an aside, etc. As I illustrate in Chapter 5, the stories that the individuals told and the metaphors they used to describe events can provide insight into how individuals represent and interact with their world (Lakoff & Johnson, 1980). Many of the more formal, extensive interviews that I conducted with my primary informants (e.g. with one of the co-founders of the program), the principals (there have been three since I began my research in 1989), the teachers I worked most closely with (two in the kindergarten, two in the first grade, one in the third grade, one in the fourth grade, and two in the sixth grade) were audio-taped and transcribed verbatim.

Not all of my data were interview data. I also collected articles about the program in which someone else interviewed the Oyster Bilingual School participants, pamphlets the school published for conferences they held at Oyster Bilingual School to illustrate their bilingual model in action, copies of presentations that the parents gave at a conference about the program, observations and transcripts of teacher and parent–teacher meetings, observations and transcripts of classroom interaction, and samples of student work. In these cases, I was not the intended audience. The consistency of the Oyster Bilingual School representations of their program across a variety of speech events to a variety of audiences supports my interpretation of and explanation for the underlying Oyster Bilingual School discourse.

I began my analysis of the interview data by looking closely at individual transcripts to understand how the Oyster educators represent and evaluate what the problem was for whom, their goals for the various target populations, beliefs about Oyster's success, etc. (see Tannen, 1993, for discussion of frame analysis). Once I had analyzed individual texts in detail, I looked across texts from a particular level of authority, e.g. the teachers' level, and began to identify recurring themes. For example, I found considerable coherence in how various individuals represented and evaluated what the problem was for LEP students in mainstream US schools, and how Oyster functioned as the solution to societal problems for language minority students. Then I looked across the levels of authority and at official policy statements and other site documents (e.g. newspapers, curricular materials, conference papers, etc.) produced and/or distributed by Oyster, and again identified coherence in the text representations and evaluations about what made Oyster's bilingual program successful with its linguistically and culturally diverse student population. I am not claiming that there was no variation in the Oyster educators' discourse about their practice. Rather, I am claiming that there was considerable coherence in themes they identified and in the way they represented and evaluated what contributed to Oyster's success. My intertextual discourse analysis of the data described in this section allowed a collective understanding of Oyster's *ideal* plan.

Analysing classroom discourse

To understand how the language plan was *actually* implemented on the classroom level, I spent one year (1989) in the sixth grade and another (1990) in one of the kindergarten classes as a participant-observer. In addition to working with the students and the teachers in a variety of ways (e.g. as an ESL, math, and writing tutor, as a classroom aide) and taking extensive fieldnotes about my participation and my observations, I taped and transcribed classroom interaction, and I collected samples of student work. My analysis of classroom discourse concentrated on identifying patterns of language use and intergroup relations which I compared to the ideal plan. As part of my ongoing interviews/conversations described earlier, I regularly asked the teachers whom I was working with about my interpretations, which either confirmed what I was finding or pushed me in other directions to further my investigation. To ensure that the patterns of interaction and interpretation that I identified in the kindergarten and the sixth grade were representative of those throughout the school, I conducted spot observations in pre-K, first, third, fourth, and fifth grades over the course of my study. When I finished my analysis, I submitted my findings (Freeman, 1993) to the school. In 1994, I returned to Oyster to talk to the administrators about my work; they both confirmed my interpretations and informed me of ways they were working to address many of the discrepancies between the ideal plan and actual implementation that I had identified and that I describe in detail in Chapter 8.

My approach to analysing classroom discourse incorporates insights and methodologies from the ethnography of communication, interactional sociolinguistics, conversation analysis, and social psychology into a critical discourse orientation. The process that I undertake to describe the classroom texts requires several stages. Consistent with an ethnography of communication approach, my analysis proceeds from the macro-level to the micro-level, and I change what I take to be the relevant unit of analysis as I progress.

The first level of my classroom discourse analysis involves identification of speech situations, which are in some recognizable way bounded or integral to the participants (Hymes, 1974). Identification of speech situations is very straightforward, because participants mark speech situations as distinct from one another by some verbal or non-verbal discourse markers. The speech situations that are relevant to this study are the individual classes or segments of classes that teachers and students explicitly name (e.g. math, journalwriting).

I proceed from identification of the particular speech situations to analysis of the speech event or speech activity (I use these terms interchangeably). According to Duranti (1988), the basic assumption of speech-event analysis is that an understanding of the form and content of everyday talk in its various manifestations implies an understanding of the social activities in which speaking takes place. He argues that speech events are not merely accompanied by verbal and non-verbal interaction, they are shaped by it. Hymes (1974) proposes a preliminary list of features or components of communicative events that can be remembered by the acronym SPEAKING: S (situation: setting and scene); P (participants: speaker/sender, addressor, hearer/receiver/ audience, addressee); E (ends: outcomes, goals); A (act sequence: message form and message content); K (key: e.g. sarcasm, seriousness); I (Instrumentality: channel, forms of speech); N (Norms: norms of interaction and interpretation); G (Genre: e.g. lecture, essay, discussion group). I use Hymes' SPEAKING grid as a checklist of parameters to distinguish one speech event or activity from another.

Once I have identified the speech situations and speech events within the text that I am working with, I return to the beginning of the transcript again for another look. At this stage in the analysis, I take the utterance as the relevant unit and determine its **participation framework**, which Schiffrin (1985: 243) summarizes as 'the set of positions which individuals take in relation to an utterance'. As Goffman (1981) discusses, delineation of the participation framework of an utterance requires more than the identification of speaker and hearer. For example, an individual can be a speaker, a ratified listener, an unratified listener such as an overhearer. Following Goffman (1981), I identify, for example, whether the teacher is talking to one student or to the whole class, and whether a student is talking to the teacher, to the entire class or to one student.

After looking closely at the participation framework of each utterance, I take another look at the transcript in its entirety and, following Edelsky (1981) and Philips (1983), I investigate **floor distribution**. In trying to understand who has the floor, Edelsky recognizes the difference between 'turn', an on-record speaking behind which lies an intention to convey a message which is both referential and functional (1981: 403) and 'floor', the 'acknowledged 'what's going on' within a psychological time and space' (1981: 405). She differentiates between floors developed by one person at a time, and collaboratively developed floors. Philips' (1983) analysis of classroom interaction distinguishes the 'official' floor (sanctioned by the teacher) from the 'unofficial' floor (not sanctioned by the teacher). Since it is difficult to determine exactly what 'sanctioned by the teacher' means, unless the teacher explicitly says that certain talk is not permitted (in which case the analyst knows that the talk was not sanctioned), my criteria for distinguishing official and unofficial floor revolves around topic identification, with attention to topic maintenance and topic shift by teacher and students, as well as to participation frameworks sanctioned by the teacher. I mark my transcripts for 'official' and 'unofficial' floor distribution, and take note of which utterances are part of which floor.

Because of the teacher's powerful socializing role in the classroom, an understanding of **teacher ratification** strategies is very important to the analysis. Philips (1983) builds on Goffman's (1981) notion of ratified *versus* unratified speakers and listeners in her description of means of teacher ratification: (1) direct, (2) substitution of pronouns, (3) expansion, and (4) repetition. She recognizes that the teachers also fail to ratify students' contributions through (1) rejection, (2) providing the correct response, and (3) non-incorporation of the students' utterance by repetition of the teacher's previous utterance (Philips, 1983: 86–7). Philips (1983: 89) claims:

> it should be evident that while turn economies and participant structures are designed to equalize students' access to the floor, the teacher's response patterns are not. Instead the teacher's response patterns selectively incorporate student's utterances heard and judged to be appropriate or correct and ignore those that are incorrect and inappropriate.

Because the Oyster educators emphasize student-centered interaction which encourages students to interact directly with each other, I investigate **students' ratification** of each other's contributions as well as teachers' ratification of students' contributions to identify what are considered appropriate classroom participation patterns.

After marking the overall floor distribution, I again look much more closely at what is going on in the interaction, but at this stage in the analysis I am concerned with the unit of the speech act. The basic premise of **speech act theory** is that people use language not only to describe the world but also to change it by relying on public, shared conventions (Austin, 1975; Searle, 1975). Consistent with the notion of speech act analyzed by ethnographers of communication, yet distinct from the notion of speech act commonly analyzed by linguists, I take the position that interpretation of speech acts depends on features of the context and interaction. How does language uttered by speakers and interpreted by hearers in contexts perform action? More specifically, how does the teacher's interactional work socialize the students into acquiring their social roles relative to each other in the classroom and school discourse? To begin to answer these questions, I turn to work in **ethnometho-**

dology and **interactional sociolinguistics**, both of which assume that conversation is an interactional achievement.

Although neither the ethnomethodologists nor the interactional sociolinguists specifically talk about speech acts, their micro-level discourse analytic approaches contribute to an understanding of how some utterances function in the interaction. Following the ethnomethodologists' conversation analytic approach, I investigate what the participants in the interaction are doing that affects the speaker's utterances (e.g. Schegloff, 1988). For example, I analyze how sequencing contributes to the participants' understanding of the function of some utterances as speech acts, e.g. after a question participants expect an answer. I also investigate how the turn-taking mechanism works, for example, the role of pauses in allocating the next turn, and the supportive interactional work that back channel cues such as 'Uhhuh' and 'Oh really?' provide.

Gumperz (1982), one of the originators of the interactional sociolinguistic approach, argues that conversational involvement, or an observable state of being in coordinated interaction, is the basis of all linguistic strategies. Without involvement, there is no shared meaning. Following Gumperz, Tannen (1989) investigates linguistic strategies that achieve interpersonal involvement with emphasis on the joint construction of meaning by conversational partners. She argues that the more work hearers do to supply meaning, the deeper their understanding and the greater their sense of involvement with both the text and the speaker. For example, her work illustrates how repetition facilitates production and comprehension of language, connects speakers to the discourse and to each other, and helps accomplish the social goal of managing the business of conversation. She argues that these functions of repetition simultaneously provide an overarching function: that of coherence and interpersonal involvement. In her work on conversational style, Tannen (1986) demonstrates that interruption is not necessarily negative, and that overlap often shows involvement. Consistent with their interactional sociolinguistic approach, I investigate how linguistic features contribute to interpersonal involvement. Given my assumption that communication is more complex among students of diverse backgrounds, understanding how they involve themselves in the negotiation of meaning is crucial.

As I mention in Chapter 3, I follow Vygotsky in assuming that less capable individuals learn to participate appropriately in activities through the guidance of a more capable peer. Useful to my analysis is Vygotsky's notion of the 'zone of proximal development'. According to Wertsch (1985),

> Vygotsky defined the zone of proximal development as the distance between a child's *'actual developmental level as determined by independent problem solving '* and the higher level of *'potential development as determined through problem solving under adult guidance or in collaboration with more capable peers'*. (Vygotsky, 1978: 86, cited by Wertsch, 1985: 67–8; emphasis in original)

This notion of the 'zone of proximal development' provides an analytical tool for understanding some of the interactional work the teacher does in socializing the student through the classroom discourse, as well as the interactional work the students do to socialize each other.

In sum, my intertextual analysis of classroom discourse begins with individual texts of classroom interaction, and investigates how the linguistic features and discourse strategies that I identify function together to provide educational opportunities to all of the Oyster students. I continually relate my close analysis of individual classroom texts to each other in order to make the underlying norms of interaction and interpretation that guide behavior at Oyster Bilingual School explicit.

As mentioned earlier, my analysis is informed by my ongoing conversations with teachers and students about what they do and why, and these conversations often suggest directions for further inquiry. Because my goal is to investigate how the dual-language plan functions in its sociopolitical context, my micro-level analyses (presented in Chapters 9 and 10) are constantly informed by my understanding of the macro-level sociopolitical struggle that I described in Chapters 5–8.

I do not pretend that my study is exhaustive. I aim to describe the language plan and implementation from as many directions as possible. The validity of such a study comes from the identification of patterns that are repeated throughout the discourse (student, teacher, classroom, administrator, parent, and policy statements) that work together to make one explanation plausible, and to rule out rival hypotheses. The fact that all the participants on all the levels identify similar influences as contributing to the success of the plan is what supports my argument.

THE DYNAMIC NATURE OF DUAL-LANGUAGE-PLANNING AT OYSTER BILINGUAL SCHOOL

The diagram of my research design (Figure 9, below) locates the situational level of the classroom interaction within the institutional level of Oyster Bilingual School within the societal level of mainstream US discourse. I want to emphasize the dynamic interrelationships among problem identification, planning, and implementation on the different planning levels that I identified at Oyster, as well as how these processes interact with sociopolitical factors. According to Fairclough (1989), one possible relationship among levels of context is reproductive. That is, the language used in the micro-level, face-to-face classroom interaction can reflect and help reproduce the existing macro-level social order in schools and in society. This is the case that many ethnography of communication studies conducted in schools document, in which the language minority students' subordinate social role is reflected in and perpetuated by mainstream US educational discourse (e.g. Scollon & Scollon, 1981; Heath, 1983; Philips, 1983). This, however, is not the only possiblity. Another is that the language used in the micro-level, face-to-face classroom interaction can challenge and potentially transform the macro-level social order. This is the implicit

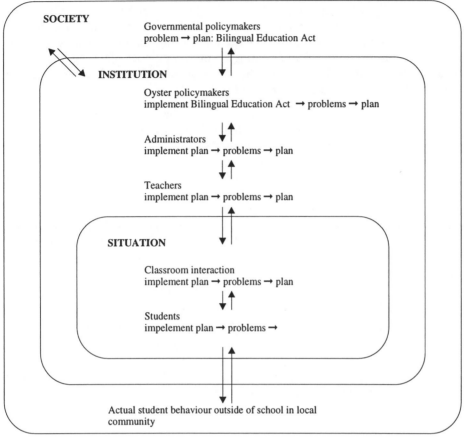

Figure 9 The dynamic, multi-level, multi-directional nature of language-planning and implementation at Oyster Bilingual School

goal of the dual-language-planning and implementation efforts at Oyster Bilingual School. As Figure 9 illustrates and as I discuss in detail throughout Chapters 5–10, Oyster's bilingual plan was made in response to a societal plan to implement the Bilingual Education Act. The response to this plan on the institutional level involved decisions on the part of policymakers, administrators, teachers, and parents. Their decisions interact in dynamic ways with plans and problems on the situational level the classroom.

The diagram of my research design (Figure 9) illustrates the levels of institutional authority and the interactions among those levels that I identified at Oyster Bilingual School. There is dialogue concerning planning, implementation, and outcomes between levels. The changes that one level makes in order to be able to implement another level's plans are fed back to that level in the form of problems that require new plans. The greatest amount and most complex interaction occurs at the situ-ational level between Teachers and Students in the Classroom interaction. The majority of my efforts therefore focused on gaining an understanding of the dynamics within these levels and relating them to the upper planning and imple-mentation levels; that is to relate the micro-level situational context to the macro-level institutional and societal contexts.

I would like to stress at the very beginning the multidirectional, dynamic interaction of influencing factors. My ethnographic/discourse analytic experience has taught me that an educational language plan and its implementation cannot be realistically discussed in terms of a simple causal equation, as was the case with the Bilingual Education Act's earlier equation of English language proficiency and equal educational opportunity (see Chapter 2 for further discussion). Rather, the implementation of a language plan in an educational setting with the goal of providing equal educational opportunities to a linguistically, culturally, and socioe-conomically diverse student population is a complex sociolinguistic situation that requires a complex response. My discussion of Oyster's dual-language-planning and implementation therefore concentrates on identifying, describing, interpreting, and explaining the influences that the individuals within Oyster Bilingual School expressed as contributing to the program's success.

Although language-planning discussions tend to be primarily problem-oriented, there has been some concern for the development of a theoretical framework for the field (e.g. Haugen, 1983; Neustupny, 1983; Cooper, 1989). A word of caution is in order here in that regard. The factors that I argue contribute to Oyster's 'successful' program are based on the language-planners' (at all levels) identification of those factors within their particular sociopolitical situation. These factors therefore can provide guidelines for the investigation of another educational language plan and implementation in its distinct sociopolitical context. In addition, an ethnographic/ discourse analytic approach can provide a methodology for undertaking another such study (see Chapter 11 for discussion). The specific factors that I describe as contributing to Oyster's success in its local context, however, are not meant to contribute to the development of a more general theory of educational language-planning. As Duranti discusses with reference to Hymes' (1974) SPEAKING grid (an acronym for components that provide a preliminary framework for ethnogra-phers of communication to investigate speech events),

> the grid, in its various versions, has always maintained an etic status and was never accompanied by a (general) theory of the possible relationships among the various components. Such a theoretical discussion, in Hymes' program, seemed to be possible only at the local level (i.e. with respect to particular communities) and not within a more global, comparative framework. (Duranti, 1988: 219, emphasis in original)

Similarly, because of the complex interaction of particular sociopolitical factors with the contextualized language plan, it may be that a more general theory of dual-language-planning is not possible, especially at this stage in our understanding of language-planning processes. Identification of factors that contribute to the successful implementation of one dual-language plan is, however, a step in the direction of developing a framework for investigating and ultimately understanding educational language-planning processes on the local level.

CONCLUSION

This chapter has provided a general description of how I related Oyster Bilingual School's dual-language plan to the larger sociopolitical context, and a detailed description of how I gained access to the school, my role in the research process, and my data collection and analysis methods. This discussion was intended to address issues about the validity and reliability of my research, as well as to facilitate replication of this approach in another context. I turn now to a detailed ethno-graphic/discourse analysis of dual-language-planning and implementation at Oyster Bilingual School. I move from analysis of the ideal plan (Chapter 5) to actual implementation (Chapters 6–10). This case study demonstrates how the Oyster educators translate their assumptions about and expectations for their students into a dual-language program that provides more or less equitable educational opportu-nities to all of their students. It also illustrates the tension between Oyster's alternative educational discourse practices and the mainstream US discourse prac-tices that it opposes.

CHAPTER 5

The Need for an Alternative: The Oyster Perspective

The purpose of this chapter is to begin to make explicit the abstract underlying ideology that structures Oyster's discourse about language use, minority participation rights and intergroup relations. My intertextual analysis links the Oyster educators' stories and policy statements to each other and locates them in relation to mainstream US educational discourse. This analysis illustrates the Oyster perspective on the problem for language minority students in mainstream US discourse and the Oyster perspective on the solution to that problem. The chapter concludes by introducing the underlying social identities project that I argue informs and explains Oyster's program and practices.

Before I move to my analysis, I want to suggest how educational researchers and practitioners can use my presentation of the Oyster Bilingual School program and practices to think about how any school provides educational opportunities to their target populations. As I mentioned in Chapter 1, the specific details of an ethnographic study are not intended to be directly translatable to another context. However, educational researchers and reflective practioners can use the questions that I have used to investigate how the Oyster educators organize their dual-language program to critically analyse educational programs for minority students in another context. This chapter, for example, asks what the Oyster educators believe the problem is for their target populations, and what they believe the solution to that problem is. I encourage researchers and practitioners to ask what other educators and/or they themselves believe the problem is for language minority students, and what they believe the solution to that problem is. Do they believe, for example, that language is a problem for language minority students, and that language instruction is the solution to that problem? Or do they believe, for example, that systemic discrimination is a problem for language minority students, and that bilingualism and cultural pluralism are solutions to that problem? I encourage researchers and educators to think critically about how local assumptions and expecations about students, their needs, their abilities, and their strengths position language minority students relative to language majority students at school, and to ask whether this is an equitable construction of social relations. As I argue throughout this book, the assumptions and expectations that educators have about their students have serious implications for the ways they organize educational programs and practices, and for the educational opportunities they provide their students. I turn now to a detailed analysis of the Oyster perspective on the problem for language minority students at school and of their solution to that problem.

MAKING OYSTER'S PERSPECTIVE EXPLICIT: AN INTERTEXTUAL ANALYSIS

The intertextual analysis presented in this section reveals the Oyster perspective on language minority students' experiences in mainstream US schools; this perspective can be understood as their justification for creating an alternative educational discourse at the school. My analysis illustrates how surface linguistic features (e.g. story structure, metaphor, lexical choice, participant role, modality, etc.) that I identified in the Oyster texts provide traces of the abstract, underlying, ideological Oyster discourse.

Before I begin my intertextual analysis of the Oyster educators' stories, policy statements, and other site documents, a word of qualification is in order. My discussion of the reasons underlying the Oyster program could be interpreted as suggesting a coherent Oyster collective who all have the *same* reasons for opposing mainstream US educational discourse practices. Such an argument, however, would be absurd. The people associated with Oyster, from policymakers to students, all have different experiences (schemas/texts) that they draw on as they talk about the world and interact with each other. Some, for example, have personally experienced discrimination as language minority children being socialized through mainstream US educational discourse. Many of these individuals describe their experiences with what they perceived to be forced assimilation as motivating their goals with the language minority children at Oyster. Others were born outside of the United States, immigrated as adults, and use two or more languages in their linguistic repertoire on a regular basis. These individuals see bilingualism as a resource that they want to develop in the individual Oyster students as well as in US society. Still others are native Standard English-speaking middle-class people who, for whatever combination of experiences, speak of discriminatory practices in the United States. These educators want to socialize the language minority and majority students at Oyster differently than mainstream US schools generally allow. Others, like the children, may have no experience in other educational institutions, and have only the school's messages and the messages they get outside of the school, e.g. through the media or in their neighborhood, to draw on. This list is by no means exhaustive of the diverse experiences represented in the school.

While there is considerable variation in the personal experiences of the individuals associated with Oyster, it is possible to abstract a general Oyster perspective on language minority students' experiences in mainstream US schools as compared with the alternative experience that Oyster offers to language minority and language majority children. I begin my presentation of that perspective with a story that Señora Ortega, the principal of Oyster at the time I began this study (1989), related to me about her personal experience as a native Spanish-speaking Mexican American student in monolingual English schools in Texas. I then relate other Oyster texts that I collected to Señora Ortega's story in order to demonstrate coherence throughout the Oyster educational discourse. I conclude this section by presenting the underlying story that emerged from my intertextual analysis. This story can be understood as Oyster's reason for constructing its alternative educational discourse.

One day in conversation, Señora Ortega told me a story about how she had been made to feel ashamed of her name and ashamed of her language at school, and that this experience motivated her work at Oyster. Segmenting Señora Ortega's narrative according to the structures that Labov (1972) identifies, with close attention to her representation and evaluation of her experience, provided a useful starting point for analysis as story structure can provide a systematic means of relating one text to another.[1] I have also underlined metaphorical language use on the transcript because, as I discuss in more detail later, coherence in metaphorical language use provides another means of linking texts.

ORIENTATION 1:

as a child … and I'm talking about personal experience

COMPLICATING ACTION 1:

one of the problems I had was that I never felt good about my race because it was never talked about … my name … I was so embarrassed … I remember … because no one could say /ele'na/ … I was always called /ili'na/ /e'lena/ or /e'len/ … and I always felt like they all knew that the teacher was pronouncing it wrong

RESOLUTION 1:

so I was so embarrassed all the time … I hated my name for years

ORIENTATION 2:

and it wasn't until I grew older

COMPLICATING ACTION 2:

that I started saying … well there's nothing wrong

RESOLUTION 2:

and *I actually started going back to my culture*

With Complicating Action 1, Señora Ortega identifies a problem she had in her youth: *I never felt good about my race because it was never talked about*. She draws a causal connection between not talking about her race and the negative evaluation of her race. Tannen (1993) identifies omission among her list of linguistic features that provide surface evidence for underlying frames. In other words, omission is evaluative. One interpretation of omission is that whatever is omitted goes without saying and therefore does not warrant mention.

Other interpretations of omission can be found in critiques of mainstream social practices that regularly omit minority contributions and perspectives. For example, feminists argue that women have not been equally represented in government, the medical field, the legal field, and that their voices have not been heard in these domains. This omission is explained by the patriarchal structure of mainstream society in which women have not been defined as legitimate participants in these discourses (see e.g. Cameron, 1990, for a review of this issue). Proponents of multicultural education also contend that mainstream US discourse regularly marginalizes or omits minority contributions from the curriculum content (see Chapter 8 for further discussion). Perhaps, in Señora Ortega's public school experience (or more generally within mainstream US society) race was not discussed because race is not considered a legitimate topic of conversation within mainstream US educational discourse.

Alternatively, the omission of a particular topic can be interpreted as an effort to avoid a taboo subject. Feminist critics (e.g. Butler, 1990) cite mainstream US society's reluctance to discuss sexuality, and especially homosexuality, as examples of omission that suggest the unspeakable. Applying this critique to Señora Ortega's story, her public school's omission of discussion of her race, like mainstream US public schools' omission of discussion of race in general, perhaps suggest that race was defined as unspeakable. Whatever the interpretation, Señora Ortega represents this omission as causing her to feel negatively about her race. As we see throughout Chapters 6 to 10, this concern with including and positively evaluating topics that have traditionally been excluded, marginalized, or otherwise negatively evaluated in mainstream US schools and society has important implications for how Oyster's program and practices are organized.

Metaphorical language use is also evaluative. According to Lakoff and Johnson (1980), metaphors that people use in their everyday speech and writing reflect the way that people conceptualize abstract ideas. For the purposes of an intertextual analysis, coherence in metaphorical language use across texts provides another means of linking texts to make underlying ideologies explicit. In Resolution 2, Señora Ortega employs a metaphor of movement in her utterance — *and I actually started going back to my culture* — which presupposes that she *had left* her culture. She represents the minority language (Spanish) and the minority culture (Mexican) as places that a language minority child can leave behind and possibly return to at a later time.

Such metaphorical representation of language, culture, and identity is common-place at Oyster. For example, Señor Xoci, the sixth grade Spanish-dominant teacher, used similar metaphors of movement (underlined on the transcripts below) in his description of his experience as a native Spanish-speaking Mexican American who attended monolingual English public schools in the southwest United States. Notice that this excerpt from my conversation with Señor Xoci echoes Resolution 2 of Señora Ortega's story:

> *I came back to my roots* when everything else had fallen apart ... you start looking around for something to hold onto and then you realize who you are ... and you finally get a grip ... this is *where I come from* ... this is *where I tie back into* ... so you sort of *go back into it*

Señora Rodriguez, one of the Spanish-dominant kindergarten teachers, also uses metaphors of movement away from and back to the minority language in response to my asking whether she thought the native Spanish-speakers would maintain their Spanish throughout their lives:

> I think *they'll recapture their Spanish* ... they'll realize exactly *where they fit* ... but society begins to teach them ... that there is a difference ... and there is a discrepancy ... and that there is ... and the fact that they are controlling their success or failure ... and they will start to realize that ... how much their culture ... *where they really come from* ... and *they'll begin to realize and go back to it.*

The Oyster educators' use of this metaphorical language to describe language minority students' experiences with the abstract notions of language, culture, and identity reflects a conception of language, culture, and identity as objects or places that a language minority child can leave behind while the individual then moves someplace else without them. Such representations of language, culture, and identity suggest that these notions are thought of as static and separable from the individual. In each of these accounts, the return to the native language, culture, and/or identity is positively evaluated, which implies a negative evaluation of the language minority student leaving the native language, culture, and identity. I want to emphasize that these static representations of language, culture, and identity stand in opposition both to the theoretical notions of language, culture, and identity discussed in Chapter 3, as well as to the empirical evidence that I documented at the school. As I illustrate throughout Chapters 6–10, the alternative educational discourse that Oyster has constructed demands a more dynamic, multiple, situated, negotiated, and negotiable understanding of language, culture, and identity in order to explain the options they make available to their minority students and majority students at school.

It is important to emphasize the representation of the language minority students' participant role in the assimilation process because we also find coherence across accounts at this level. Señora Ortega, in Complicating Action 1 and Resolution 1 (which is actually a complete story in itself), does not represent herself as having much choice. Her utterances — *I never felt good, it [my name] was never talked about* — and — *I was so embarrassed* — suggest that other students' actions were responsible for her negative evaluation of herself and for her leaving her culture. It is not until Complicating Action 2 that Señora Ortega represents herself as taking responsibility for actions, for example in her utterances — *I started saying ... well there's nothing wrong* — and — *I actually started going back to my culture*. Echoing the theme that minorities perceive of themselves as having no choice in the assimilation process, one of the co-founders of the Oyster bilingual program, Señor Estevez, provided the following description of immigrants' being forced to abandon their native language and identity in order to succeed in mainstream US society:

> the big problem in the United States ... years back ... that is not related to bilingual education ... it is related to the acquisition of any other language than English ... I just want to tell you two things ... first of all ... a problem of immigrants ..they have to find the identification of being an American in the dominance of a language ... and your allegiance your patriotism ... years back ... not well founded ... was the sooner that I forget the old country ... the more American I am

Señor Estevez's use of the modal *have to* reflects the obligation he attributes to immigrants to *find the identification of being American*. He represents immigrants as having no choice in the assimilation process: In order to be more American, the immigrant must forget the old country. Señor Estevez makes his negative evaluation of this mainstream ideology explicit in his utterance, *not well-founded*.

Shortly after Señora Ortega told me the story discussed earlier, she provided what I interpreted in Labov's (1972) terms to be the coda, or the way she returns from the stories she was telling to the present time. I have italicized the part that reflects her construction of the Oyster experience for students, and underlined the part that reflects her construction of the mainstream experience for students.

> **CODA**: you see what I'm saying ... *they're being prepared for something that is making them a better human being ... it's amazing ...* **as opposed to this discrimination and bigotry when they're out there**.

Señora Ortega uses this coda to relate her personal experience stories to the more general *discrimination and bigotry* in mainstream US educational and societal discourse. She also explicitly contrasts the *discrimination and bigotry* of mainstream US discourse with Oyster, which suggests her construction of Oyster as non-discriminatory and therefore the solution to the problem.

The following excerpt from the paper that Oyster parents presented to the NABE conference visitors in 1980 also describes Oyster as an alternative to mainstream US schools because of the negative effects of those schools on native Spanish speakers. I have italicized their construction of the mainstream US school experience and their construction of the Oyster experience is in bold italic.

The Director of EDC [Educational Development Center] pushed hard for integrated dual-language education involving English and Spanish speakers. *She felt that transitional bilingual education had isolated Hispanic students.* In DC [Washington, DC] *the philosophy placed emphasis on maintaining language and culture.* (Oyster Bilingual School, 1980)

In this account, Oyster is represented as the solution to the problem for the *isolated Hispanic students*. As in the other accounts we have seen, the Hispanic students are attributed little choice in the process. The conception of language and culture as static is also reflected in the lexical choice *maintain*.

Identifying coherent representations and evaluations of language minority students' experiences in mainstream US schools in these and other texts that I collected at Oyster enabled me to make explicit the following underlying story that I present as Oyster's reason for constructing its alternative educational discourse. The parts of the story are based on Señora Ortega's account, which provided for me the most complete and concise telling of the language minority students' story in mainstream US discourse.

ORIENTATION:
(1) Minority student goes to mainstream US school.
COMPLICATING ACTION 1:
(2) Minority student is made to feel bad/inferior about being different.
RESOLUTION 1:
(3) Minority student abandons negatively evaluated minority language, culture, and identity.
COMPLICATING ACTION 2:
(4) Minority individual later in life realizes that minority language, culture, and identity is OK.
RESOLUTION 2:
(5) minority individual returns to minority language, culture, and identity, now positively evaluated.
CODA:
(6) Goal of school: to provide an alternative to the minority and majority students alike: the development of positive minority identities whose linguistic and cultural differences are expected, tolerated, and respected within the educational discourse.

Oyster's underlying story can be understood as a story within a story, with the first story consisting of the Orientation, Complicating Action 1, and Resolution 1. In Complicating Action 1, the minority student is represented as having no choice in the process; he/she is *made* to feel bad/inferior about being different in the mainstream school. The resolution to this problem, abandoning the native language, culture, and identity, can be understood as the only choice if the minority student wants to participate and achieve in the mainstream US discourse. Another choice for the minority student is to opt out of mainstream US educational and societal disourse with its required assimilation strategy, which is perhaps a partial explanation for the disproportionately high minority drop-out rate from US public schools. It is important to mention that for many minority students, Resolution 1, either assimilating to mainstream ways of speaking and interacting or dropping out of mainstream US educational and societal discourse, is the end of the story.

I propose, however, that the Orientation, Complicating Action 1, and Resolution 1 can be understood as the Orientation to the second story that the Oyster educators told. In the second story (Complicating Action 2 and Resolution 2), the minority student is represented as later in life realizing the possibility of positively evaluating the minority language, culture, and identity, and therefore returning to that language, culture, and identity. The coda presents Oyster's goal for its language minority students. These educators have recognized discriminatory practices against language minority students in mainstream US schools and society, rejected this discourse, and have attempted to construct an alternative educational discourse at Oyster Bilingual School which socializes language minority and language majority students into seeing themselves and each other as equal participants in school.

Before moving to analysis of Oyster's Philosophy Statement, it is important to mention that the Oyster educators are not alone in their perspective on the problem for language minority students in mainstream US schools and society. This is a story that I have repeatedly heard from language minority students in other contexts, and that is gaining increasing currency among (language minority and language majority) educators who work with language minority populations in the United States. Thus, this perspective makes an important contribution to the conversation about how to provide equal educational opportunities to an increasingly diverse student population, a conversation that until recently has been dominated by the unquestioned assumption that assimilation was the only available option to members of linguistic and cultural minority groups. As I emphasize throughout the book: just as there is always more than one option available to language minority students, so too there is always more than one option available to US schools that serve language minority populations.

LOCATING THE PHILOSOPHY STATEMENT IN THE LARGER SOCIOPOLITICAL CONTEXT

In order to demonstrate how Oyster Bilingual School's dual-language education program interacts with the larger sociopolitical context of US schools and society, I begin with analysis of official school policy. This section presents an intertextual analysis of the Oyster Mission Statement, and draws on our understanding of societal discourses surrounding bilingual education in the United States (Chapter 2), language minority students in mainstream US schools (Chapter 3), and the underlying story outlined earlier in this chapter as possible meanings that are available for interpreting Oyster's ideal. I begin my discussion of the two-part Oyster Mission Statement by mentioning that the *Teachers' Handbook* is written almost entirely in

English. The exceptions are the Mission Statement and the Philosophy Statement (part 2 of the Mission Statement). Both of these statements are presented on the top of the page in English and on the bottom in Spanish. Such code-switching in the *Teachers' Handbook* is evaluative because of the school's policy with respect to the use of Spanish and English in official school documents.

All documents sent home to parents are to be written in Spanish and in English with no page numbers, and the official letterhead is to appear on both sides of the page so that one language is not represented as having priority over the other by virtue of its being first. When I wrote to the parents requesting permission for their children to participate in this study, the permission letter had to follow the same format. This policy is undertaken in an effort to include all of the parents in the school's decision-making processes, not only those who speak English. Similarly, the booklet that Oyster distributed to NABE visitors is written in Spanish and English. Such a policy symbolically reflects the school's dedication to being bilingual and inclusive, and to elevate the status of Spanish within the school. Because of this policy, I would have expected the entire *Teachers' Handbook* to be written in both Spanish and English, but this is only the case for the Mission Statement and the Philosophy Statement. The use of Spanish in these two documents exclusively marks the importance of their content for the writers as well as for the intended audiences.

My discussion here of the two-part Mission Statement will be limited to an intertextual analysis of the Philosophy Statement because the Philosophy Statement provides Oyster's reasons for their dual-language program. I have included only the English version of the Philosophy Statement here, and I have added sentence numbers before each sentence for ease of discussion.

Philosophy
1 We believe that every Oyster School child has an inherent right to an education which will enhance the development of maximum capability, regardless of sex, ethnic, economic, social, or religious background. 2 We believe that every child has the ability to learn, and that we must build upon this positive assumption. 3 We believe that every child has an inalienable right to the tools which facilitate the achievement of personal goals and the fulfillment of obligations to society. 4 A child's learning ability, employment potential, and cultural interests are enriched by achieving competency in a language beyond his/her own, in a classroom where children from various cultures learn and share together. 5 We believe that children from Hispanic cultures will learn to perform better in English in an atmosphere where their native language is respected and where continued growth in their native language is provided. 6 In addition, native English speakers will have their educational experience enriched by achieving competency in a second-language, at an age when achieving such a competency is easiest.

7 Therefore, the Oyster School staff pledges itself to meeting this challenge by providing a comprehensive bilingual educational program in an atmosphere that is open, concerned and responsive to the needs of students and the community.

8 We believe that the educational program at Oyster must provide an environment in which all students are afforded the opportunity to obtain competencies which will help them survive as individuals and as members of society. 9 We believe that the racial and ethnic richness and diversity of the Oyster student body are the bases through which we will enrich and further promote the goals of building a culturally pluralistic society.

10 To this end we are committed to the establishment of practices and programs which will insure the intellectual, physical, emotional and aesthetic well-being of all our students.

The Philosophy Statement, like any text, assumes a voice or a speech role and projects an audience role. This statement is directed to two different groups which affects the speech and audience role of the text. On the one hand, the Philosophy Statement is distributed as part of the *Teachers' Handbook*. In this case, the text assumes an inclusive *we* speech role, which functions to immediately involve the teachers in the discourse as a part of *we*. The beliefs represented are taken to be, in this case, the same as the beliefs of the audience. On the other hand, the Philosophy Statement is reproduced in literature that the school distributes to visitors or takes to scholarly conferences. To these audiences, the text assumes an exclusive *we* speech role. In this case, *we* is limited to the teaching and administrative staff of Oyster which stands as a collective. The beliefs expressed in the Philosophy Statement may or may not be the same as the audience's beliefs. In this latter case, the use of *we* also functions to implicitly involve the audience in the Oyster collective's beliefs.

The speakers' or writers' attitude towards the propositional content of a text can be revealed by investigating the linguistic features of modality, tense, negation and lexical choice (Halliday, 1985; Labov, 1972; Tannen, 1993). The clause *we believe*, which introduces sentences 1, 2, 3, and 5 in paragraph 1 and sentences 8 and 9 in paragraph 3, establishes the writers' certainty about the ideational content of these propositions:

(1) *that every Oyster School child has an inherent right to an education which will enhance the development of maximum capability, regardless of sex, ethnic, economic, social, or religious background;* (2) *that every child has the ability to learn, and that we must build upon this positive assumption;* (3) *that every child has an inalienable right to the tools which facilitate the achievement of personal goals and the fulfillment of obligations to society;* (5) *that children from Hispanic cultures will learn better in English in an atmosphere where their native language is respected and where continued growth in their native language is provided;* (8) *that the educational program at Oyster must provide*

an environment in which all students are afforded the opportunity to obtain competencies which will help them survive as individuals and as members of society; (9) that the racial and ethnic richness and diversity of the Oyster student body are the bases through which we will enrich and further promote the goals of building a culturally pluralistic society.

The repetition of the clause *we believe* emphasizes the text's commitment to that value-orientation. Note that the majority, but not all, of the sentences in the Philosophy Statement are introduced by this value-orienting clause which suggests the writers' assumption that these beliefs are not held everywhere as general truths. That is, the writers reflect their awareness of other voices in the larger educational discourse community that may have different beliefs. In contrast, sentences 4 and 6, for example, do not begin with the clause *we believe*:

(4) *A child's learning ability, employment potential, and cultural interests are enriched by achieving competency in a language beyond his/her own, in a classroom where children from various cultures learn and share together; (6) In addition, native English speakers will have their educational experience enriched by achieving competency in a second-language, at an age when achieving such a competency is easiest.*

In these sentences, there is no explicit value-orienting stance, which makes these sentences read as unquestioned assumptions by all, i.e. as general statements of fact. Recall from our discussion of the evolution of the Bilingual Education Act in Chapter 2, however, that these propositions have not been seen as unquestioned truths; they have in fact only recently been proposed as possibilities for language minority and language majority students.

Note also that the writers have chosen the simple present tense to express the majority of the propositions, which further reflects the writers' attitude that these propositions are truths. Of the 24 verbals in the text, only nine express modality, in these cases through the lexical choice of either *must* or *will*. The use of the modal *must* in sentence 2, *We believe that every child has the ability to learn, and that we **must** build upon this positive assumption* and in sentence 8, *We believe that the educational program at Oyster **must** provide an environment in which all students are afforded the opportunity to obtain competencies which will help them survive as individuals and as members of society* (my emphasis) strongly encodes a social or moral obligation to fulfilling these beliefs. The use of the modal *will* in sentences 1, 5, 6, 8, 9, and 10 can be understood as either representing a future state of affairs, or as a promise that these processes as they describe will happen. In either case, the choice of the modal *will* marks the writers' attitude as other than a simple statement of fact.

The textual organization of the Philosophy Statement provides a clue to answering the question, What is the reason for the Oyster program? The use of the conjunction *therefore* that introduces paragraph 2 allows the reader to understand that the beliefs expressed in paragraph 1 function as reasons underlying the Philosophy Statement and by extension the program.

People always have a choice in what they say or do not say and how they say it. It is therefore evaluative that the statements in paragraph 1, which can be interpreted as reasons for action, are included (and not others) because they suggest that the writers believe that these statements do not go without saying, according to the writers, these statements are for whatever reason not self-evident. At the time of writing to all people who may read the document. The reasons for action that I identified in the Philosophy Statement can be grouped into the following themes: (1) educational rights of diverse student populations, (2) language-as-resource orientation, (3) 'learning and sharing together' versus segregation, and (4) additional reasons requiring an alternative educational discourse. These themes organize the following discussion of the reasons for Oyster's dual-language program.

Educational rights of diverse student populations

As Skutnabb-Kangas (1984) advises, language-planning researchers need to understand language-planners' explicit and implicit goals for the various populations that will be affected by the language plan in order to begin to understand how the language plan interacts with its sociopolitical context. The reasons that the Philosophy Statement includes begin to reveal these explicit and implicit goals.

The choice of subject in each of these sentences immediately reveals that the underlying reasons for the Oyster program are student-centered:

(1) *every Oyster School child*
(2) *every child*
(3) *every child*
(4) *a child's learning ability, employment potential and cultural interest*
(5) *children from Hispanic cultures*
(6) *native English speakers*

There is no differentiation among populations of children within the school's philosophy in sentences 1, 2 and 3; the subject of each of these sentences is *every child*. This is consistent with the school's explicit policy of equal treatment for all children regardless of their linguistic, cultural, or socioeconomic background. In sentence 4, the writers chose to use a singular subject, *a child's learning ability, employment potential, and cultural interest,* rather than *every child* which was used in the preceding sentences. The focus is now on the individual, rather than on the collective.

Sentence 5 provides the first concrete referent of what subpopulations the writers refer to, *children from Hispanic cultures*. Note that the writers did not say *Hispanic children*, which would have been simpler, and instead said, *children from Hispanic cultures*. The use of the prepositional phrase introduced by a preposition of location focuses on the students' difference as a matter of place: from Hispanic cultures, rather than as a different kind of children: Hispanic children. *Cultures* is also plural, representing Hispanic as more than one and reflecting the writers' assumption that Hispanic culture is not homogeneous. Recognition of variety in Hispanic culture stands in opposition to mainstream discourse in which 'Hispanic' is considered more or less homogeneous.

The second subpopulation referred to is *native English-speakers*. It is noteworthy that *children from Hispanic cultures* are referred to first and that *native English-speakers* are referred to *in addition*. The Philosophy Statement reflects the recognition of two distinct groups of children. Within those groups, the *children from Hispanic cultures* are the primary concern, and the *native English-speakers* are an additional concern.

I would like to draw attention to the writers' lexical choice; *inherent right* in sentence 1, *every child has an **inherent right** to an education which will enhance the development of maximum capability, regardless of sex, ethnic, economic, social or religious background,* and *inalienable right* in sentence 3, *we believe that every child has an **inalienable right** to the tools which facilitate the achievement of personal goals and the fulfillment of obligations to society* (my emphasis). This lexical choice contributes to the cohesion within the text, and evokes the discourse of political philosophy and constitutional law. Evoking constitutional law in this way functions to provide a legitimate, legal basis for the Oyster beliefs.

The preposition *regardless of* means not taking into account (sentence 1). There are many other qualities that the authors could have chosen to follow the preposition 'regardless of'. The inclusion of the qualities *sex, ethnic, social, or religious background*, and not others is evaluative, leading the reader to infer that the writers assume that somewhere at some time, these qualities *are* taken into account and in some way interfere with a child's *inherent right*. It is noteworthy that language is not even mentioned, given that the majority of Civil Rights and Bilingual Education legislation about how to provide equal educational opportunities to students defined as LEP focuses on language. Perhaps this is because language is assumed by the authors to be included in one of these other categories, for example as a part of social background. Or perhaps language is not conceptualized as a problem. In any case, the inclusion of this sentence can be interpreted as a reflection of the writers' belief that within the larger educational discourse not *every child* is currently being provided an *education which will enhance the development of maximum capability.*

The fact that *children from Hispanic cultures* are mentioned first, and *native English speakers* are mentioned *in addition* suggests the writers' belief that it is the *children from Hispanic cultures* who have been denied these rights, and that the *native English-speakers* have had their rights to education fulfilled, so they can be considered *in addition.* In Chapter 6, I provide a relatively in-depth investigation of the Oyster answer to the question, What is a student? and I will elaborate on the policymakers', administrators', and teachers' explicit and implicit goals for the various populations there.

Language-as-resource orientation

The difference between how language is defined at Oyster Bilingual School and in mainstream US schools and society is key to understanding Oyster's opposition to the mainstream US evaluation of language minority individuals and groups. Sentence 4 provides the first mention of language, and is the first sentence that is not introduced by the value-orienting clause *we believe: A child's learning ability, employment potential, and cultural interests are enriched by achieving competency in a language beyond his/her own, in a classroom where children from various cultures learn and share together*. In this sentence, *language* is represented as an asset and as a source of enrichment. Note that there is no distinction among children at this point; *achieving competency in a language beyond his/her own* is represented as a resource for all children. The nominal *competency* is modified by the prepositional phrase *in a language beyond his/her own*. The writers could have chosen to write *in a second-language*, which is the unmarked way of describing language acquisition. But instead they subordinated *beyond his/her own* which reflects the assumption that language is a part of the individual, suggesting a close relationship between language and identity.

Sentence 5, *Children from Hispanic cultures will learn to perform better in English in an atmosphere where their native language is respected and where continued growth in their native language is provided*, offers additional attributes that Oyster associates with language; it is something that can be *respected* (or not), and something that is capable of *continued growth* (or not). The sequencing of these clauses connected with the coordinating conjunction *and* could be interpreted to mean that in an atmosphere where continued growth in the native language is not provided, there is no respect for the native language. The lexical choice *better* evokes a comparison with some other environment, and the inclusion of sentence 5 as one of the reasons for the program suggests the writers' assumption that such a respecting environment that fosters continued growth is not in existence everywhere.

Given my assumption that the meaning of mainstream US educational discourse is an available meaning, specifically to these writers as well as generally to the entire Oyster discourse community, it seems reasonable to suggest that sentence 5 evokes and rejects the most common mainstream US educational solution for LEP students. In transitional bilingual education or pull-out ESL instruction, no *continued growth in their native language* is provided (and perhaps no respect for the native language?). As discussed in Chapter 3, mainstream US educational discourse defines the native language of the language minority child as a handicap that needs to be overcome in order to perform better in English. And as we saw previously, the Oyster parents argued that transitional bilingual programs had *isolated Hispanic students*. In contrast, Oyster's language-as-resource orientation defines the native language of the language minority child as an *asset,* a source of *enrichment*, and something to be *respected* to foster *continued growth* so that the child can *perform better in English*.

The inclusion of the clause, *children from Hispanic cultures will learn to perform better in English* (sentence 5) presupposes the school's goal of English competency. This proposition refuses the discourse of conservative groups like 'English Only' that bilingual education is a threat to the learning of English (see Chapter 2 for further discussion). Oyster's dual-language model does not question the goal of all students' learning English, the stated goal of the Bilingual Education Act of 1988:

> Recognizing that, regardless of the method of instruction, programs which serve limited English proficient students have the equally important goals of developing academic achievement and English proficiency. (PL 100–297, Section 7002.4)

Since bilingualism is not constructed as a problem but as an asset within the Oyster discourse community, there is no threat to the learning of English.

Sentence 6 is represented as an additional reason, *In addition, native English speakers will have their educational experience enriched by achieving competency in a second-language*. The semantic quality of the verb *enrich* demonstrates the writers' assumption that their bilingual program offers the language majority students more than traditional educational discourse offers. In other words, Oyster's dual-language program is more than a solution to a problem for language minority students. The program involves and benefits language majority students. In this sense, the dual-language program can be understood as addressing a larger problem in mainstream US society, that of limited second-language resources in general.

'Learning and sharing together' versus segregation

A distinct yet related reason underlying the Oyster program that emerged from my intertextual analysis of the Philosophy Statement and the conversations/interviews with the different levels of educators was the Oyster rejection of segregation of language minority students as a solution to providing equal educational opportunities to all students. Sentence 4, *A child's learning ability, employment potential, and cultural interests are enriched by achieving competency in a language beyond his/her own, in a classroom where children from various cultures learn and share together,* can be interpreted in relation to mainstream US educational practice in which the students defined as LEP are segregated, because segregation makes their learning and sharing together impossible.

It is important to mention that segregation is also recognized as a problem by the Bilingual Education Act of 1988:

> the segregation of many groups of limited English proficient students remains a serious problem. (PL 100–297, Section 7002.12)

The majority of programs that received federal funding at the time of this study, however, were those which continued to segregate LEP students, and therefore exacerbate this problem. As mentioned in Chapter 2, it has only been recently that the Bilingual Education Act has funded dual-language programs.

Conversations with Señora Ortega also make explicit her assumption that the Oyster program can be understood as in opposition to mainstream US educational segregation of language minority students in either pull-out ESL classes or in transitional bilingual programs. She described one of the reasons for beginning the program as follows:

> This program started as a way to address the needs of the Hispanic children that came here in the community because of the fact that ... they were just sitting in ESL classrooms for a year and finally mainstreamed two years later with exit criteria that were for the birds ... so the teachers say why should they sit there when they could be acquiring an education ... right? ... something they can transfer later on.

Señora Ortega's lexical choice functions to evoke the transitional model: *ESL classrooms, mainstreamed two years later,* and *exit criteria* are all terms used in the bilingual education discourse community to describe early-exit transitional programs.

Consistent with the parents' previous description of the transitional model's isolating effects on Latino students, in this account Señora Ortega provides a picture of Latino students segregated in ESL classrooms within the transitional bilingual program and then exited after they have presumably acquired English. Her negative evaluation of the transitional model she has evoked is revealed in her representation of the process *they were just sitting in ESL classrooms for a year.* The listener gets a picture of students who are not actively involved in the learning process, but *just sitting.* She represents the circumstances of the mainstreaming process: *with exit criteria that were for the birds,* revealing her attitude that the evaluation procedure was not appropriate for the students either.

Note that Señora Ortega's criticism of the early-exit transitional model is similar to Cummins (1992) claim that it takes longer than two to three years for LEP students to acquire the academic English necessary for equal educational opportunities in the all-English mainstream US educational programs (see also Adamson, 1993, for a discussion of academic competence). There is a concern that emphasizing early-exit from transitional bilingual programs (represented by Señora Ortega in her use of the time element *two years*) does not adequately prepare students to compete as equals in mainstream US educational programs.

Additional reasons requiring an alternative educational discourse

The inclusion of sentence 2, *We believe that every child has the ability to learn and that we must build upon this positive assumption* leads the reader to infer the writers' belief that elsewhere not every child is believed to have the ability to learn. Sentence 4 also makes reference to *a child's learning ability.* The words *ability to learn* and *learning ability* echo the words *learning disabled* within special education discourse. A common critique of mainstream US educational practices is that very often students who are somehow different are labeled as learning disabled and segregated from the mainstream US classroom. The Bilingual Education Act refers to the problem of misplacing LEP students:

> Recognizing that reliance on student evaluation procedures which are inappropriate for limited English proficient students has resulted in the disproportionate representation of limited English proficient students in special education, gifted and talented, and other special programs. (April 1988: PL 100–297, Section 7002.19)

This passage from the Bilingual Education Act, however, does not state which groups have a disproportionately high representation in which kinds of classes and conversely which groups have a disproportionately low representation in which kinds of classes. It is important to mention that the populations in learning disabled classes include a disproportionately high representation of other than Standard English-speaking, white middle-class students, and the populations in gifted and talented programs include a disproportionately low representation of other than Standard English-speaking, white middle-class students, suggesting that what is labeled learning disabled might be systemic racism (Oakes, 1985). The segregation of learning disabled students in special education classes parallels the segregation of students defined as LEP in the transitional bilingual programs or in pull-out ESL classes in which Other is taken out for some different treatment.

Sentence 2 continues, *we must build on this positive assumption*. The choice of the word *positive* evokes its counterpart 'negative'. They could have simply said *assumption* without changing the referential meaning. The use of positive *assumption,* however, suggests that the writers believe that the negative assumption, that *not every child has the ability to learn*, is currently in practice somewhere in the educational discourse. Their certitude in their moral obligation as expressed in the clause *we believe that we must build upon this positive assumption*, functions as a demonstration of their opposition to educational discourse practices in which the negative assumption holds true. Recall from Chapter 2 that only very recently have explicit statements about LEP students' abilities to achieve high standards been made.

It is possible to continue this way throughout the rest of their beliefs in paragraph 1 that they present as reasons for their course of action. Including sentence 3, *we believe that every child has an inalienable right to the tools which facilitate the achievement of personal goals and the fulfillment of obligations to society* as a reason underlying their program allows the interpretation of the writers' assumption that not every child is *gaining the tools to facilitate the achievement of personal goals and the fulfillment of obligations to society*. This proposition evokes criticisms of current educational practice that students are not equipped with critical thinking and problem-solving skills that are necessary for them to participate in the workplace. This belief is concretely substantiated by disproportionately high drop-out rates for students from other than white middle-class backgrounds. The phrase, *fulfillment of obligations to society,* presupposes that students do in fact have obligations to society that must be fulfilled, which stands in opposition to complaints of an apathetic generation that is described by critics of contemporary educational practice as lost and disinterested.

In sum, an intertextual analysis of the Oyster Philosophy Statement makes clear that the Oyster educators reject the language and cultural difference-as-problem orientation that characterizes the mainstream US schools' treatment of language minority students because of their assumption that the mandatory assimilation to majority norms strategy is discriminatory. Instead, the Oyster educational discourse is characterized by a language and cultural difference-as-resource orientation that sees bilingualism and cultural pluralism as resources to be developed by language minority and language majority students alike. The following discussion explores this orientation as expressed in the Philosophy Statement in greater detail.

The Oyster challenge

The discourse marker *therefore* that introduces paragraph 2 signals to the reader that the reasons outlined earlier require the following course of action, or produce the following consequences. Paragraph 2 consists of one sentence: *Therefore, the Oyster school staff pledges itself to meeting this challenge by providing a comprehensive bilingual program in an atmosphere that is open, concerned and responsive to the needs of students and the community.* With respect to the social function of the text, the verbal *pledges* suggests that the text can be understood as a promise to do whatever follows in the rest of the text. The lexical choice *pledges* reflects the seriousness of the staff's commitment to its constructed obligation.

The subject of this sentence, *the Oyster school staff,* is the first specific referent of the *we* that has been used throughout the Philosophy Statement. The use of the specific referent at this point makes the *we* much more formal, which is consistent with the formal lexical choice of the verbal *pledges*. What does the Oyster staff pledge to do? They pledge to meet *this challenge*. The word *this* is anaphoric with all of the beliefs outlined in paragraph 1, which I argue earlier represents the writers' reasons for action. That their action is represented as a *challenge* further supports my argument that the writers believe that equal educational opportunity for all is not happening everywhere in educational discourse.

Since Chapters 6–8 present a relatively in-depth exploration of the parts of the Oyster cultural system and their interrelationships, I will limit my intertextual analysis here to the Philosophy Statement in relation to mainstream US educational practices. I understand the Oyster pledge, as expressed in the remainder of the Philosophy Statement, to be the basis of and legitimization for the alternative educational discourse they have constructed.

The preposition *by* in the embedded clause *by providing a comprehensive bilingual program* makes explicit the circumstantial relationship of manner and demonstrates that what follows is to be understand as the answer to the question, how? The bilingual program is to be instrumental in *meeting this challenge*. The prepositional phrase, *in an atmosphere that is open, concerned and responsive*, begins to describe the attributes of their comprehensive bilingual program. Since the writers express their obligation as a *challenge*, the reader can infer the writers' belief that their solution is different from what other programs offer; otherwise there would be no challenge. In the Oyster construction, bilingual programs that are not comprehensive and that do not respect the native language are not represented as open, concerned, and responsive, but perhaps the opposite: closed, not concerned and not responsive.

Understanding the participant roles of the students and the teachers/school relative to each other within the comprehensive bilingual program is central to understanding the implementation of the dual-language education program. The verbals and derivative forms that the writers chose to represent the processes that the students and teachers/school participate in begin to reveal their (ideal) participant roles relative to each other.

As we saw earlier, students are represented as the central concern of the Philosophy Statement, so I begin my discussion of participant role with the students. The students are referred to in the following sentences:

Sentence 1:	[students']	*development of maximum capability*
Sentence 2:	[students']	*ability to learn*
Sentence 3:	[students']	*achievement of personal goals*
	[students']	*fulfillment of obligations to society*
Sentence 4:		*a child's learning ability*
	[a child's]	*employment potential*
	[a child's]	*cultural interests*
	[students']	*achieving competency*
		children learn and share together:
Sentence 5:		*children ... will learn to perform*
Sentence 6:	[students']	*achieving competency*
Sentence 8:		*students ... obtain competencies*
	[students]	*survive*

Notice that the semantic quality of these verbals and derivative forms all encode agency. The students are represented as actively involved in the learning process.

This representation of the students as agents responsible for their own learning, achievement, development, and survival stands in contrast to the participant role of students in mainstream US educational discourse, in which students are represented as recipients of information. In the Oyster construction, *every child*, i.e. *children from Hispanic cultures* and *native English-speakers,* is equally represented as an agent in the educational process. This stands in contrast to minority populations who are often not constructed as having choice, for example, in being *forced to assimilate* (see earlier), or being denied equal educational opportunities because of cross-cultural differences in discourse strategies (e.g. Heath, 1983; Philips, 1983).

Either the teachers, the school, or education in general are referred to in the following sentences:

Sentence 1:	*education which will enhance the* [students'] *development*
Sentence 2:	*we must build upon this positive assumption*
Sentence 3:	[teachers/school provide] *tools which facilitate the* [students'] *achievement*
Sentence 4:	[students' ability etc.] *are enriched by* [education]
	[school provides] *classroom where children ... learn ...*
Sentence 5:	[school provides] *atmosphere*
	[students'] *native language is respected* [by atmosphere]
	continued growth in [students'] *native language is provided* [by atmosphere]
Sentence 6:	[students'] *educational experience will be enriched* [by teachers/school]
Sentence 7:	*The Oyster School staff pledges to meeting this challenge*
	[school] *provides a comprehensive bilingual program*
	[school provides] *atmosphere that is ...*
Sentence 8:	*the educational program ... must provide an environment*
	students are afforded the opportunity [by environment]
Sentence 9:	*we will enrich*
	we will further promote the goals of building
Sentence 10:	*we are committed to the establishment*
	practices and programs which will insure

The semantic quality of these verbals and derivatives represent the teachers and the school as instrumental in the educational process. This construction of teacher as instrumental stands in contrast to the mainstream US educational construction of teacher as central, in control, and the agent in the educational process.

Paragraph 3 can be interpreted as part of the Oyster pledge. Both sentences of paragraph 3 begin with the clause *we believe*, contributing to the cohesion of the text and further establishing the text's certainty about the beliefs that underlie their pledge. I restate the entire paragraph here for ease of reference.

8 We believe that the educational program at Oyster must provide an environment in which all students are afforded the opportunity to obtain competencies which will help them survive as individuals and as members of society. 9 We believe that the racial and ethnic richness and diversity of the Oyster school

student body are the bases through which we will enrich and further promote the goals of building a culturally pluralistic society.

Paragraph 3 is concerned with describing the attributes of the comprehensive bilingual program that Oyster *must provide*. The choice of the modal *must* reflects the moral or social obligation to fulfill this pledge. We can infer that the attributes that the writers present are attributes that they assume are not found in other educational programs that work with *children from Hispanic cultures*.

The lexical choice within this paragraph is evaluative. Sentence 8, *all students are afforded the opportunity to obtain competencies which will help them survive as individuals and as members of society,* illustrates Oyster's belief that this is a struggle for at least some of the population. We can infer from the first referent of *every child* that *children from Hispanic cultures* is the subpopulation that the writers believe must struggle because they have not traditionally been afforded equal opportunity. The word *afforded* raises the notion of cost. In the case of Oyster, the 'cost' of providing an environment in which all students have equal educational opportunity is something they can and must *afford*.

Racial and ethnic differences are defined as *richness*. The *diversity* of the student body is referred to by the singular nominal *student body;* it is an integrated whole (however, since student body is a relatively formulaic expression, not too much weight should be given to this meaning). *Racial and ethnic richness* and *the diversity of the student body* are additionally defined as instrumental in achieving what is unquestioningly stated as their goal; *to enrich and further promote the goals of building a culturally pluralistic society.* This goal is not modified by a belief or any kind of stance; it is rather presented as a truth. As discussed in Chapters 1–3, within mainstream US educational and societal discourse, assimilation and not cultural pluralism has been the more common goal. This statement represents further opposition to the value orientation of the mainstream US educational programs and practices for language minority students.

Paragraph 4, which is introduced by the discourse marker *to this end* functions as a statement of action that the Oyster staff takes: *we are committed to the establishment of practices and programs which will insure the intellectual, physical, emotional, and aesthetic well-being of all of our students.* The lexical choice here reflects the degree of their commitment. The semantic quality of the verb *insure* represents their value orientation towards their bilingual program as unquestionably certain. We saw in Chapter 1 that the writers of the Teachers' Handbook describe the Bilingual Program as 'unique in the city and country', which presupposes a comparison with other bilingual programs and practices; i.e. the transitional model or less than a comprehensive bilingual program. The reader can infer the writers' belief that other than a comprehensive bilingual program does not *insure the well being of all of the students.* The Oyster program is represented as reaching *all of the students,* not just some.

THE SOCIAL IDENTITIES PROJECT AT OYSTER BILINGUAL SCHOOL: AN INTRODUCTION TO THE IDEAL

The intertextual analysis of Oyster educator stories, policy statements, and other site documents presented in this chapter makes explicit Oyster's perspective on language use, academic participation rights, and intergroup relations. As opposed to mainstream US educational discourse's language-as-problem orientation, Oyster's educational discourse is characterized by a language-as-resource orientation. That is, as opposed to requiring *language minority* students to transition to monolingualism in Standard English in order to participate and achieve in school and society, Oyster requires *all* students to become bilingual and biliterate in Spanish and English. This analysis, however, has also revealed that limiting discussion of Oyster's work with its linguistically and culturally diverse student population to language alone would only allow a superficial understanding of how the dual-language program functions. Discrimination against the Spanish-speakers in the United States is a recurring theme that underlies the Oyster educators' work. I therefore argue that the Spanish–English language plan is one part of a larger social identities project that aims to promote social change by socializing children differently from the way children are socialized in mainstream US educational discourse.

Fasold (1984) discusses the notion of identity-planning in connection with language-planning efforts, stating that a successful language-planning policy will include measures to influence a person's self-identification, making the identity of the target language population desirable. The Oyster social identities project, however, is not restricted to measures to influence a person's self-identification. It is a policy of action. The Oyster social identities project attempts to provide the students not only with the ability to speak a second-language, but in the case of the minority students, techniques for asserting their right to speak and to be heard in a society that, at least in the Oyster construction, regularly refuses minority populations such rights. By socializing the majority and minority students to see themselves and each other as equal within the Oyster educational discourse, the Oyster social identities project aims to promote social change from the bottom up.

CONCLUSION: RECONSTITUTING SOCIAL RELATIONS AT SCHOOL

This chapter has provided an intertextual analysis of Oyster Bilingual School's Philosophy Statement that relates their ideal policy to larger mainstream US educational and societal discourses about language use, minority participation in schools and society, and intergroup relations. This analysis suggests that Oyster Bilingual School is organized to provide an alternative to mainstream US educational discourse in order to provide equal educational opportunities to all of the Oyster students. But, as Lemke (1989: 41) writes:

A single text voice may work to reconstitute these relations, but only the emergence of a stable intertextual formation in its community can finally do so.

In order to reconstitute the social relations so that language minority and language majority students see themselves as equal relative to each other, and as agents, with choices, and ultimately responsible for their own achievement, the implementation of the discourse on the classroom level must be coherent with the discourse constituted in the philosophy statement.

Chapters 6–10 investigate how this ideal is translated into action by looking closely at clasroom discourse practices at Oyster Bilingual School. As we saw in Chapter 3, conceptualizing schools as cultural communication systems provides an integrated means of understanding how social identities are jointly constructed through the norms that structure local definitions of teaching and learning at school. The next three chapters focus on the different parts of the alternative educational discourse system that the Oyster Bilingual School educators have developed. Chapter 6 provides a detailed discussion of the social identities of students and teachers at school, and shows that the Oyster educators have very different assumptions and expectations about their students than are traditionally held within the mainstream US educational discourse system. Chapter 7 argues that the Oyster educators' ideological beliefs about their students requires a very different organization of teaching and learning than is found in mainstream US schools. Chapter 8 looks closely at the norms that structure the curriculum content and classroom interaction to describe how minority social identities are negotiated through the Oyster Bilingual School discourse system.

While it is artificial to take apart the components of any discourse system because they are interrelated and they mutually inform each other, it is useful for analytic purposes. I encourage educational researchers and practitioners to analyse other educational discourse systems to see how they define language minority students relative to language majority students at school. The questions that I pose to investigate how the Oyster educators have constructed their alternative educational discourse can be used by other educational researchers and reflective practitioners to see how assumptions and expectations about language minority and language minority students at school translate into actual educational programs and classroom practices, and to see what opportunities those discourse systems make available to all of the students. I turn now to a detailed analysis of the Oyster Bilingual School system.

Note

1   Many of the stories that emerged in my interview data technically do not fit into Labov's (1972) definition of a narrative. For example, Señora Ortega's story is more of a summary of multiple experiences using basic narrative syntax instead of the traditional narrative of one past experience. Since my concern here is not in defining or identifying what a narrative is, but rather finding a systematic way of relating one account to another, the basic issue for Labov of what constitutes a narrative is not a problem for me. Using the narrative structures that Labov identifies as tools for analysis, I identify consistency in thematic content within these structures across (narrative and non-narrative) accounts.

CHAPTER 6

'It's Like a Community that Crosses Language, Cultural, and Class Lines'

Discourse communities have choices in how they define themselves, their members, and their relations to each other. This chapter presents Oyster Bilingual School's definitions of students, teachers, and school. Intertextual analysis of the Oyster educators' assumptions and expectations about students, teachers, and other community members relative to each other highlights Oyster's opposition to mainstream US assumptions of a homogeneous student population that should behave according to white middle-class Standard English-speaking norms in order to participate and achieve at school. Instead, the Oyster educators assume that their students, teachers, and parents come from linguistically, culturally, and socioeconomically diverse backgrounds, and that they have a wide range of ways of interacting with the school. Therefore, rather than seeing diversity as a problem that can and should be overcome, Oyster positively evaluates itself as 'a community that crosses language, cultural, and class lines' (Oyster parent). Its diversity is represented as a natural fact of life, and is drawn on as a resource in the school's efforts to provide equal educational opportunities to all of the students. Oyster Bilingual School can thus be understood as a community not of homogeneous individuals, but of diverse individuals who are unified by their common educational goals and common social practices.

WHAT IS A STUDENT?

This section provides Oyster Bilingual School's definition of a student, and accounts for similarities as well as differences among the Oyster educators' assumptions and expectations about the strengths and needs of their diverse student population. The collective answer to the question, What is a student? can be seen to underlie the

Oyster program. Likewise, individual educators' answers to this question, which are based on their own experiences as students and teachers, can be seen to underlie their particular practices.

Recall from Chapter 3 that mainstream US educational discourse is based on the assumption that the student population is homogeneous and that it behaves according to language majority norms (i.e. white middle-class native English-speaking). Under this model, linguistic and cultural diversity is considered a problem to be overcome. Any student who is 'Other' than language majority is expected to assimilate to language majority norms in order to succeed in mainstream US schools and society. In the mainstream US educational system, students are considered recipients of content information and academic skills from their more knowledgeable teachers. Because students are assumed to come from similar linguistic and cultural backgrounds, they are expected to interact with and learn the curriculum content and academic skills more or less in the same way.

It is immediately obvious that the Oyster educators do not consider their student population to be homogeneous. A superficial look at the Oyster perspective on their students might lead to the understanding that there are two kinds of students at the school — native Spanish-speakers and native English-speakers. Of these two populations, the Limited English Proficient (LEP) native Spanish-speakers seem to be the Oyster educators' primary concern. Support for this interpretation is readily available. For example, the school's dual-language policy addresses native Spanish speakers and native English speakers through Spanish and English. There are two teachers in every class, one Spanish-dominant and one English-dominant. In addition, the Mission Statement describes two groups of children: *children from Hispanic cultures* and *native English speakers.* While *Hispanic cultures* is represented as plural, analysis of the Mission Statement suggests that the policy is primarily concerned with the singular group *children from Hispanic cultures* because this is the group represented as not having equal educational opportunities in mainstream US educational discourse (see Chapter 5 for discussion).

The Oyster educators' assumptions and expectations about their students' strengths and needs, however, are more complex than this. First, conversations with teachers and administrators and continued observations of the curriculum content and its implementation in the classroom interaction reveal that the category *native Spanish-speaking* is not assumed to be unitary. For example, while the majority of the native Spanish-speaking student population is Salvadoran, the teachers represent a wide range of Spanish-speaking countries, cultures, and languages (see next section for further discussion of this variation). The principal, Señora Ortega, expresses her belief that including different varieties of Spanish not only legitimizes the variety but also the speaker of that variety:

> and it's all because it's a different variation of Spanish ... so all of this is an education for them ... and the message is very clear ... all languages ... all cultures ... are equal ... they are just as good and they have a lot to offer

Oyster's assumption of diversity in the category *native Spanish-speaking* stands in opposition to the mainstream US assumption of hispanic as homogeneous.

The Oyster educators assume and expect diversity not only in the native Spanish-speaking population, but across the entire student body. The following excerpt from the 'Racial and Ethnic Differences Statement', also found in the *Teachers' Handbook*, reflects this assumption:

> Oyster Bilingual School places a strong emphasis on the richness and diversity of its student and parent populations. The staff and friends of Oyster build upon this racial and ethnic diversity, enrich it, and further promote the goals of building a culturally pluralistic society.
>   Our student body encompasses children from many different cultures. They are viewed as assets and resources; their diverse backgrounds and experiences are incorporated into classroom and school-wide activities in all subject areas. (Oyster Bilingual School, 1988)

This official policy statement presupposes racial and cultural diversity within Oyster's student body. Note that in this statement the emphasis is on *many different cultures,* which stands in contrast to the Mission Statement's emphasis on *children from Hispanic cultures.* Given the diverse Oyster student population (see Chapter 1), and the increasingly diverse and rapidly changing US population (see Chapter 2), attention to diversity in general rather than any one cultural group in particular seems essential.

Mrs Washington, the sixth-grade English-dominant teacher, echoed this concern for students from all backgrounds. Mrs Washington's goals were to provide equal educational opportunities to all students through an emphasis on academic skills development:

> I don't care if they are black, white, green or yellow ... that child is going to work in my class ... and that child is going to get the skills to make it out there

In addition to skills development, Mrs Washington emphasized the need to incorporate an understanding and appreciation of the African heritage of the African American students into the curriculum (to be discussed in more detail in Chapter 8). Perhaps because she is an African American who has experienced discrimination against African Americans within United States society, she was concerned not only with the Latino students but with all minority students who may experience discriminatory treatment in US society. In fact, she occasionally criticized the Spanish-dominant educators for too much emphasis on Latino students and issues because it excluded other groups similarly to the ways that Latino students and concerns have been excluded in mainstream US discourse.

The Racial and Ethnic Diversity Statement positively evaluates the racial and cultural backgrounds of the students, whatever they may be, through such lexical choices as *richness, asset,* and *resource.* This positive evaluation stands in opposition to the mainstream US educational evaluation of difference as a handicap that requires special treatment to be overcome. Within Oyster, the students' diverse backgrounds and experiences are incorporated into classroom and school-wide activities in all subject areas (see Chapters 8–10 for illustration of this point). Oyster's inclusion of discussion of racial and ethnic diversity as part of the curriculum content (to be discussed in Chapter 8) legitimizes those topics in the educational discourse, and by extension legitimizes the various minority groups at the school. In addition, this statement evokes and opposes the mainstream US practice of segregating 'Other' until they have assimilated at which time differences across their backgrounds would be more or less neutralized. At Oyster, there is no need for the minority student to assimilate to majority ways of speaking and interacting. Rather, the minority student has the right to participate.

Señor Estevez, like the official policy on racial and ethnic diversity, describes the child's individual background in positive terms:

> tell me your strong points and I'm going to tell you … you know … where I'm going to start building … you have to start building on something that exists there

This focus on *strong points* presupposes that every child has some strong points, and stands in contrast to the mainstream US educational focus on a child's differences as deficits that need to be corrected. Focusing on strong points rather than deficits implies a radically different definition of the minority child in relation to the educational discourse. The minority child does not need to be 'fixed' at Oyster. The minority child, just like the majority child, needs to be nurtured in order to grow.

The fact that the children's *strong points* have to be made explicit presupposes that the children have different strong points, which can be at least partially related to their different sociocultural backgrounds. A third-grade English-dominant teacher told me her basic assumption about differences as follows, 'never assume that all the children know anything … their backgrounds are too varied'. Such an emphasis on the students' different backgrounds was a very common theme at Oyster. There was an assumption that teachers needed to understand these differences in order to be able to provide equal educational opportunities to all of the students, i.e. to know what *exists there* in order to know where to *start building* (see Chapter 7 for further discussion of this point).

Part of understanding what a student is includes being aware of and understanding differences in value systems. According to Señor Estevez,

> so again … we have to train you to understand the value system … what's going on with them … so those are the things again … and sometimes you see teachers talking to strangers … and here is where the cultural clash takes place

Señor Estevez's pronoun *you* in the second line can either be understood as referring to me specifically as a white middle-class native English-speaking teacher, or, more generally, to any white middle-class native English-speaking teacher who works with students from culturally diverse backgrounds. If the teacher does not expect and understand differences in the student population, communication is likely to break down. Without effective intercultural communication, the minority child is unlikely to be able to achieve to his or her full potential.

The Oyster assumption of difference can be contrasted with the mainstream US educational assumption of homogeneity. In the mainstream classroom, in order for the transmission model to be effective, the teacher must assume the students have common background knowledge and that the students are at the same developmental level so that the content the teacher presents can lead to the learning of that content. Operating under the assumption of homogeneity among students and teachers means that teachers do not need to be aware of the students' different background knowledge, value systems, ways of communicating, and strengths and weaknesses in different activities at school. Thus, the Oyster perspective offers a radically different orientation to students from the mainstream US educational orientation.

Within the school, there is the assumption that the differences among the children which affect their participation and academic achievement cannot be attributed exclusively to linguistic, racial, or ethnic background. Socioeconomic class distinction is repeatedly described as a problem in the teachers' ability to meet the students' diverse educational needs. For example, Señora Rodriguez, the Spanish-dominant kindergarten teacher, told me, 'it's more class than anything else but here Hispanic is poor and black and white is rich'. Señora Rodriguez makes explicit her assumption that socioeconomic class distinctions run along ethnic lines within the Oyster community. This correlation of ethnicity and socioeconomic condition can confuse the issue of how to provide equal educational opportunities because it makes problem identification more complex. Moreover, it is reasonable to assume that a more complex problem will require a more complex solution.

Similarly, in a meeting I attended in which the Spanish and English-dominant kindergarten and first grade teachers were coordinating the skills and promotion requirements between levels, one of the English-dominant first grade teachers stated her concern with the low-income students as follows:

> social and emotional stuff is a problem for me ... we don't have a middle class here ... we have rich and poor ... finally I said to hell with the rich ... I'll work with the poor ... my answer to the rich is ... there's a lot of private schools

Later in the meeting, this same teacher revealed her assumption, consistent with the others presented thus far, that the Latino population is the poor population in the school:

> the social and emotional problems are usually Hispanic ... this school is for the Hispanic ... we have that infusion from over the bridge ... that's what this school is about ... we can't brush them aside

Over the bridge refers to the neighborhood that the majority of the low-income Latino students live in. This teacher makes her assumption very clear that the low-income Latino is the primary concern. Her utterances, *this school is for the Hispanic*, and *that's what this school is about*, demonstrate her belief that the implicit goal of the entire school, and not just her personal goal, is to meet the educational needs of the low-income Latino students.

I provide one final rather lengthy example of a teacher's assumptions about diversity in the student population. There are several reasons for my paying so much attention to this example. First, this teacher's assumptions about Latino-Anglo differences can be seen to underlie his classroom practices (see Chapter 10). In addition, as I discuss later, this description of Latino-Anglo differences, if correct, helps explain negative stereotyping of Latino students I encountered in other Spanish–English (transitional) bilingual schools in the northeast coast of the United States. And finally, this explanation finds parallels in other aspects of the discourse that I describe later. In sum, I present this tentative explanation of Latino-Anglo differences as an area for further investigation.

The sixth-grade Spanish-dominant teacher, Señor Xoci, reflected his assumption of Anglo-Latino differences in perceived questioning rights in a series of conversations we had. In one conversation, Señor Xoci explained to me (utterances about Latino students are italicized):

> the Anglo kids already know how to ask for things ... they are demanding and pushy and always ready ... they already know what they're going to do ... they want to be a lawyer ... drive a BMW ... live up on the Hill ... they've got it all planned ... *the Latino kid is more laid back ... **man** (changes register throughout boldface) ... **I'm going to get me a job ... maybe I'm going to hang out ... take it easy** ... their goals are entirely different* ... the Anglo kids are pushy ... they know how to play the game ... *the Latino kids just lay back* ... then a teacher says hey ... I'm not going to help that child if he doesn't want to work ... it's not that ... *they don't know how to ask*

Interested in obtaining more information about his assumptions about these Latino/Anglo differences, I asked Señor Xoci a follow up question:

Rebecca: remember the other day when you told me the Anglo kids know how to ask ... and the Latino kids don't know how to ask? what did you mean by that? that the Latino kids don't know how to ask?

Xoci: uhm ... yeah ... uh see that kid over there (points to Latino student)

Rebecca: yeah

Xoci: he's a real smart kid ... he can get anything he wants from his friends or on the street or whatever ... but in class he's real quiet ... just sits there and takes it all in real passively because he doesn't ... he doesn't think he should ask

The conversation continues and Señor Xoci tells me a story about how his father, a low-income Chicano living in Texas, did not know how to ask for medical services because he thought it was a privilege, not a right. Señor Xoci concludes the story about his father with the following generalization about Latinos:

> when they don't know how to ask they can't get access … they have a right to proper access to equal opportunity … they need to see access as a right and not just a privilege … access will only be given when you ask

These accounts reflect Señor Xoci's assumptions that (1) Latino youth will ask their peers for things and about things; but (2) Latino students will not ask questions of the teacher because they assume questioning to be a privilege, not a right. These different assumptions are reflected in his classroom organization and teaching strategies (illustrated in Chapter 10).

If Señor Xoci's assumptions about Latino and Anglo differences in perceived questioning abilities and rights is correct, it helps explain some Anglo teachers' possible misinterpretation of Latino participation styles. In the first story here, Señor Xoci explained how the Latino students' not knowing how to ask affected their Anglo teacher as follows:

> then a teacher says hey … I'm not going to help that child if he doesn't want to work

Señor Xoci's construction of the teacher's response echoes statements that one of the Anglo teachers made to me about Latino student participation in PS 22, the transitional bilingual program in Perth Amboy, New Jersey that I referred to in Chapter 3. She said, 'the Hispanic students are just lazy … they really don't care about being here' and 'I don't get it … if they don't understand … why don't they just ask'.

Señor Xoci's explanation is that it is not that the Latino kids do not care, as interpreted by these Anglo teachers through their cultural frames. Rather, it may be that the appropriateness conditions governing participation rights in questioning within the educational domain are different in Anglo and Latino cultures. Because cultural differences are generally below the level of consciousness, one group interprets the other group's behavior through their own culturally conditioned frames, which can lead to misunderstandings, in this case to negative stereotypes that have potentially damaging consequences for the Latino students' ability and right to participate equally in the academic discourse.

I want to stress that I do not know if this is *the* explanation. In fact, I think it is probably too simplistic to be *the* explanation. Several points, however, are relevant here. First, with respect to Oyster, Señor Xoci's assumption about Latino/Anglo differences in questioning strategies informs his practice. Second, further support for this explanation can be found in another Spanish-dominant teachers' comments about differences in Latino/Anglo parental participation styles, discussed later. And third, although Philips' (1983) Warm Springs study identified a different set of discourse strategies that led to misinterpretation of student participation and academic achievement, the outcome — teacher stereotypes based on different participation preferences that negatively define the minority student relative to the mainstream institution — is the same.

This section, although by no means exhaustive, reveals the knowledge schemas the Oyster educators have for students. The teachers express their expectations of linguistic, cultural, and socioeconomic diversity in their students' home lives which they believe influences the students' knowledge base and ways of interacting in the classroom, as well as the social, economic and emotional problems that students bring with them to the school. Chapter 8 describes and Chapters 9 and 10 illustrate how policymaker, administrator, and teacher assumptions of their students' diverse backgrounds, needs, and interests are incorporated into the design of the language plan, and of the implementation of that plan on the classroom level.

WHAT IS A TEACHER?

Within mainstream US educational discourse, there is one teacher in every classroom. On the one hand, she (most mainstream US teachers are white middle-class native English-speaking women) is considered an agent in the educational process, and retains the majority of the power in the classroom. On the other hand, she is not generally involved in planning decisions, but is instrumental in implementing the policy handed down from above. The Oyster definition of teacher stands in contrast to this mainstream US notion.

By every account, the teachers are considered integral to the Oyster program's success. In fact, most successful educational programs attribute much of their success to 'good teachers', and Lindholm (1990) lists high-quality instructional staff as one of the criteria for an effective dual-language program. This section provides a picture of who the Oyster teachers are based on the policymakers', administrators', and teachers' talk and supported by my own observations. These accounts construct teachers as valuable resources who work together to solve the problems that arise in their classrooms, who positively represent and evaluate minority students, and who are very committed to the education of all of their diverse student population. Since Oyster is an elementary school, it is the first educational experience for most of the students. Therefore, the Oyster definition of a teacher makes an important contribution to the development of the students' knowledge schema for who a teacher is and what a teacher does.

According to the ideal policy, there are two teachers in every room, one Spanish-dominant and one English-dominant, and the teachers are defined by the policy statements as instrumental in the children's education. Teachers in the instrumental role can be understood as in opposition to the mainstream US notion of teachers in the agentive role. I will return to a discussion of what a teacher does in Chapter 7 as I provide the Oyster answer to the question, What is teaching? Although it is somewhat artificial to separate the two, I want to begin by emphasizing who the people are relative to each other.

According to Señor Estevez, the teachers make or break a program. Although I was not there when the program began, and my analysis is primarily concerned with description, interpretation, and implementation of the Oyster program betweem 1989 and 1991, a few excerpts from Señor Estevez's interview that provide his representation of the initial planning stages are useful to emphasize the central role of the teachers in this planning process:

* you want to start with the teachers ... the children have a remarkable ability to learn ... adults have a remarkable ability to forget ... so I get those teachers ... so the first aspect of the training had nothing to do with the languages ... it was an explanation of the objectives ... what is this work about
* and it was first to put ... to make out of a conglomerate of teachers a group ... and out of the group a team ... because it was done through two team teachers
* **Estevez:** we did the ... uh first was to accept each other
  Rebecca: as teachers?
  Estevez: no ... as human beings ... and that uh ... to listen to each other's experiences ... good or bad
* so later we started to slowly to work with the teacher ... and that you will have to be self sufficient ... that you are the biggest resource ... that it's not a book ... it's not Professor such and such ... it's you

Because the implementation of the plan is *done through teachers*, they have to be included in the planning process. Señor Estevez's accounts provide us with a picture of teachers working together and taking responsibility for solving their own problems. Teachers are defined as *self-sufficient*, and the *biggest resource*. His lexical choice, moving from *conglomerate* to *group* to *team*, reflects the need for a *collective* effort among the teachers to socialize the children differently. This representation of teachers as central to the planning process stands in contrast to mainstream US representations of educational planners as not including teachers. The notion of teachers working together to solve their problems also can be contrasted with mainstream US educational practices in which teachers are often isolated from one another with no time to plan and collaborate together.

A cornerstone of the Oyster approach is that there are two full-time teachers in every classroom, one Spanish-dominant and one English-dominant. According to the principal, Señora Ortega, this distinguishes the Oyster program from other bilingual programs, and is crucial to the plan:

so part of the thing that you find in this program ... and this has been for years ... that you don't find in other bilingual programs nationally or internationally ... is that you have two teachers in every classroom ... not teacher aides ... but two full-time teachers in every classroom ... two full-time teachers in every class-

> room ... one that is Spanish-dominant and one that is English-dominant ... and
> it's not a translation of what one teacher does for the other teacher ... equal time

Señora Ortega's repetition of *two full-time teachers in every classroom* reflects her evaluation of the importance of there being full-time teachers who have *equal time*. Her utterance *not teacher aides* reveals the importance associated to symbolically representing both the Spanish-dominant and English-dominant teachers as equals. This can be contrasted with many ESL programs in which schools hire teacher aides who speak the native language of the children in the class, and who help the teacher, but who do not have the same status as the regular teachers. By giving equal time to Spanish and English teachers, the school is symbolically saying that Spanish and English are equal to fulfill the educational function.

Oyster emphasizes the practical and symbolic ramifications of the teachers selected to work within the school. Because of their diverse backgrounds, the teachers bring a variety of approaches and materials to the Oyster program that a homogeneous group of teachers could not offer. Señora Ortega describes the practical implications as follows:

> so you're talking about programs ... teaching strategies ... materials ... uh
> cultures ... that's brought in ... literature from Argentina, from Mexico, from
> Chile from all these places ... it's very different ... and also for the students ...
> to see that there are different varieties of Spanish ... and it's OK ... it's not just
> Spanish from Spain ... that is the way ... absolutely not ... that is *not* the way
> here in the States [her emphasis]

Señora Ortega's concern for the symbolic implications for the students is evident in her utterances *to see that there are varieties of Spanish and it's OK*. Her belief that all varieties of Spanish are not viewed as equal in the mainstream, and that Spanish from Spain (Castellano) is considered to be superior to Latin American varieties of Spanish, is clearly expressed and rejected.

To give an idea of the diverse languages, cultures, and identity groups that the Oyster teachers represent, I summarize where the teachers are from and what languages they speak later. I obtained this information from a handbook introducing the Oyster program that the student journalists of the Oyster bilingual newspaper *Oyster Writes/Oyster Escribe* compiled and distributed to the 1990 NABE conference visitors. The students had interviewed all of the teachers in the school and contributed their short interviews to the NABE bulletin. The description of each teacher provided information about where the teacher was from, how many years they had been teaching, how many languages they spoke, educational background, and, in some cases, a short quote about what they thought of the Oyster program.

Before I present the teacher information, I want to draw attention to the importance of the student question about how many languages the teachers speak. First, the inclusion of this question reveals the expectation of bilingualism. Second, this question is one of only five questions that the students asked of each teacher, which reflects the importance both to the student interviewers as well as to all of the readers of the bulletin of making explicit the multilingual, multicultural resources that the teachers bring to the program.

The information on the Spanish-dominant teachers is written in Spanish and the information about the English-dominant teachers is written in English in the NABE bulletin. Since neither the Spanish nor the English descriptions are translated, anyone who wants to read the entire bulletin must have reading ability in Spanish and English. This too sends a message that Spanish–English bilingualism is expected in order to participate fully in the Oyster educational discourse.

As the following summary demonstrates, the teachers provide considerable linguistic and cultural resources for the program. Of the Spanish-dominant teachers, four are from Puerto Rico, two are from Argentina, two are from Peru, and one each is from Cuba, Columbia, Guatemala, and El Paso, Texas. All of the Spanish-dominant teachers speak Spanish and English. One of the Peruvians also speaks Quechua. Of the English-dominant teachers, three are from Washington, DC but one of those adds that her family is from Puerto Rico, and one each is from Tennessee, New York, New England, Missouri, Louisiana, New Jersey, Pittsburgh, and California. Of the 11 English-dominant teachers, one speaks five languages (one of which is Spanish), three speak Spanish and English, one is an English–French bilingual, and six are monolingual English speakers. Of the six resource teachers, one is a native Spanish speaker from Columbia who speaks English and Spanish, one is a native English speaker from Baltimore who speaks four languages (including English and Spanish), one is from Washington, DC and speaks Spanish and English, and three are monolingual English speakers; one from Florida, one from Missouri, and one from North Carolina. The principal the first year I was there was from El Paso, Texas, a native Spanish speaker who speaks Spanish, English, and French.

The fact that the Spanish-dominant teachers and students represent a wide range of countries and corresponding varieties of the Spanish language makes Oyster's dual-language program somewhat different from many other dual-language programs in the United States which serve Spanish-speaking students from the same national background. As Heyck (1994: 162–3) writes,

> Ethnicity is both a primordial tie and a mechanism for imagining community, because for the Latino the term 'community' has little meaning without the qualifiers 'Mexican', 'Puerto Rican', 'Cuban', or 'Dominican'. With these adjectives, the term 'community' comes to life.

In response to this diversity, the Oyster educators create an artificial pan-Latino community which unifies the Spanish speakers as an authentic sub-group within the larger Oyster community.

Because I was interested to learn how Oyster prepared teachers to work in Oyster's dual-language program, I asked Señora Ortega about the teacher training.

She explained that the program's success could not be attributed so much to *training per se,* but to the commitment the teachers have to their job:

> so in the Spanish part we don't have openings hardly ... so the training per se is really a commitment they feel ... and they get it from the teachers who are here ... they do a lot of observing ... like Señor Xoci coming in ... just in observing ... it was explained to him what it is ... but the only way he can learn is by seeing the commitment ... and you feel it in the air when you see what these teachers put out

In the context of Oyster Bilingual School, the *commitment* that the teachers have is not only to individual students, but to their working together in order to promote social change so that all groups can participate more or less equally.

In fact, teachers identified the following qualities as necessary for a teacher in a bilingual school on a questionnaire that I distributed to them, which echo Señora Ortega's description of the teachers' commitment:

> Must think of heterogeneity as something to maintain — isn't something to diminish.

> Needs to be patient, accepting, caring, sensitive, never shocked, never make assumptions, never stereotype, be flexible, open to new ways of doing things, careful not to impart the attitude that 'this way is best'.

These teachers' responses include a number of things to do as well as a number of things not to do. As mentioned earlier, negation is evaluative and can reveal people's assumptions and expectations. Their utterances *never be shocked, never make assumptions, never stereotype, careful not to impart the attitude that 'this way is best', (heterogeneity) isn't something to diminish,* reflect assumptions that some-where these processes are happening, presumably in mainstream US educational discourse. These utterances also reflect their negative evaluations of such practices.

In sum, the Oyster collective describes teachers as an integral part of the program's success. They are constantly expected to do needs analysis and to plan and solve problems accordingly. They need to expect diversity, value diversity, be emotionally and socially sensitive, and committed to the students and to the community. This stands in contrast to the mainstream US educational definition of a teacher, and as we will see in Chapter 7, structures the definition of learning and teaching at Oyster Bilingual School.

WHAT IS SCHOOL?

The Oyster educators talk and write about their school as one linguistically and culturally diverse community all working together to educate the children. Evidence for Oyster's inclusive notion of 'community' can easily be found. For example, administrators and policymakers claim that their school-wide bilingual program originally began as a grass-roots community effort involving community activists, parents, and teachers (see Chapter 1). The parent organization is referred to as the 'Community Council', and is very active in all aspects of school management. Parents, whether active members of the Community Council or not, are expected to and do volunteer their services throughout the school on a regular basis. Students wear t-shirts that say 'Oyster Community Bilingual School'. One parent told me, 'you know, the great thing about this school is it's like a community that crosses language, cultural and class lines'.

This constructed notion of co-membership in the Oyster school/community is central to understanding Oyster's success with their linguistically and culturally diverse student population. As Erickson and Schultz (1982: 17) point out in their discussion of co-membership in counselor/student interactions, 'attributes of status such as ethnicity or social class do not fully predict the potential co-membership resources', in this case for co-membership in Oyster Bilingual School. The common goal of educating the children is the attribute that ties these individuals from diverse backgrounds into one Oyster community that they recognize and explicitly refer to. In other words, the Oyster community has chosen to define themselves as one community with common interests and goals as opposed to several distinct communities (e.g. Salvadoran, African American, European American) that are often in conflict with each other in mainstream US society.

Oyster Bilingual School provides an example of language minority (Spanish-speaking) educators collaborating with language majority (English-speaking) educators to design and implement programs and practices that meet the needs of their linguistically and culturally diverse student population. As such, the Oyster School study makes an important contribution to the language-planning literature because most studies document language-planning efforts by the language majority community for the language minority community. Language-planning at Oyster Bilingual School, however, did not begin with equal support from the language minority and language majority populations. As the following discussion highlights, creating co-membership in a community among people who have very different assumptions and expectations, for example about bilingual education and language minority participation, can require considerable effort on the part of the community members.

By all accounts, Oyster's bilingual program began as a grass-roots effort coordinated by an active Latino community struggling to meet the needs of an increasing Latino population in Washington, DC. For example, according to the March, 1993 Oyster Bilingual School Fact Sheet, Oyster's program was created 'by a coalition of Hispanic leaders, parents, and educators who pushed the Superintendant to replace the traditional, underenrolled program at Oyster with an innovative two-way bilingual program' (p.1). Reflecting Oyster's assumption that teachers are an integral part of every level of planning and implementation, 20 experienced native Spanish-speaking teachers from a variety of Latin American countries were recruited to help transform Oyster from a traditional monolingual English program to a dual-language program. However, as Señor Estevez described, the principal and teachers at (monolingual) Oyster were originally reluctant, and did much to discourage the idea of a dual-language program in their school. In response,

> the parents and bilingual teachers launched a public-relations effort in the community arguing for the advantages of an enrichment program for all its students. They argued for stability in real estate values of both the Woodley Park and Adams Morgan communities with a quality program in its elementary school. They argued for integration along racial, cultural, and socio-economic lines through an educational program that would give equal weight to learning two languages well for all its students. (Oyster Bilingual School, 1993, p. 2)

It is interesting to note that in Oyster's historical overview, and in my interviews with Señor Estevez, the arguments presented in support of the school-wide bilingual program focused on economic and security benefits to the community rather than on the benefits of bilingual education or any moral commitment to the equal educational opportunities of the native Spanish-speaking students. This suggests the bilingual program advocates' sensitivity to the various interests of the populations who would be affected by the dual-language program.

In all accounts of the history of Oyster's bilingual program, as in other examples of problem identification and resolution that I observed at Oyster (see later for further discussion), the Oyster educators do not describe a school as a place where policy is handed down to administrators and teachers to implement uncritically. Rather, teachers, parents, and other community members are represented as actively involved in the decision-making, reflecting the dynamic, multi-level, multi-directional nature of dual-language-planning at Oyster Bilingual School (see Chapter 4).

Señor Estevez relates his personal goal of building a sense of co-membership that emphasizes what the students have in common. Since Señor Estevez was one of the co-founders of Oyster's dual-language program, his goals can be considered to reflect the ideal of the original dual-language plan:

> we have overemphasized in general in the US what separates people and not what puts them together ... I start always saying ... you know ... that you and me are the same ... so let's look for the common aspect

At first this seemed like a contradiction to me. On the one hand, the school claims to celebrate diversity and include it as a part of the curriculum content (see Chapter 8 for further discussion). This inclusion of diverse languages, cultures, histories, literatures, etc. could be interpreted as focusing on difference. Yet here, one of the co-founders emphasizes concentrating on what the children have in common. As I discuss later, the underlying social identities project provides an explanation for this apparent contradiction.

Instead of emphasizing differences between the students, Señor Estevez expects the teachers *to build on* [the children's] *strong points, on something that exists there* (see previous discussion). Although he does not state it explicitly, in the context of Oyster's goal of cultural pluralism, which sees the students' racial and ethnic diversity as instrumental in achieving that goal, we can understand part of the students' strong points to include their racial and ethnic backgrounds and experiences. Including discussion of the children's differences then allows the students to understand that these differences are legitimate to talk about. By extension, the various minority identity groups within the school are legitimated. When differences are legitimated, they do not function as barriers that separate groups nor do they force the minority students to assimilate to majority ways of speaking and behaving. In such an educational discourse, it becomes possible for the children to see that they have more common qualities than differences. Talking about difference then becomes instrumental in highlighting similarities.

The following excerpt from my interview with Señor Estevez presents his construction of the relationship between the school and the community, and an environment that is conducive to learning. This excerpt very concisely presents the relationship between the school and the community that I observed throughout Oyster. According to Señor Estevez:

Estevez: the schools are the schools ... if the environment is receptive and is conducive to learning ... you can do a lot of things there

Rebecca: when you say environment ... do you mean the institution and the community ... or just the school

Estevez: the three ... the school is the hub and the things go around the school ... if the environment is conducive to learning ... if the parents are motivated ... if poverty is not so objectionable ... you know it's conducive ... if the school is safe ... it's conducive ... if the teacher has a nice attitude towards the job ... it's conducive to learning ... if the parents believe in delayed gratification ... it's conducive to learning ... all those things is a matter that some families have it ... and bring it with the children those values ... some families will acquire it in the environment of the school ... that's why you have to bring the community

In response to my request for clarification of what he meant by *environment*, Señor Estevez provides a relatively detailed picture of what is involved in creating what he repeatedly refers to as *an environment (that) is conducive to learning*.

First, Señor Estevez's emphasis on the creation of an environment that is conducive to learning further supports the construction of the school as in the instrumental role and the students as in the agentive role. Consistent with the Mission Statement and the Philosophy Statement constructions (see Chapter 5), Señor Estevez represents the school as under the obligation to accommodate students. This representation stands in opposition to mainstream US educational discourse in which the language minority student is under the obligation to assimilate to the school.

Señor Estevez represents the school metaphorically with his utterance *the school is the hub and the things go around the school,* providing an image of the central role of the school but with other factors closely involved. The rest of the excerpt provides Señor Estevez's construction of what those *things* that *go around the school* are, as well as what he means by *an environment that is conducive to learning.* Señor Estevez's attitude towards what makes a school successful is illustrated through his use of the conditional as he includes features that are part of an environment that is conducive to learning. In order of presentation, the themes of these clauses are *the parents, poverty, the school, the teacher, the parents.* Three out of five of these conditions are related to home influences.

First, I briefly mention the two conditions that are not related to the home: *if the school is safe* and *if the teacher has a nice attitude toward the job.* With respect to the school, at the time of this study, the representations of the school as successful, including my description of parents lining up outside of the school to enroll their students, gives an image of a school that is definitely safe. And in the previous section, we saw the attitudes of the teachers as concerned about the particular students and their successes.

Here is a list of the conditions related to home that Señor Estevez expresses as contributing to an environment that is conducive to learning.

- *if the parents are motivated*
- *if poverty is not so objectionable*
- *if the parents believe in delayed gratification*

With respect to poverty, at another point in the interview, Señor Estevez mentions that *bilingual education does not cure poverty.* And as we saw earlier, the teachers represent low-income (and the problems associated with that social position) as one of their greatest problems in providing more or less equal educational opportunities to all of their students. This leaves two home conditions that the school can influence in order to create an environment that is conducive to learning. The remainder of the excerpt provides Señor Estevez's representation of the process related to these two home conditions, which I repeat here:

> that some families have it and bring it with the children those values ... some families will acquire it in the environment of the school ... that's why you have to bring the community

This excerpt reveals Señor Estevez's expectation of different home values with respect to the conditions, *if the parents are motivated and if the parents believe in delayed gratification,* as well as his expectation that if the parents do not have motivation and a belief in delayed gratification, then it is the school's obligation to socialize the parents into acquiring these values. In Señor Estevez's construction, the school has an obligation to the students, which includes an obligation to socialize the parents into developing the same expectations about participation in the school as the school has for the students. In this way the students ideally receive consistent messages about their participation in the educational discourse from both the school and the home.

What is parental involvement?

Because parents are considered central to Oyster's success, I turn now to a discussion of what parental involvement means at Oyster Bilingual School. Oyster parents, like all other members of the Oyster community, have obligations to their children, to the teachers, and to the school. These parents also have rights in the decision-making processes and management of the school's affairs. As the following discussion illustrates, parents are involved in a variety of ways in the multiple levels of educational planning and implementation at Oyster Bilingual School (see Chapter 4 for discussion and a diagram of planning and implementation levels).

Señor Estevez described parental involvement in the early planning stages of the program. He emphasized the need to train teachers and parents so everyone would understand and support the school's objectives:

Estevez: the first thing was the training of the teachers ... the explanation of the objectives ... and training parents
Rebecca: that's what I was going to ask you
Estevez: it's a very important thing ... you cannot do any project in education without parental support

According to Señor Estevez's description of the early planning days, teachers, parents, administrators, and community activitists met with linguists who consulted on language teaching and learning issues, and with an expert on group dynamics to help them understand how to work together as a team. He emphasized:

> I wanted the community involved ... to involve the community is a very tedious problem ... but the community have to understand what do you mean by bilingual ... what do you mean by ESL ... what do you mean by this ... what do you mean by the other thing ... the most literate will read a book so you recommend it to them ... the others might not know because they might not be well educated ... they have to understand that you are not doing an experiment with their children ... that it is proved ... that it works in some places ... that if they have any doubt to come to you and .... but above all ... it was the teachers who have to work with the parents

While I have no way of knowing whether Señor Estevez's account of what happened in 1971 was what *actually* happened, his representation of the planning process is consistent with administrator and teacher representations of parental involvement at the time of my study. According to the Oyster educators, parents need to understand what is involved in their children's education if they are expected to be involved and supportive. Communication between parents and teachers is crucial to develop this understanding and joint commitment to the children's education. Because the parents' backgrounds are so varied, Señor Estevez mentions that the school does not expect all parents to relate to the school in the same ways. He argues that it is the school's responsibility, and especially the teachers' responsiblity, to bring parents into the school in whatever way works for everyone involved.

As mentioned earlier, the Community Council is the offical parent teacher organization at Oyster Bilingual School. The following description of the Community Council appears in the *Teachers' Handbook*, and offers an idea of the range of activities that the parents participate in and are responsible for.

Community and Parental Involvement

Community/parental involvement is an integral and welcome component in the life at Oyster School. The community (neighborhood) is receptive to and interested in school programs and projects. It readily donates goals and services on our behalf.

Parents have long been recognized as a part of our 'team'. Our parent body works on a continuous basis in all phases of school life. We have attempted to communicate effectively with all sectors of our community and to form a cohesive bonding of the home, school, and student body. Parents work actively as volunteers and tutors and underwrite/sponsor many school events and expenses. They participate in the planning and implementation of school activities and serve as ready resources whenever and wherever needed.

Our parent organization is the Oyster School Community Council. Financial support from this group helps to provide additional human, material, and physical resources of benefit to the entire school. These resources include:

* hiring a music teacher and a science resource teacher,
* providing classroom funds,
* underwriting the cost of subway and bus fares for field trips,
* purchasing texts and library books, not available through system allotments, and funding the RIF program and the student newspaper.

Parent and Community Volunteers number well over 100. At the beginning of the school year, all parents are polled to determine the type of school service which they wish to offer to the school. Suggested areas include classroom assistance, tutoring, fund-raising, school-wide programs, and clerical support. Options vary so that parents can choose convenient schedules and projects that can be done at home, in school or elsewhere. In addition to parents, many community persons come to school to serve as tutors and to assist in various other areas, as needed.

The Oyster School Community Council holds two general meetings each year and monthly Board meetings. The Council consists of elected officers, twelve board members, teacher representatives, and the principal.

> We view our role in improving education as a team effort. Parents are made to feel needed and wanted as a part of this team and encouraged to help and communicate with us in the way most comfortable and convenient for them. (Oyster Bilingual School, 1988)

Notice the emphasis on collaboration in the lexical choice to describe parental/school relations: For example, they use the terms *a team, a cohesive bonding of the home, school, and student body.* The parents from *all sectors of our community* are *made to feel needed and wanted as part of this team.* This representation of Oyster supports Señor Estevez's construction of the Oyster community, and stands in contrast to many mainstream US schools that have not established close coordination with the parents in the child's education.

An important question to address is: Why wouldn't parents be involved in their children's education? There are numerous potential reasons, some of which could be especially relevant to the low-income Latino population, which makes up about half of Oyster's population. For example, if the parent does not speak English, the language of the school, it is very difficult to establish such a *team* effort. To address this problem, Community Council meetings are co-facilitated by one native Spanish-speaker and one native English-speaker, and are conducted in both languages so that proficiency in English is not required for parental involvement in Community Council Meetings. And there are two teachers in each class, one Spanish-dominant and one English-dominant, so that proficiency in English is not required for parents to talk to the teachers either. In addition, all documents sent home are written in both Spanish and English.

Another potential problem is that the parent may not feel that he or she has the right to be involved in the school's decisionmaking process, perhaps because of cross-cultural differences in assumptions and expectations about appropriate parental involvement in school affairs. The concluding statements of the policy statement make explicit Oyster's recognition of differences in parental participation: *Parents are encouraged to communicate with us in the way most comfortable and convenient for them.* As I discuss in more detail later, the school recognizes that just as students' diverse linguistic and cultural backgrounds may affect their participation in class, diverse parental backgrounds may affect their participation in school and in the child's education.

The *Teachers' Handbook* description of the Community Council provides an image of parents and teachers and administrators sharing power in the decisionmaking process and in the day-to-day running of the school. This image is also reflected in a paper that the parents presented at NABE in 1980 entitled 'The History and Politics of Oyster Bilingual School':

> As early as 1972, parents were strongly involved in the school. Parents took a hand in selecting a new principal for the school. Candidates for principal were interviewed in parents' homes. The person subsequently chosen was approved by the parents, the bilingual office and the school officials downtown. (Oyster Bilingual School, 1980)

Similarly, when I was conducting research at Oyster in 1991, the parents represented on the Community Council were actively involved in the recruitment of the new principal, Señora Mendoza. These accounts together provide a coherent picture of parents sharing power with the school to jointly determine what is best for the children, at least according to official and policymaker accounts.

The Oyster educators also describe considerable parental involvement on the administrative, teacher, and classroom levels. Señora Mendoza emphasized that sometimes parents take initiatives to effect change through the Community Council, sometimes teachers do, and sometimes administrators do. Whatever the case, the goal is to enlist support of the other groups and to find ways to accomplish the initiatives. A current example (the Peace Works Project) that Señora Mendoza provided illustrates this group process very clearly. Señora Mendoza described Oysters' concern that the children have been talking and playing much more aggressively in the last few years, and that this behavior is a reflection of the increasing aggression, discrimination, and violence in schools across the country and in society overall. This concern, she says:

> gave way to a committee that essentially was started by parents ... and the teachers weren't that much involved in it ... which was called The Cultural Diversity Committee ... that happened four years ago ... now.. it took four years of writing proposals starting small ... checking out this ... doing that

According to Señora Mendoza, the Cultural Diversity Committee did research on all the companies and agencies in the United States that worked on conflict resolution. She continued:

Mendoza: together with the parents and the teachers ... we decided on this company from Florida because they do it bilingually ... and we had all the money from the Restructuring Team ... not all the money but ... the Community Council put in funds ... the Restructuring Team put in funds ... we got a grant from the Local Advisory Neighborhood Commission to support the initiative etc ... and we did three days of intensive training of teachers ... of stud ... on the the program that goes from Pre-K through sixth grade ... on these uh ... for the students in fourth, fifth and sixth grade that we trained as peer mediators in conflict resolution ... and for the parents ... and the parents was how to fight fair at home

Rebecca: and so like a model? ... how to fight fair among themselves ... and with their children?

Mendoza: and with their children ... and in the case of the parents ... for example ... we got it in both English and Spanish ... and the training was in English and Spanish

Rebecca: How many parents participated

Mendoza: Well they did it for a 100 ... we figured we would never get a 100 ... and we got a 150

Rebecca: wow
Mendoza: we have 300 kids here

Notice Señora Mendoza's emphasis on involving all parts of the community in their effort to reduce violence and discrimination in the school. The parents from the Community Council initated the process, the administration supported their efforts, and both of these groups obtained funding. The training process involved all of the groups in the community: the teachers, the parents, the local neighborhood commission, and the students so that students would receive consistent messages about conflict resolution. Also notice that Señora Mendoza's description of the communal effort involved in the Peace Works initiative parallels Señor Estevez's description of the communal effort involved in the original planning process. The Oyster educators believe that no educational innovation can be successful without parental involvement, and that if the parents are expected to be supportive and involved, they have to understand the objectives. This often involves group training.

The Peace Works project is an example of a project that the parents on the Community Council initiated and then enlisted support of the other members of the Oyster community to carry out. According to Señora Mendoza, this is not always the case. Sometimes teachers initiate the effort, as was the case in their earlier move towards a more cooperative learning model. And sometimes the administrators initiate the effort, as is the case in their current emphasis on improving science and math instruction throughout the school. Whatever the case, the ideal is for all of the groups to communicate with each other to reach a common understanding of the objectives, and then to work together as a team to achieve them. It is important to mention that, as in any organization, competing interests are involved and there are inevitable tensions and struggles and conflicts. Microanalysis of these team-building efforts is an important area for further research.

Because many US schools are currently experiencing difficulties involving parents in their children's education, I provide the following discussion of how Oyster teachers and administrators successfully involve the Oyster parents. According to Señora Ortega, the principal when I began my study in 1989, the parents must get involved when the children enroll in school. This view was supported by a parent whom I met at the 1991 Black History Celebration who told me: 'You really don't have any choice, they let you know from the beginning that you have to be involved in the school and your child's schooling.'

But simply asking parents to get involved at the beginning of the year is not enough, especially when working with a community as linguistically and culturally diverse as Oyster. As mentioned earlier, one strategy the Oyster educators use to get all parents involved is to produce everything for the parents in Spanish and English so that they can read important school information and so that they can participate in Community Council Meetings etc. However, simply using Spanish and English is not enough. Teachers and administrators talk of the importance of recognizing different cultural assumptions and expectations that native Spanish-speakers and

native English-speakers have about parents' relationships to the school. The following example illustrates how a teacher's assumption about cross-cultural differences
on the parental level affects her relationships with the diverse groups of parents.

According to the policy statement, Community Council is a relatively active
organization made up of students' parents, and is one of the volunteer efforts the
parents can provide, but in this case on an elected basis. In addition to the elected
officials who have voting privileges in, for example, the election of the principal,
parents are all encouraged to attend the monthly meetings. The meetings are to be
held in Spanish and English so that no parents are excluded. Community Council is
to be representative of the Oyster community which, as one middle-class Latino
parent said 'crosses language, cultural, and class lines'. Therefore, one would expect
approximately the same demographic distribution as in the student population.

The Community Council meeting that I attended, however, had a noticeable
absence of low-income Latino parents whose children constitute a large proportion
of the student body. According to the people at the meeting, the attendance was
approximately the same as at all of the meetings. My question was: Why was the
low-income Latino population not present at the Community Council meeting?

A tentative explanation is that the low-income Latino parents could not attend
the Community Council meetings because they had to work. The explanation may
not be so simple, however, because a different meeting that I attended which Señora
Rodriguez, the Spanish-dominant kindergarten teacher, had organized for the Latino
parents of her students was well attended and both meetings were scheduled for 6:00
in the evening. There had to be some explanation for why the low-income Latino
parents attended one meeting organized by the school but not another.

Señora Rodriguez, who had also attended that Community Council meeting, and
I were discussing the different Latino parent participation. She explained the
absence at the Community Council meeting in terms of cultural differences governing participation rights in the educational domain:

> if a child goes home and says my teacher punished me … the Hispanic parent
> will say I'll bet you did something wrong … the Anglo parent will come the
> next day and says … why um so and so told me that he was punished yester-
> day … can I know what happened … and I'm not saying that one is right and
> the other one is wrong what I'm saying is that they're different values

Señora Rodriguez describes the difference in participation as cross-cultural differences in preferences for parental role in decisionmaking in the educational domain.
In the Anglo case, the parents are expected to get involved in the school's decision-
making, and to question what they do not understand. In the Latino case, the parents
are expected to leave the decisionmaking to the educator, because that is the
teacher's area of expertise which the Latino parent respects. Señora Rodriguez
explains:

it's a different culture ... in Latin America the top four people are mayor teacher doctor priest ... the teacher is responsible for all the education ... so it's a problem when they come here

She explained the Latino parental participation in the other meeting that she had personally organized by saying 'if I ask a Hispanic parent to come and do something for me, they are always there'. She concludes a story about Latino parental participation with the utterance, 'Because I *asked*, the teacher *asked*' (her emphasis). Señora Rodriguez assumes that the Latino parents will respect her authority in the educational domain and leave the decisionmaking to her. If she as teacher, however, asks for the Latino parents' help, she assumes they will be there to work with her, and they are.

Notice the similarity in Señora Rodriguez's assumptions about parental participation and the sixth-grade Spanish-dominant teacher, Señor Xoci's assumptions about student participation discussed earlier. Señora Rodriguez assumes there are Latino/Anglo differences in perceived parental participation rights in the educational discourse. Señor Xoci assumes there are Latino/Anglo differences in perceived participation and questioning rights in the classroom discourse. And just as Señor Xoci's assumption about Latino/Anglo differences in perceived participation rights helped explain negative stereotypes that Anglo teachers may have about Latino students (see previous discussion), Señora Rodriguez's assumption about Latino/Anglo differences in perceived parental participation rights helps explain a negative stereotype about Latino parents that I heard from an Anglo teacher at PS 22, the transitional bilingual school in which I had conducted research:

the Hispanic parents never come to the PTA meetings ... they really don't care about what their kids are doing here

I heard similar complaints from teachers in a transitional bilingual school in a low-income Puerto Rican/Dominican community that I worked in in 1985 in Brooklyn, New York. If Señora Rodriguez's explanation is accurate, it potentially has very serious consequences for school/community relationships. That is, what may be considered respect for teachers' authority by the Latino parents could be interpreted as not caring by the Anglo teachers. This observation has serious implications for cross-cultural misunderstanding since the US public school system is run, generally speaking, according to Standard English-speaking, white middle-class expectations, and public school teachers often interpret the Latino parents' behavior through their own cultural frames. Therefore, in order for teachers and parents to be able to work together to help educate the children, teachers need to be aware of the potential for cross-cultural miscommunication in the perceived parental role.

This view on cross-cultural differences in parental participation rights was supported by other teachers in the school, and informed the way that they worked with the different parental populations. On the administrative level, Señora Mendoza supported the idea that the school needs to work differently with the Latino parents and the Anglo parents. She said that when they have a general parent meeting, the Anglo parents and the middle to upper class Latino parents attend. But when they have a training or a meeting for only Latino parents, the low-income Latino parents that they had had trouble reaching showed up en masse. Therefore, she says, Oyster has two lines on the budget for parent training — one for general training done in Spanish and English, and one for Latino parents done exclusively in Spanish. The teachers and administrators have found this strategy effective in bridging the cross-cultural differences in assumptions and expectations about parental involvement in the school, and an effective means of bringing in a large population of parents that many schools seem to have trouble involving.

Parental involvement at Oyster Bilingual School adheres to the principles that Ovando and Collier (1985) argue are required for successful home–school relationships in multi-cultural communities. These principles are first, educators must learn about community language use, resources, strengths, values and desires. Second, parents must learn about school procedures and pedagogy, and they must reinforce academic development at home. And third, a balance must be maintained between the parent's power to determine the form and content of the school program based on community needs and values, and the school's power to prescribe the form and content of the school program based on professional expertise. Ultimately, parents come to see themselves as partners in, rather than spectators of, their children's education.

In sum, the Oyster definition of school can be understood as a community made up of people from diverse linguistic, cultural and socioeconomic backgrounds. What gives this community a sense of co-membership is their dedication to the education of all of the children. Although there are diverse interests, conflicts, and struggles within the school, there is an attempt to take the interests of all of the different groups that the school serves into consideration, and to share in the rights and responsibilities within the school.

Señor Xoci summarizes what kind of an education Oyster Bilingual School's socializing discourse provides for the students as follows:

> I I mean ... the feeling there is that ... you don't have a model culture teaching the ideas ... you're having a a a a a a ... you have a variety of individuals ... of all colors ... from all countries ... from all experiences ... built in different shapes ... different bodies..different attitudes ... but everybody is sort of working towards that same end ... and everybody understands that the goal of this institution ... is to teach the kids ... now the fact that we have native speakers of Spanish and native speakers of English adds even more ... because now what's happening is that both of these individuals seem confident in their own languages ... don't have to sit there and struggle to prove anything ... because that's the way it is ... it's just the normal course of their experience ... so what ends up happening is that these children pick up on that.

The educational discourse that the Oyster Bilingual School educators have constructed provides their students a very different experience than either language minority or language majority students have in mainstream US schools.

CONCLUSION

We have seen in this chapter that the Oyster educators reject the mainstream US assumption and expectation of a homogeneous student population that should speak Standard English and that should interact according to white middle-class Standard English-speaking norms. They also reject the assumption that linguistic and cultural diversity is a problem that language minority students have to overcome. Instead, the Oyster educators assume that their students come from a wide range of linguistic, cultural, and socioeconomic backgrounds. Linguistic and cultural diversity are seen as resources to be developed, and the goals of bilingualism, academic achievement, and intercultural communication skills are the same for all of the students.

According to the concluding passage of the *Teachers' Handbook* statement on 'Racial and Ethnic Differences',

> Oyster Bilingual School's focus is on the development of bilingualism, biliteracy and biculturalism for every student through the mastery of academic skills, the acquisition of language and communicative fluency, the appreciation of differences in racial and ethnic backgrounds, and the building of a positive self concept and pride in one's heritage. (Oyster Bilingual School, 1988)

The inclusion of this statement is evaluative, reflecting the Oyster assumption that *the appreciation of differences in racial and ethnic backgrounds*, and *the building of a positive self concept and pride in one's heritage* are not readily available in mainstream US discourse. Although the students come from very different backgrounds, the school has the same high expectations for all of them. Students are constructed as central to the educational process, and as agents in the processes *develop, acquire, appreciate,* and *build.* The teachers and school, both through who they are, and how they interact with students and with each other, can be understood as instrumental in facilitating students' efforts to meet these expectations. I provide a detailed discussion of the Oyster definitions of teaching and learning in Chapter 7.

Oyster can be understood as a 'community that crosses language, cultural and class lines'; a community that is unified by a common educational goal for all of the children. Creating a community out of diverse individuals, however, requires ongoing effort. This chapter has presented many examples of how the Oyster educators assume that people will have very different assumptions and expectations about school, as well as about their participation rights and obligations relative to each other at school. As a result, these educators emphasize that ongoing communication is necessary for them to negotiate how to work together to develop a shared understanding of what their common goals are, and then about how they can work together to reach those goals.

For example, Señor Estevez described how the original dual-language planners brought parents, teachers, and administrators together in the early development of the program so that they would all understand how the dual-language program would work and so they would share the same objectives for the children. Señora Rodriguez and Señora Mendoza assume that there are cross-cultural differences in how the Latino and Anglo parents understand their rights and obligations relative to the school, so they work very differently with these populations in order to involve all of the parents in the education of the children. Señor Xoci expects his Latino and Anglo students to prefer different ways of interacting in the classroom, and organizes his classroom interaction so that all of the students can participate and achieve more or less equally (see Chapter 10 for illustration). These individuals recognize that linguistic and cultural diversity influences people's understanding of themselves, each other, and the social world, and that ongoing communication makes it possible for them to jointly negotiate meaning.

I argue that discourse communities have choices in how they define themselves, their members, and their relations to each other. We have seen two competing definitions of students, the mainstream US definition that was presented in Chapter 3 and the Oyster Bilingual School definition presented in this chapter. I encourage educational researchers and reflective practioners to look critically at local assumptions about who the students are relative to each other at school and in the community, and for educators to look for ways to understand and value what the students bring with them to school as potential resources to draw on. Perhaps even more importantly, I encourage educators to seriously ask themselves what their expectations are for their students' achievement, because teachers' expectations matter. When teachers assume that their low-income Spanish-speaking students, for example, come from backgrounds that do not prepare them to achieve at school, or that their students really do not have the potential to attend the university if they choose to, it is very difficult for these students to achieve. If teachers assume that there is little that either they or the school can do to facilitate these students' academic achievement, more than likely the students will not achieve. While education cannot cure poverty, educators can look for ways to identify the individual and community resources that they can build on, and work together to help students from a wide range of backgrounds participate and achieve at school (see Moll, 1995, for ways that educators can identify and build on local 'funds of knowledge').

I also encourage researchers and practitioners to consider local definitions of teachers and of schools. How do the members of the school see themselves and each other in relation to the educational planning process? Do teachers and parents see themselves as having the right and obligation to be actively involved in the decision-making process? Are administrators actively involved in both the classroom and the community? Do the various groups communicate with each other? Do they share an understanding of their educational objectives? When they have competing interests or interpretations, what happens? Do they try to find ways to negotiate a shared understanding and goal, or does communication break down? While the Oyster educators' definitions of students, teachers, and school are based on their local circumstances, the assumption that a school is made up of people with diverse assumptions and expectations is generalizable. The expectation that these individuals will need to communicate regularly so that they all understand and share the same objectives is also generalizable.

According to Carbaugh (1990), we can understand how a particular 'cultural identity' is negotiated and displayed by analysing the 'cultural frames and forms for performance' within the cultural communication system (see Chapter 3). This chapter has provided a detailed discussion of local definitions of student, teacher, and school within the Oyster educational discourse community, and has offered a series of guiding questions for reseachers and practitioners to use to explore definitions of student, teacher, and school in another educational discourse system. I turn now to a discussion of Oyster Bilingual School's definitions of teaching and learning.

CHAPTER 7

Learning and Teaching at Oyster Bilingual School

As described in Chapter 3, 'cultural frames and forms for performance' (Carbaugh, 1990) are sequences of talk that members of a particular culture can and do identify. It is through these frames and forms that individuals negotiate and display their social identities. Research into language socialization and social identity construction suggests that people not only display but also construct their understanding of who they are relative to each other through their participation in language-mediated activities (see Chapter 3). The ways that communities organize their discourse practices vary cross-culturally, and this has implications for social identity development in different cultural contexts. Specifically, the manner in which a particular school organizes its learning and teaching opportunities for language minority and language majority students has implications for the students' understandings of their capabilities, which in turn affects academic achievement. This chapter presents Oyster Bilingual School's answer to the questions: 'What is learning?' and 'What is teaching?'

Recall from Chapter 3 that the mainstream US educational notion of teaching involves the transmission of a standardized curriculum content to what is assumed to be a homogenous student population who speak Standard English and behave according to white middle-class norms. In this model, learning is understood as the reception and then demonstrated mastery of that content, primarily through standardized tests. The educational atmosphere is often competitive with an emphasis on individual achievement, reflecting the mainstream US educational and societal belief that competition among individuals encourages the best results. Since the student population is assumed to be homogeneous, the students who are labeled Limited English Proficient (LEP) are taken out of the regular all-English classes and provided at least ESL instruction. Where there is a sufficient number of students from the same language background, LEP students are segregated from other

150

students in transitional bilingual educational programs. In order for language minority students to learn in mainstream US schools, they are encouraged to transition to monolingualism in English and assimilate to white middle-class norms. Language minority students who do not assimilate tend to fail at school.

As we saw in the last chapter, the Oyster educators do not assume a homogeneous student population, and they reject assimilation to monolingualism in English as an option for their students. These two socially-constructed facts require alternative organizations of learning and teaching. The Oyster assumptions about who their students are, what their varied needs are, and how to prepare them all to achieve academically are reflected in Oyster's bilingual education/learning/teaching practices. Students are socialized through these discourse practices to understand what they are capable of achieving at school.

WHAT IS LEARNING?

The primary goal of Oyster Bilingual School is to provide equal educational opportunity to all of its students. Because of its perspective on what is involved in achieving this goal for its diverse student population, Oyster has the additional goals of (1) bilingualism in Spanish and English for all of its students; and (2) a culturally pluralistic environment that expects, tolerates and respects differences among the students and in society. Additive bilingualism and cultural pluralism can be understood as instrumental in fulfilling the primary goal of academic achievement for all students. The goal of bilingualism relates to the students' developing the *ability* to speak a second-language, and the goal of cultural pluralism relates to the students developing the *right* to participate in the discourse. In other words, students' socializing experience through Oyster's alternative educational discourse ideally enables students to develop the ability and the right to participate in the educational discourse and to achieve academically. Accomplishing these same goals for students from very different backgrounds requires the design and implementation of several complementary plans.

Gaining the ability to speak two languages

First of all, as with any program designed to serve the needs of LEP students, the Oyster dual-language program includes an English language acquisition plan. As reflected in the following excerpt from my interview with Señor Estevez, Oyster emphasizes the students' learning to use language in context for real purposes:

Estevez: now I … I am a strong believer that languages cannot be taught in the absence of a context or a content … that is … just to acquire a language for the sake of knowing another language without expressing a thought … so that's why I believe a lot in math and sciences

Señor Estevez's use of the negative in his utterance, *I am a strong believer that languages cannot be taught in the absence of a context,* explicitly rejects mainstream

US models of language teaching that focus on decontextualized grammatical form. In contrast to traditional approaches to teaching ESL instruction, Oyster takes a content-based ESL approach, in which the LEP students are taught to speak English as a second-language by using English for the real purpose of learning content-areas and developing academic skills. This approach is consistent with any content-based ESL program (see Brinton *et al.* (1989) and Richard-Amato & Snow (1992) for detailed discussions of content-based second-language instruction).

Second, Oyster's dual-language plan includes a Spanish-language acquisition plan for the limited Spanish Proficient students. According to Señora Ortega, Oyster decided to offer the native English-speaking students the opportunity to acquire Spanish through a content-based Spanish-language curriculum:

Ortega: but we were saying ... what do they get in return ... what about the English speakers ... we were saying ... you know politically ... it's got to be equal in order to buy into it right? ... so they said ... well ... they can learn Spanish right? ... and ... so it's like an enrichment program

In order to provide equal educational opportunities to the English-speaking and Spanish-speaking students, Oyster's explicit goals include additive bilingualism for all students.

To fulfill the goals of bilingualism in Spanish and English for all students, Spanish and English are to be equally distributed throughout the students' day, week and academic experience. There are two full-time teachers in each class; the English-dominant teacher ideally speaks and is spoken to only in English and is responsible for teaching half of the curriculum in English, and the Spanish-dominant teacher ideally speaks and is spoken to only in Spanish and is responsible for teaching the other half of the curriculum in Spanish. Since the primary goal of this educational program is academic skills development and mastery of content, there is no problem if the students need to use their first language to aid in each others' comprehension (see later for further discussion of distribution of languages, content, and skills). The 50%/50% distribution of languages ideally provides the students sufficient comprehensible input in the second-language, which is considered a necessary condition for second-language acquisition (Dulay *et al.*, 1982). In this way, the non-native English-speaking students and the non-native Spanish-speaking students have the opportunity to develop the ability to speak English and Spanish as second-languages respectively. In the case of students who speak neither English nor Spanish, they have the opportunity to develop the ability to speak both English and Spanish as additional languages.

The motivating principle behind the dual-language acquisition plan is need, which revolves around the English-dominant and the Spanish-dominant students and teachers in the classroom. The English-dominant teacher and the native English-speaking students can be understood as instrumental in fulfilling the

English-language acquisition planning goal for the native Spanish-speaking students, because they provide the need for the Spanish-speaking students to communicate in English in class and the resources for their acquisition of English. In the same way, the Spanish-dominant teacher and the native Spanish-speaking students are instrumental in fulfilling the Spanish-language acquisition planning goal for the native English speakers. Oyster's dual-language plan relies on the assumption that if the students find the need to use both languages, and if they have resources available to acquire their second-language, they will. Conversely, if the students do not find the need to use the second-language, or if they do not have the available resources, they will not acquire it. Señora Ortega explains the importance of this policy:

Ortega: which is why it's very important that our teachers in that classroom be Spanish-dominant ... native Spanish-dominant ... because people from Southwest ... and I'm guilty ... and Señor Xoci is guilty ... we grew up in a very bilingual community ... we codeswitch all the time ... and if we do that in the classroom the kids are going to say ... I don't need to learn Spanish I don't have to use Spanish to talk to Señor Xoci or Señora Ortega because she's English dominant ... and you can't expect a child to use another language if he doesn't find a need for it

Señora Ortega's negative evaluation of code-switching in the classroom is evident in her use of the adjective *guilty* to describe her and Señor Xoci's tendency to codeswitch. In order for the model to work, the ideal policy assumes that the teachers strictly adhere to the plan.

The Spanish component of the Oyster program can also be understood as a Spanish-language maintenance plan. Because 50% of the day is dedicated to content-area instruction in Spanish, the native Spanish speakers need to maintain and develop their Spanish in order to achieve academically in the Spanish content-areas. Oyster's emphasis on native language maintenance and additive bilingualism can be understood in contrast to the mainstream US educational and societal emphasis on subtractive bilingualism in transition to monolingualism in English. Language at Oyster is a resource to be developed by all students, rather than a problem to be overcome.

The goal of the dual-language acquisition plan is for all of the students to develop the necessary ability, or communicative competence, to achieve academically in content-areas in both Spanish and English. Following Canale and Swain (1980), communicative competence consists of (1) linguistic competence (accuracy), (2) sociolinguistic competence (appropriacy in the speech event), (3) discourse competence (appropriate genre selection and use), and (4) strategic competence (ability to compensate for any weaknesses in the above three areas). Oyster's emphasis on academic competence in the second-language can be contrasted with bilingual education programs in the United States that are criticized for not enabling LEP students to develop the necessary academic competence to compete as equals in the all-English classes (Adamson, 1993). Chapter 8 presents examples of activities that I observed and emphasizes how they can be understood to develop various aspects of the children's ability to communicate competently.

Gaining the right to participate in the educational discourse

As I argue throughout this book, Oyster's dual-language program is about much more than language in the traditional sense. Consideration of the sociolinguistic context in which Oyster is situated enabled me to see the underlying social identities project that informs and explains Oyster's program. Understanding the social stigmatization of the Spanish language in the United States requires that the Spanish language-planning component additionally be considered an example of educational status planning. Because of the close relationship between language use and social identity, if students are socialized to see Spanish as legitimate to fulfill the official educational function, by extension Spanish speakers are seen as legitimate participants in the educational discourse. Viewed from the perspective of the underlying social identities project, the goal of teaching Spanish is not only to develop and/or maintain students' abilities to use Spanish, but also to strengthen the symbolic social identities of Spanish speakers for both native and non-native Spanish speakers. Ideally, the students all come to see Spanish speakers as having the right to participate equally and achieve at school.

Oyster's dual-language education program can be understood in contrast to mainstream US educational discourse in which LEP students are segregated from the regular classes until they have acquired enough English to participate. At Oyster, the Spanish-speaking LEP students do not have to wait until they acquire English to participate. Because both native English-speaking and native Spanish-speaking students are learning all content-areas in both their first and second-languages together at the same time, the native Spanish-speaking LEP students have the right to participate in the Oyster educational discourse from the moment they enter the school.

Notice that the Oyster definition of equal educational opportunity is quite different from that employed in mainstream US educational and societal discourse. As Señora Ortega stated earlier, *it's got to be equal in order to buy into it.* The Oyster notion of equal educational opportunity goes beyond the Bilingual Education Act's mandate of English language proficiency for all students. In the Oyster alternative educational discourse, 'equality' means bilingualism in Spanish and English for language minority and language majority students, not monolingualism in English. Rather than assuming a homogeneous student population and treating all of the students equally in English, the Oyster educators assume a linguistically and culturally diverse student population, and treat them differently in order to provide them all the opportunity to meet equally high expectations (see Chapter 9 for illustration). Since equal treatment in mainstream US educational discourse generally leads to the subordinate role of language minority students (see Chapter 3), the Oyster educators' unequal treatment yet equally high expectations for their language minority students makes it possible for these students to develop social identities whose differences are expected, tolerated, and respected in the educational discourse.

Translating the ideal into actual classroom practice

The question is, how is this ideal translated into classroom practice? Given (1) the assumed diversity among the students' knowledge bases and ways of interacting, and (2) the difference between the teachers' and the students' backgrounds, as well as (3) the impossibility of any teacher *knowing* the background of every single student, especially the subtle cross-cultural differences in ways of interacting, the question becomes, What kind of a classroom interaction can teachers of diverse student populations organize in order to provide all students opportunities to gain the ability to speak Spanish and English, as well as the right to participate more or less equally in the educational discourse?

As a solution to this question, Oyster has adopted the cooperative learning model. According to the Oyster educators, cooperative learning organizations contribute both in symbolic and practical ways to the Oyster dual-language and social identities project goals: through a variety of cooperative learning organizations, the students improve their ability to speak both Spanish and English as either first or second-languages (or sometimes third or fourth). In addition, because students from diverse backgrounds are working together and learning from each other, the minority and the majority students alike learn to see the minority students as having equal rights to participate in the educational discourse (see Kessler, 1992, for further discussion of cooperative learing).

The physical organization of the classroom social space reflects and perpetuates the definitions of students as agents in the educational process, and of teachers as instrumental to that process. Figure 10 is a diagram of the Oyster social space. It is intended to be a general diagram of any first-through sixth-grade classroom organization in Oyster, rather than the organization of any one particular class.

The organization of the desks into groups of four or six in the cooperative learning model symbolically represents the central role of the students. This organization opposes the mainstream US classroom organization in which all of the students' desks face the teacher (see Figure 6, Chapter 3).

There are a variety of student organizations that utilize this social space. For example, sometimes the entire class is divided in half with the Spanish-dominant teacher conducting class in Spanish on one side while the English-dominant teacher conducts class in English on the other side. Sometimes either the Spanish-dominant teacher or the English-dominant teacher conducts the entire class in either Spanish or English respectively. In this case, the teacher who is not the official teacher may be outside of the class doing something else, or may be in the classroom. Sometimes the unofficial teacher does independent work on the side, or sometimes s/he assists the official teacher and circulates to work with individual students or small groups. Within the Spanish and English content-area classes, there are also a variety of organizations. The students may all be working with the teacher together, or the students may be working in small groups which the teacher oversees, or the students may be working independently. The students change their particular groupings and the organization within the class quite frequently to do a variety of activities in any one subject area. The fact that students are learning through a wide range of activities and organizations increases the possibility that everyone's individual and/or cultural learning preference is accommodated at some time. In addition, the regular changing of activities, and changing from one teaching and learning style to another, contributes to the students' flexibility.

I include a few of the teachers' comments about the benefits of cooperative learning which were written in response to a question about the advantages and disadvantages of cooperative learning on a questionnaire that I administered. One teacher responded:

> Cooperative learning allows for more conversational time for the students in whichever language during content instruction. They need more chances to speak than student–teacher only interaction would allow.

This teacher mentions the benefits of the cooperative learning organization with respect to the language acquisition plan because such student-centered organization provides the students more opportunity to use the second-language. In small groups, the students have the opportunity to, for example, question and answer each other on a regular basis. The variation in classroom organizations allows students to use language to perform a greater variety of language functions, facilitating their development of communicative competence. Since they are working through the second-language to develop academic skills, they are gaining the necessary academic competence to achieve in content-areas in the second-language. In addition, the students are actively negotiating meaning through the second-language, which provides increased opportunities to make second-language input comprehensible, thus aiding second-language acquisition (Pica *et al.*, 1987; Pica, 1988).

Another teacher provided the following response to the same question, which stresses the central role of students in developing academic skills through a second-language:

> I think it has its place in any classroom, but especially in a bilingual setting. Often peers can explain something to a child who is weak in whichever particular language we're using at the time more succinctly than an adult can.

This teacher positively evaluates the students' abilities to explain difficult concepts to each other, again emphasizing the agentive role of the students in their learning. Vygotsky's notion of the 'zone of proximal development', in which the more

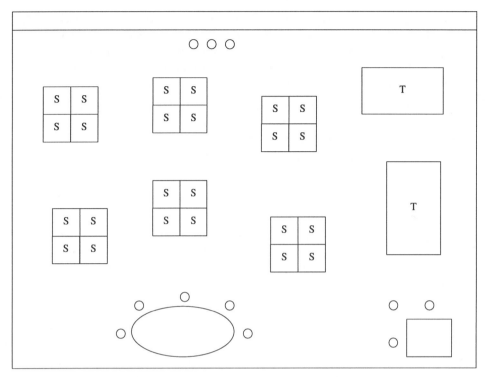

Figure 10 Classroom space at Oyster Bilingual School

capable peer helps the less capable peer accomplish a particular task, underlies the teacher's comment. Valuing student–student talk as educational can be contrasted with a mainstream US teacher-centered classroom, in which such student interaction is often considered disruptive and off-task, especially if the language used is not the official language of the classroom.

In addition to contributing to the language acquisition and academic skills development goals, cooperative learning organizations contribute to realizing the goals of the underlying social identities project. The sixth-grade Spanish-dominant teacher had been sent by Oyster to attend a 'Master Teacher' conference on cooperative learning and share what he learned upon his return with the other teachers. He gave me a handout he had obtained at the conference which contrasted three types of classroom situations: (1) cooperative, in which students work to-gether; (2) competitive, in which students avoid each other or obstruct each others' efforts, and (3) individualistic, in which students are not supposed to interact at all. The handout provides a summary of the major research findings of Johnson *et al.* (1981). I repeat the first point because of its relevance to the Oyster social identities project:

> Cooperative learning experiences result in more positive student–student rela-
> tionships which are characterized by mutual liking; positive attitudes toward
> one another; and mutual feelings of obligation, support, acceptance, and respect.
> This is true regardless of the ethnic background, social class, and ability of
> students. (*Master Teacher*, 1990).

These attributes, *positive student–student relationships, mutual liking, positive
attitudes toward one another, mutual feelings of obligation, support, acceptance
and respect* are consistent with the Oyster social identities project goal of developing
positive minority identities whose differences are expected, tolerated, and respected
in the educational discourse.

The same sixth-grade teacher who gave me the handout likens the cooperative
learning organization to a community:

> that's why they come up with alot of these strategies in cooperative education
> you know … studying just basic um traditional um relationships in in in
> community and … in family … and in working together where children feel a
> sense of accomplishment as a group

And as we have seen throughout, the creation of a Oyster community that crosses
linguistic, cultural and socioeconomic boundaries is an important goal of the
program.

In sum, cooperative learning groups provide organizations in which the students
are positioned as central to the educational process. The assumption is that groups
of children working together in small groups provides students opportunities to
negotiate meaning among themselves, which not only facilitates their acquisition of
language skills, their understanding of content-areas and their development of
academic skills, but also leads to a sense of connectedness to the group. When the
members of the group come from diverse socioeconomic, racial, and ethnic backgrounds, students are to develop a frame for understanding groups to have such
diversity, and to develop strategies for communicating within such groups. Ideally,
the students are socialized into expecting and respecting diversity, and will learn to
treat 'other' as equal. Ideally, by socializing children differently from mainstream
US educational practices, the children will be prepared to promote change in
mainstream US society from the bottom up.

WHAT IS TEACHING?

Based on my conversations with the Oyster educators about their practice and my
observations of that practice, I would say there are two related answers to this
question. The first has to do with what an individual teacher does to enable an
individual student to develop the ability to speak two languages and the right to
participate in the academic discourse as the means of facilitating that student's
development of academic competence. The second response is 'team-teaching'. I
begin this section by discussing qualities that the Oyster educators attribute to a

teacher working with diverse student populations. I then proceed to a discussion of their team-teaching approach.

The combination of the Oyster definition of students as linguistically, culturally, and socioeconomically diverse, their assumption that this diversity influences the learning process, and their dedication to a student-centered approach has implications for the ways individual teachers interact with the individual students. The teacher's agenda requires much more than presentation of content for the students to all receive equally, as the mainstream US educational model seems to assume. According to Señor Estevez, in order to be able to communicate with the children, it is crucial for the teachers to be aware of cross-cultural differences:

Estevez: I go back to the training of teachers ... there is a big difference between the school culture and the home culture ... and sometimes it's a contradiction sometimes it's a contradiction ... and you have to understand at least how ... the values of the other child has ... and to understand your own value system ... and see where they conflict and where they overlap

The Spanish-dominant kindergarten teacher, Señora Rodriguez, explained what these expectations about students required of her as a teacher:

you have to know every family ... and you have to know every background of every child ... don't tell them to work..make them understand why they want to work ... give them the reason to do the work

Compare Señora Rodriguez's rejection of one approach in her utterance, *don't tell them to work* with the approach she advocates in the utterances, *make them understand why they want to work, and give them the reason to do the work.* In the first utterance, the teacher is represented as the agent in the process 'teacher tells student to work', which she rejects. This representation is consistent with the mainstream US educational representation of the teacher as agent and more powerful. Her alternative approach in the next two utterances positions the students as agents in the process 'they want to work'; these utterances advocate student choice. The teacher's role is to provide reasons, and to encourage the student's choice.

The same construction of students as agents in determining their own success and teachers as instrumental in developing the child's awareness of that potential is reflected in the following excerpt from one of the Spanish-dominant first grade teachers:

I see the emotional situation increasing every year ... you scratch inside that child and you see a very talented individual ... if you work with them ... and show them they can be successful ... they can make it

In this account, even the children who on the surface have problems can be taught to see themselves as successful. The teacher's job is instrumental, to facilitate the child's recognition and development of potential, or to position the student to position him/herself.

Several interesting questions are raised here. First of all, is there a contradiction in the fact that the teacher is the one with the power to position students to position themselves? I argue that there is no contradiction at all because of the nature of speaking roles assigned to people by society. The teacher has the more powerful role in the classroom, and can use that power in any number of ways. In a cooperative learning environment, the teacher uses that power in a way that enables the students to question each other as well as to question the teacher. The student-centered classroom organization stands in contrast to a more teacher-centered organization in which the teacher questions the students or the students question the teacher. For example, as we saw in the last chapter, Señor Xoci assumes that the Latino students will question each other but not the teacher. Therefore, if his assumption is correct, the cooperative learning environment the teacher creates is more conducive to providing both Latino and Anglo students equal opportunity to participate (see Chapter 10 for illustration).

Secondly, what are the implications of this methodology, positioning students to position themselves as having the right to participate, for the shyer, more reticent students in the class? Although I will not address this question in detail here, briefly the answer seems to lie in the teacher's respecting the students' participation styles and in providing a variety of classroom organizations. If the student prefers not to speak, but the teacher can see that the student is actively participating and is learning from the class, often that student is allowed to be silent. When the normally quiet student volunteers to participate orally, the teacher seems to be more supportive than usual, emphasizing that all, regardless of style, are encouraged to contribute. Also, the students are regularly organized into small groups to work on a project. In this environment, a student who is normally shy in front of the entire class has the opportunity to collaborate in the smaller group, receiving reinforcement for his/her contributions. Through this peer ratification, and group presentation rather than individual presentation of ideas, the shy student can contribute. Furthermore, there are many activities in which the entire group must participate. For example, as Chapter 10 illustrates, all of the sixth-grade students are encouraged to share poems that they had written. By gaining practice and support in sharing their ideas with the class, even the shyer students can participate more actively.

As discussed earlier, central to the implementation of the dual-language acquisition plan is use of native language models; in each classroom there is one Spanish-dominant teacher and one English-dominant teacher. Since there are two teachers in each classroom, Oyster has adopted a team-teaching approach. The team teachers share the responsibility for facilitating the students' active learning process, and help develop autonomous students who make choices, and take responsibility for their learning. We have already seen the teachers' description of what individual qualities this requires: openness, flexibility, awareness, and respectful of difference. It remains for me to discuss their description and interpretation of team-teaching.

Señora Ortega provides the following description of the team-teaching approach, which I understand as the ideal:

> they work with their partner ... the two teachers in every class have got to plan together ... they've got to coordinate ... so that they're not ... one talking about apples and the other talking about oranges ... so the child sees there's connections ... it makes more sense..the puzzle comes ... you know ... together

In Señora Ortega's construction, the teachers coordinate everything together for the benefit of the students. In this way, the Spanish-dominant teacher and the English-dominant teacher's lesson planning in Spanish and English respectively ideally serves to reinforce the underlying concepts that the students are learning and academic skills they are developing in both languages simultaneously.

Señor Xoci also expressed benefits of the team-teaching approach for the students, but the reasoning he reflects in this excerpt has less to do with presentation of the material in two languages and more to do with there being two adults in the classroom with whom the students interact:

> a lot of it has to do with the fact that ... I think a lot of it is going into more practical turf ... I think a lot of it has to do with the fact that you have two teachers in the classroom ... you have more supervision ... you have less room for the child to sort of goof off and stray ... you have more actual follow up

A bit later in our conversation, Señor Xoci continues:

> well that's ... this is the backbone ... this is the skeleton all right ... and you've got teachers ... you've got teachers who really do care ... and a lot of that has to do with the fact that you have less ... again it all leads down to the fact that ... in my opinion ... the kids are still ... they're more accountable ... that's what it is ... they're more accountable ... and there're more adults to communicate with them ... and there are more adults around to say **Buenos días, ¿cómo estás?** [Good morning, how are you?] ... **pórtense bien** [behave yourself] ... **cállate** [be quiet] ... **siéntate** [sit down] ... **párate** [stop that] ... **vete** [come here]

Señor Xoci here attributes much of the success of the program to the fact that there are two teachers in every class which makes the children *more accountable* with *less room for the child to sort of goof off*. Notice that in both of these reasons, the children are represented as agents with choices and who take responsibility; they can either *goof off* or be *more accountable*. The role of the two teachers is to provide more supervision, i.e. to be instrumental in helping the children make the right choices and take responsibility for those choices that they have made.

In response to the questionnaire question about the advantages and disadvantages of the team-teaching approach, one teacher wrote:

(1) Avoid the isolation other teachers in other schools feel — having another adult to talk to; lack of this wears on other elementary teachers.
(2) Keeps me on my toes — can fake it to the kids but not to the partner — like having 24 hour informal observation.
(3) Opportunity to discuss specific learning/behavior problems of specific kids; 'yes, he has the same problem in Spanish', 'yes she failed her Spanish spelling test this week also'.

This teacher explicitly evokes mainstream US educational practices in the first part of her response, positively evaluating the Oyster team-teaching approach and negatively evaluating the mainstream US teaching approach because of the emotional well-being of the teacher. The team-teaching approach fulfills three interrelated functions for the teacher; companionship, increased accountability, and consulting about student learning. Given the Oyster definition of teaching as requiring the teacher to know the backgrounds of all the children so they know what to build on and how best to do that, the consultant role is quite important. In a mainstream US classroom, where the students are considered more or less homogeneous, the consultant role would not be as relevant. Another teacher responded to the same question on the questionnaire as follows:

The two clearest advantages of team-teaching for me are:
(1) class size is reduced by 1/2,
(2) a co-professional for constant consultation on lesson effectiveness, ideas to help individual students, and, in the case of Oyster, *native* language models for students [emphasis in original]. A less important advantage is splitting the drudgery of paper work.

Both of these teachers' comments suggest that the two members of the team cooperate with each other in their attempts to meet the educational needs of their students. This requires cooperation in distributing and coordinating the content-areas as well.

Señora Ortega provided the following description of that distribution of content and coordination among the team-teachers, which I take to represent the ideal.

here the teachers … like I said before … they both have to teach reading..language arts and math … both to all the kids in English and Spanish … right? … we have to do that … in addition to that they have to teach science..social studies..geography..computers..art … OK … first semester one teacher will say … OK I'll do science in English and the other teacher will say … OK I'll do social studies in Spanish to the whole class … OK … second semester they'll say … OK … my turn to do social studies in English and your turn to do science in Spanish

Señora Ortega's use of the modals *have to* in the beginning of her description of the distribution of content makes explicit that there are some requirements handed down from above (presumably from the school district), which she lists: reading, language arts, math. However, she also represents the team-teachers as having a considerable amount of autonomy in determining the actual distribution of language through content-areas on the classroom level. Señora Ortega follows the district's requirements for content distribution with another list of content-areas that must be taught. Her constructed dialog between the team-teachers, *OK I'll do science in English, OK I'll do social studies in Spanish, OK my turn to do social studies in English and your turn to do science in Spanish* iconically represents the ideal of dialog and cooperation among the team-teachers.

One of the first-grade English-dominant teachers provided the following response to the question concerning distribution of languages in the classroom, which is similar to Señora Ortega's construction of the ideal,

> Reading is given equal time in both languages. All science in English, all social studies in Spanish. Math switches languages by semester.

The difference is that these first-grade teachers prefer to teach one or the other subject, social studies or science, the entire year in either Spanish or English rather than switching everything each semester. That the team-teachers describe choice and flexibility reflects the autonomy of the teachers in implementing the plan.

Similarly, one of the third/fourth-grade English-dominant teachers provided the somewhat more detailed response to the same question about distribution of languages in the classroom:

> We organized everything such that 50% of each child's day is in each language. We divided the class in two groups for one hour each language instruction; the third hour of the morning was generally for math — this language of instruction switched by semester. For all group activities (math word problems done in cooperative groups; reading to class; creative writing; journals; handwriting practice; we switched language by day or by week). We taught one semester in each language for science and social studies — with the other language teacher free to help groups (we did a lot of cooperative activities) and especially ESL or SSL students in the class (i.e. as English teacher, I'd help SSL students during Spanish science classes).

This teacher's description of the method that she and her team-teacher worked out is consistent with the ideal that 50% of the instruction is to be in Spanish and 50% in English, and that math and language arts be taught in both languages. In addition, her description provides an image of two teachers closely cooperating together in order to implement the plan, not only with respect to distribution of content-areas and language, but also with respect to supporting each other and providing extra help to students who may be having difficulty in their second-language, either

English or Spanish. She also emphasizes the group, cooperative learning activities referred to in the last section.

Not only is it important to have equal time for the subject areas, but equal materials for the subjects are also necessary. According to Señora Ortega, this has been a problem, because of lack of Spanish language materials on the market:

Ortega: material … we're far behind with Spanish … as far as what's available on the market … so you find that teachers make alot of their own materials … um um … the uh curriculum has been translated … at least language arts and reading has been translated into Spanish by some of the teachers here

Rebecca: so everything is developed internally

Ortega: so that we have credibility within the system we had to do CBC

Rebecca: I don't know what that means

Ortega: the competency-based curriculum within the district … so that you can justify that teacher paid by DCPS [District of Columbia Public Schools] budget … he has to be accountable for carrying out the curriculum in the district … and they do … what the Spanish teachers do is add more to it … because you have to add more language to it … more grammar to it … in terms of verbs in Spanish … you know what that is

Consistent with Señora Ortega's description, I saw Spanish materials obtained from a variety of sources. For example, the kindergarten teachers had made many books in Spanish, some of which were translations of English texts. One method of teaching the students to read in both languages was to read the same story to them in English and in Spanish. The assumptions underlying this approach were also language in context and transferal of skills. In addition to making their own materials, I also observed that the teachers had collected, for example, books from their countries that they brought to school. In this way, the students were exposed to literature from many different Latin American countries, which provided them with a variety of cultural perspectives.

The school's goals include mastery of skills in both languages. This too assumes cooperation among the teachers so that they are aware of the skills requirements of the team-teacher. In this way, the ideal plan is for the students to perceive consistency in expectations for performance in Spanish and English. Such cooperation across expectations for skills levels was evidenced in a meeting that I observed of the kindergarten and first grade teachers. The teachers were discussing skills levels in each of the first grade classes in each of the languages so there would be consistency across the first grade and so that the kindergarten teachers could know the first grade expectations in order to best prepare the students. One of the English-dominant teachers and one of the Spanish-dominant teachers (each from a different 1st grade class) wrote a list of their expectations for a student entering first grade. A look at these lists reveals similarities and differences in explicit and implicit goals with respect to the populations. I present the English-dominant teacher's list first, followed by the Spanish-dominant teacher's list, reflecting the order they occurred in the meeting.

English-dominant teacher's criteria for first grade:

- Names of the letters of the alphabet out of sequence.
- Consonant sounds with the exception of soft c and g.
  Confusion with y and w OK.
  Basically the major consonants so they can sound it out to do invented spelling.
- I would like them to know five vowel sounds. Short vowels, long vowels — save that for first grade.
- Math — count rote at least to 10, hopefully to 20.
- Add and subtract with concrete things.
- Familiarity that there are four seasons.
- Coins — what is and what isn't a coin.
- Know that time exists.

Spanish-dominant teacher's criteria for first grade:

- Same sounds, but not all. I've seen some really bloom in a year.
- Simple two step directions. At least two. That's one of the hardest things for them to get accustomed to.
- Math — patterns. We review the numbers.
- Emotional state they are in.
- Social interaction with peers.

It is interesting to note that with respect to the list of criteria for promotion, the English-dominant teacher evidences a greater concern for skills and a lesser concern for emotional and social skills than the Spanish-dominant teacher. I want to emphasize that I am not saying that this English-dominant teacher is not concerned with the emotional or the social skills, because observation of her interaction with the teachers and the students as well as my conversations with her demonstrates her concern for these areas. Moreover, I am not saying that the Spanish-dominant teacher is not concerned with skills. What I want to point out is the difference in their criteria for promotion. This difference will be taken up again in the discussion of discrepancies between ideal plan and actual implementation in Chapter 8.

CONCLUSION

This chapter made explicit the Oyster definitions of learning and teaching, and related them to the definitions of learning and teaching in mainstream US educational discourse. The point of this discussion was to describe, interpret and explain how the students' participation in these 'cultural frames and forms for performance' (Carbaugh, 1990) works toward the goals of bilingualism for all students and the development of a culturally pluralistic environment in which all students, regardless of background, have not only the ability but also the right to participate equally in the educational discourse. Through such interactional experience, both majority and minority students ideally come to recognize the existence of positive minority social identities that are not forced to assimilate and that are not denied equal educational opportunity. The Oyster students ideally come to expect, tolerate, and respect diversity. In such a context, according to the Oyster construction, all students regardless of background are afforded equal educational opportunity.

The particulars of how learning and teaching are organized at Oyster Bilingual School are not intended to be directly translatable to another setting. However, I encourage educational researchers and reflective practitioners to examine what learning and teaching mean in another educational context. What assumptions about students are reflected in the local definitions of learning and teaching? How do these definitions position language minority and language majority students relative to each other at school? Are they positioned as agents who can make choices and take responsibility for their actions? Do all of the students have the right to participate in the educational discourse? Or are some of the students segregated until they acquire the necessary skills (i.e. abilities and rights) to participate in the academic program? These kinds of questions are intended to help researchers and practitioners look closely at specific educational programs and practices to understand how their local organization defines minority students.

Chapters 5, 6, and 7 provided an ethnographic understanding of how and why the Oyster Bilingual School social identities project functions the way that it does on the local level. Consistent with Carbaugh (1990), however, I believe that in order to more fully understand the discourse system under study, in this case the Oyster educational system in relation to mainstream US educational and societal discourse systems, it is necessary to look more closely at the 'structuring norms'. Chapter 8 provides such an analysis.

CHAPTER 8

A Focus on Inclusion

This chapter presents an explicit statement of the norms that structure discourse practices at Oyster Bilingual School. Detailed analysis of the curriculum content and of classroom practices allowed me to describe, interpret, and explain the constitutive relationship between Oyster's definitions of learning and teaching and the kinds of students that the school produces. Comparing these norms to those that structure discourse practices in mainstream US schools yields an understanding of how the micro-level classroom activities that the Oyster educators organize can offer more choices to their language minority and language majority students.

We saw in Chapter 3 that mainstream US educational discourse revolves around a relatively standardized curriculum content with standardized assessment practices that reflect an assumption of a homogenous white middle-class native English-speaking student population. Both the curriculum content and the evaluation methods can have negative effects on minority students. The minority students cannot relate to the mainstream US curriculum in the same way as the majority students because there is little positive representation of the minority students' histories, literatures, arts, or perspectives. Evaluation can also be unfair to minority students because standardized tests often contain a cultural bias against other than white middle-class populations, restricting the minority students' ability to demonstrate academic achievement.

The norms that structure the mainstream US classroom discourse can also have negative implications for minority students. In these classes, the teacher is defined as the more knowledgeable participant, with the responsibility to transmit the curriculum content to the homogeneous student body, and responsible for the evaluation of the students' mastery of that content. The teacher retains the majority of the power in the classroom including the right to delegate the students' opportunities to participate. The students therefore have considerably less power than the teacher, and must compete with each other for the relatively limited opportunities to speak and demonstrate their understanding of the content. These restricted

167

participation opportunities may affect the language minority students' abilities to develop competence in the second-language because increased opportunities to negotiate meaning can faciliate second-language acquisition processes (Pica, 1991). And since language minority students' ways of speaking and interacting are often distinct from the school's, the teacher may misinterpret the students' efforts to participate for not knowing or not caring (Heath, 1983; Philips, 1983). Such interaction can contribute to the minority student's seeing him/herself as not having the right to participate in the classroom discourse.

In contrast, Oyster's goal of developing positive minority social identities that have the ability and the right to participate requires structuring norms that focus on inclusion. My discussion of structuring norms begins with Oyster's multicultural curriculum content. Since it is much easier to understand the underlying norms of interaction through actual examples, I describe a variety of activities that I observed to illustrate representative teacher and student behavior in the classroom. The conclusion of this chapter identifies systematic discrepancies between ideal plan and actual implementation that I observed, and provides a sociopolitical explanation based on the interaction of the Oyster educational discourse and mainstream US societal discourse.

WHAT IS CURRICULUM CONTENT?

Because Oyster is a US public school, it is required to include the standardized curriculum as a part of its curriculum content, and to evaluate the students' achievement according to standardized tests (see Chapter 1 for discussion of the Oyster standardized test scores). What differentiates the Oyster curriculum from that of mainstream US educational discourse is the multicultural emphasis. My discussion of the Oyster curriculum content will therefore be limited to a description of its multicultural efforts.

The term 'multicultural' has become somewhat of a buzzword throughout the US educational discourse community recently as educators look for ways to recognize the increasing diversity of contemporary US society and incorporate this diversity into the curriculum content. Rather than try to understand what the term multicultural means elsewhere in the educational discourse community, the question to be addressed here is, what does multicultural mean with respect to the Oyster curriculum content?

I begin this chapter by presenting official policy statements that relate to the curriculum content. I then provide excerpts from administrators and teachers to reveal their interpretation of the relationship of the multicultural curriculum content to the program's goals. Examples of the implementation of the multicultural curriculum content will be provided throughout this section as well as throughout my presentation of the norms of interaction and interpretation that structure the classroom discourse.

The Teacher's Handbook provides official recognition of Hispanic Heritage Week and of Black History Month as important aspects of the curriculum, reflecting their inclusion of the Latino and African American students who make up the majority of the student population. For example, one page in the *Teachers' Handbook* is entitled Hispanic Heritage, and reads as follows:

Hispanic Heritage

A nationwide celebration is designated during the mid-week of September. In recognition of our unique student population, our celebration is extended past this week through the month of October. A culminating, sharing assembly is scheduled for early November. Appropriate instructional activities should be planned.

Hispanic Heritage Celebration

1. Biographies
    Contributions of famous Hispanics: Past
    Influences   Present
2. Hispanic poetry, literature, music, art, foods
3. Hispanic cultural studies
4. Famous Hispanic speeches, quotations
5. Capitalize upon various Hispanic countries represented by student population within class/school. Share traditions
6. Trips
7. Guest presentations

Tying the Oyster Hispanic Heritage Celebration to the national celebration illustrates to the students the importance of Hispanic Heritage not only to the school but to the country. The *unique student population* at Oyster, however, is *celebrated* not only for a week as is the case of the national celebration, but for a month and a half. Since the Hispanic Heritage Celebration begins in mid-September, which is close to the beginning of the school year, it sets the pace for how the multicultural curriculum is to be implemented and shared throughout the school.

Each class contributes something they have worked on as a class through a content-area, for example, in social studies or in language arts to the 'culminating sharing assembly'. The teaching emphasis is on incorporating students' backgrounds into the curriculum, using that background as a topic through which the students develop academic skills and acquire the second-language (either Spanish or English), and then the students share what they have learned together as a class throughout the Oyster community. The sharing and celebration of work that revolves around Latino heritage both reflects and contributes to the Latino students' pride in themselves and the students' pride in each other. In this way, all three goals of the Oyster dual-language program/social identities project — (1) academic skills development, (2) second-language acquisition, and (3) pride in one's heritage/respect for all heritages — are addressed simultaneously.

Similarly, the *Teachers' Handbook* includes a page on Black History Month, which ties the Oyster celebration to the national celebration in February, and provides suggested activities for the teachers to include in the curriculum design. And like the Hispanic Heritage Celebration, Black History Month concludes with a 'culminating, sharing assembly'. I provide the following description of the 1991 Black History Sharing Assembly that I attended to illustrate how the multicultural emphasis is incorporated into the actual classroom activities and then shared with the school.

The 1991 Black History Sharing Assembly took place all day in the auditorium. Like every sharing assembly, all of the classes participated, there were many guest presenters, and many parents attended. The Black History Celebration brochure listed the following activities which were included in the event: tie dye, listen to a storyteller, make an African drum, taste African and Carribean cooking, sing songs of Africa, wrap yourself in African cloth, taste George Washington Carver's peanut recipes, watch African dancers, watch videos about Africa, learn about the contributions of Blacks to science, look at masks, jewelry, and art from Africa, watch artists model clay into Senufo designs, watch artists paint Senufo style paintings, look at Adinkra printing and prints, make a Mousgoum village ('A Day in Black History' schedule: Friday, March 1, 1991).

As the list of activities suggests, the auditorium was transformed into a festival-like atmosphere, divided into booths and demonstration areas, and was highly interactive. Each sense was appealed to through, for example, the sound of African music or the smell and taste of Caribbean and African cooking. There were videos to watch and hands-on activities in which to participate. Many of these activities had been organized by the students as part of their content classes. For example, the sixth-grade science class in Spanish had researched the contributions of Blacks to science, and then organized an interactive demonstration of their findings in which they modeled and explained the particular scientific contributions to the Black History Celebration participants. Another class had made a Mousgoum village in their art class, and were teaching participants how to do the same as their contribution to the celebration. As with the Hispanic Heritage Celebration, the focus was on including African/Caribbean/African American contributions in their regular content classes, and then sharing their work with the rest of the school in a fun, celebratory way.

Señora Ortega expresses the importance of incorporating the students' cultural background in the curriculum content and the impact of these cultural celebrations on the student's social identity development in the following excerpt:

> do you know what I'm saying ... they feel good about themselves ... they feel stronger ... it makes them proud of who they are and where they come from ... when you give a whole presentation on El Salvador to your class ... you know how many times that is done in the district? ... when we talk about Black History Month ... we have Hispanic Heritage Month here too and we talk about the

black Hispanic also ... not just the black American ... but there's black Hispanics here too ... that's a big portion of that ... we talk about all Hispanics ... and the different countries . and the varieties . and the costumes . and the dances . and the cultures ... so these kids are feeling good about themselves and what they bring with them

Notice her mention of the *black Hispanic also*, and not just the black American because *there's black Hispanics here too*, which reflects one of the assumptions that guides their curriculum content: talking about groups that have been traditionally excluded or marginalized makes those groups legitimate; not talking about particular groups contributes to their marginalization or exclusion. According to Señora Ortega, talking about the students' cultural backgrounds and therefore legitimizing them leads to *these kids are feeling good about themselves.*

Señor Xoci expresses the importance of celebration. In one of our conversations, he had been explaining to me the importance of celebrations in the Mexican barrio and in Latin America in general, and about how Latino children have more contact with adults and celebrate rites of passage more than US children do. He thinks that this Latino cultural preference for celebrations has been incorporated into the Oyster community, and is part of their success.

Xoci: and then everybody has a good cause for celebration ... and I think that helps a lot ... and I think a lot of that sort of comes ... sort of exudes itself here at Oyster ... because here at Oyster there's a lot of fiestas ... there's a lot of celebrations

Rebecca: yeah ... you guys are always celebrating something here

Xoci: something ... and it's special ... it's incredible ... because you know ... that again reinforced alot of different ideologies ... you know

Although Señor Xoci attributes the preference for celebrating to Latino culture, the actual celebrations within the Oyster community are not limited to Latino celebrations and *again reinforced a lot of different ideologies.* For example, the *Teachers' Handbook* includes an offical statement about holidays that stresses the importance of not overemphasizing any one kind of celebration because it may exclude others, but to emphasize the holiday sharing spirit in December celebrated alternatively as Kwanza in traditional African celebration, Hannukah in Judaism, and Christmas in Christianity. In the sixth grade, the students could choose to research any one of the three traditions, preferably one they were not as familiar with, and then share their findings with the other students. In this way the three holiday traditions are included as part of the official curriculum content, exposing the students to all three as specific kinds of celebrations. Through such exposure, the students learn that all are legitimate.

I want to emphasize that although the Hispanic Heritage Celebration required the incorporation of Latino contributions into the curriculum in September and October, and although the Black History Month Celebration required the incorporation of Black American contributions into the curriculum in February, I observed materials from Latin America, Africa, and the Carribean as a regular part of the curriculum. In other words, the celebrations that I described here were extreme examples of what was actually a part of the everyday curriculum.

Since the Spanish-dominant teachers represent a variety of countries, cultures, and perspectives, the students were always exposed to Latin American geography, literature, history, politics, arts, etc. For example, the sixth-grade Spanish-dominant teacher had a collection of books written in various Latin American countries which he used on a regular basis. And since the students represented a variety of countries, cultures, and perspectives, these were also incorporated into the content-areas on a regular basis. Africa was the topic of the entire spring semester sixth-grade social studies unit that Mrs Washington, the English-dominant teacher taught, which reflects her African American background, her African pride, and her passionate interest in teaching her students to think critically about many mainstream representations of African history and African peoples. As she wrote in her paper highlighting omissions in the history of African contributions for a course she took over spring break entitled, 'An African View of the World', 'the story of Africa has not been accurately recorded. Much that is accepted today as truth will have to be changed'. This orientation informs her teaching of African history to the sixth-grade class, as she encourages the students to question what they read and to think critically. These varied historical representations, and this exposure to a wide range of countries, cultures, contributions, and perspectives require the students to open their minds, and to expect, respect, and tolerate diversity as a natural fact of life.

I include a copy of the lyrics of a song entitled 'Hear Me Out' that the third-grade read as a call and response for their contribution to the 1990 Black History Month Sharing Assembly because it seemed to me to summarize the goal of the Oyster inclusive multicultural curriculum content. Similarly, when I asked the third-grade English-dominant teacher for a copy of the lyrics, she said she had chosen this song it because 'it's what this school is all about'. For each section, a different third grader walked to the front of the stage and called out the question, and the rest of the third graders shouted out the response in unison. The person who had asked the question stepped back into the group while another moved forward to call out the next question. This format, with an individual student calling out one line and then the other students together as a group shouting in response, intensified the impact of the message. The lyrics are as follows:

Hear Me Out …
Who was the first man to set foot on the North Pole?
　　Matthew Henson — a black man
Who was the first American to show the Pilgrims at Plymouth the secrets of survival in the new world?
　　Squanto — a redman

Who was the soldier of Company G who won high honors for his courage and heroism in World War I?

Sing Kee — a yellow man

Who was the leader of United Farm Workers and helped farm workers maintain dignity and respect?

Caesar Chavez — a brown man

Who was the founder of blood plasma and the director of the Red Cross blood bank?

Dr Charles Drew — a black man

Who was the first American heroine who aided the Lewis and Clark expedition?

Sacajawea — a red woman

Who was the famous educator and semanticist who made outstanding contributions to education in America?

Hayakawa — a yellow man

Who invented the world's first stop light and the gas mask?

Garret Morgan — a black man

Who was the American surgeon who was one of the founders of neurosurgery?

Harvey Williams Sushing — a white man

Who was the man who helped design the nation's capitol, made the first clock to give time in American and wrote the first almanac?

Benjamin Bannekar — a black man

Who was the legendary hero who helped establish the League of Iroquois?

Hiawatha — a red man

Who was the leader of the first microbiotic center in America?

Micho Kushi — a yellow man

Who was the founder of the city of Chicago in 1772?

Jean Baptiste — a black man

Who was one of the organizers of the American Indian movement?

Dennis Banks — a red man

Who was the Jewish financier who raised funds to sponsor Christopher Columbus' voyage to America?

Lewis D. Santangel — a white man

Who was the woman who led countless slaves to freedom on the underground railroad?

Harriet Tubman — a black woman

The emphasis in the lyrics, as in the Oyster multicultural curriculum content, is on an inclusive history and participation of all groups.

My understanding of the multicultural curriculum content is that Oyster has an emphasis on inclusion, and that including and legitimizing one group's history, literature, arts, etc. does not mean excluding another groups. This is an important point, because critics of an Afrocentric curriculum, or any kind of multicultural curriculum, argue that emphasizing diverse groups threatens the US national identity as well as the unity of the nation (see Scott, 1992, for a discussion of this controversy). At Oyster, there seems to be an emphasis in these content-area subjects on the *people;* their relationships to one another, their struggles and their accomplishments. The students are encouraged to relate these historical or literary accounts of people to their own lives. For example, in choosing to write a biography about a famous African American, the students would be asked why they had chosen to investigate this person's story, that is, what was the significance of that person's life in the student's own life. Or the students would be asked when reading a Mexican short story which character they identified with and why, what they would have done differently, how they would have felt if they had been treated the way one character treated another, etc.

Drawing the students' attention to diverse peoples' experiences, emphasizing their struggles and their accomplishments, and then helping students relate those experiences to their own lives can fulfill several functions. Such a curriculum can offer students role models of people who were discriminated against, but who continued to struggle and made great accomplishments despite the obstacles put in front of them. These role models and their strategies would then be available for the students to draw on in their own attempts to refuse negative positioning and reposition themselves so that they can achieve. Teachers can use the multicultural curriculum content to draw students' attention to the similarity in people's experiences, and in their struggles, so that the students will learn to look for what people have in common and to work together, rather than to concentrate on what divides people. Perhaps most importantly, this type of multicultural curriculum content can be used to teach students to be aware of many different perspectives on any one topic, to think critically about what they see and hear, and to decide what to think and how to act for themselves.

WHAT ARE THE NORMS OF INTERACTION?

The section makes explicit the underlying norms of interaction that guide behavior in Oyster Bilingual School. As in the curriculum content discussed earlier, inclusion is the unifying principle. Looking closely at the level of the classroom interaction enables an understanding of how the teachers facilitate all of their students' academic achievement through Spanish and English, and how they encourage students regardless of background to see themselves and each other as equally legitimate participants in the classroom discourse. In this section, I first list the underlying norms of interaction that guide the teachers' and students' relationships to each other and to the activities they are involved in. Then I describe activities that I observed that reflect the Oyster goals for the various populations, and the theoretical and methodological assumptions on which they rely.

Before listing what I argue are the underlying norms of interaction, I want to emphasize that these norms are best understood not as hard and fast rules dictating how people must and do act, but rather as preference relations or strategies that guide what is and is not appropriate behavior within the classroom. There is always deviation from the norm, the reaction to which helps make that norm explicit. My observation of systematic deviations from the norm, or systematic discrepancies between ideal plan and actual implementation, will be taken up in the conclusion to this chapter. This list of underlying norms of interaction, in addition to describing role relationships in the Oyster classrooms, can also be applied as a set of principles to guide teachers' and students' relations in any cooperative learning organization with similar goals to those of Oyster.

Students

50% Spanish/50% English

- Students speak only Spanish to the Spanish-dominant teacher. In the Spanish content class, students speak Spanish to each other, unless they have a problem understanding, in which case, whatever language aids in comprehending the content is fine. Reciprocal policy for English.

Expect, tolerate, and respect diversity

- Everybody has the right to participate more or less equally. Just because groups have been excluded historically, and/or are currently discriminated against does not make it ok.

Think critically and solve problems

- Don't just passively accept what people say and do. Challenge what you see and hear. Come up with creative alternatives to problems you identify.

Demonstrate your agency

- Make your own choices, and take responsibility for your thoughts and actions.

Learn from each other

- Every individual has something unique and valuable to contribute. Ask each other questions, tell each other what you think, agree and disagree with each other, negotiate with each other. Think of each other as a community with common interests and common problems that require communal effort to solve.

Have high expectations for yourself

- Don't allow someone to decide for you what you are and are not capable of. Regardless of the background you come from, set high standards for yourself and find ways to build on the strengths that you have to reach your goals.

Teachers

Spanish-dominant teacher

- Speak only Spanish. Encourage students to speak only Spanish to you.

- Present yourself as a role model of a native Spanish speaker who has maintained Spanish, and who sees bilingualism as an asset.
- Bring in materials, strategies and perspectives from your native country and culture to share with the students.

English-dominant teacher

- Speak only English and encourage students to speak only English to you.

Both Teachers

- Provide comprehensible input for students to acquire the second-language.
- Expect, tolerate, respect, and celebrate diversity.
- Don't assume students know anything *a priori*. Find out what they know and what they don't know so you know how to build.
- Be supportive, caring, sensitive, open, understanding, accessible etc.
- Have high expectations for all of your students, regardless of the diversity in their background preparation.
- Provide great variety of activities that allow students to use language for different functions, in different registers, and in increasingly more complex ways so they develop the necessary communicative competence.
- Intervene when students are having problems, in either language acquisition, academic skills, content comprehension, or social relations.
- Work with your team-teacher to accomplish these things.

Notice that I have listed more principles for the Spanish-dominant teachers than for the English-dominant teachers. This discrepancy can be explained by the sociopolitical context of Oyster in relation to mainstream US society with its assumptions and expectations of monolingualism in English and assimilation to white middle-class norms of interaction. In order to (attempt to) counter these mainstream US assumptions and expectations, the Spanish-dominant teachers need to offer themselves as role models who see Spanish as an asset, since such role models are not as readily available in mainstream US society. Similarly, because of Oyster's location in the United States, materials from other countries showing other perspectives can be difficult to obtain. Therefore, the Spanish-dominant teachers also have the responsibility to supplement the curriculum.

It is important to add that the minority English-dominant teachers have similar responsibilities to the Spanish-dominant teachers by virtue of their being representatives of minority groups with positively evaluated minority social identities. Similarly, these minority English-dominant teachers offer themselves as role models of minorities in powerful positions (at least within the classroom context), and enhance the curriculum content by incorporating, e.g. an African or Caribbean perpective. This similarity between the minority English-dominant teachers and Spanish-dominant teachers' responsibilities is consistent with the underlying social identities project.

Examples of activities

In this section, I describe some of the activities that I observed, and I provide teacher descriptions and interpretations to supplement my account. The point of this section is to demonstrate how the theoretical and methodological orientations described earlier are reflected in the actual classroom activities. The Oyster educators emphasize a student-centered instructional approach in order to meet the needs of their diverse student population. They therefore emphasize student choice and utilize student interests in determining the content of actual activities which they then use as a springboard for skills (language, social, and academic) development.

The use of journal writing in every grade at some time, usually first thing in the morning or immediately after lunch, reflects this philosophy. Because I spent the most time in one of the kindergartens and in the sixth grade, I describe how journal writing is utilized in these two grades. Every day, when the kindergarten students arrive, they immediately go to their cubby holes and get paper, crayons, and pencils to write their stories. What this means changes as the year progresses, and can be understood as the students' introduction to school literacy in the case of those with no prior literacy experiences, and as literacy development in the cases of those who do have such experience. Each student draws a picture each day which can be understood as the topic of their story. Before I describe this activity, I want to mention that most of the storywriting and talking during this activity was in English. This use of English as the unofficial language among the students was typical of what I observed throughout Oyster. Sometimes the Latino students would choose to write their story in Spanish and would talk to each other or me in Spanish, but this was the exception, not the norm.

The emphasis is on student choice of a topic/picture. Sometimes the picture is copied from a book that the student selected from the class library. Sometimes the picture/story is to be a present for someone and the student therefore chooses to draw something special to either the student or the recipient of the present. Sometimes the picture/story represents what the student did the day before that he/she wants to share. Whatever the case, the student chooses the topic/picture. If the student cannot decide, sometimes the teacher or another student will help the student make a decision.

The way the activity was structured changed as the year progressed, reflecting the students' development of literacy skills as well as their understanding that they were to rely on each other and on themselves more and more. In the beginning of the year, the students were encouraged to write their names on the top of the picture/story. If a student needed help with this task, the teacher would write the student's name on a separate sheet for the student to then copy onto the top of the picture/story. Early in the year, the teachers would walk around after the students had drawn and would sit down next to each student and ask what the story was about. The student would describe the picture/tell the story. From that description, the teacher would write one sentence on a small piece of paper, read it back to the student, and the student would copy it on to the top of the picture, completing the story. As the year progressed, the teacher would provide less help, and would, for example, help the student sound out the words of the sentence so that that student could write independently. Towards the end of the year, the more advanced writers would help the less advanced writers sound out their stories. In this way the students were developing literacy skills, and relying more and more on each other and on themselves. Each week, each student would select the picture/story that he/she wanted to share with the rest of the class as part of the class display of the stories.

In the sixth grade, the Spanish and English journal writing was structured a bit more. As with the kindergarten class, every morning when the students arrived, they would take out their journals and write. One week they would write in Spanish and the next week they would write in English. Both the Spanish-dominant and the English-dominant teacher would generally write an unfinished sentence in the corner of the board, for example, 'A funny thing happened the other day … ', or 'I felt so bad when … ', or 'What I really hate about school is … '. The students had the choice of using the unfinished sentence to stimulate their writing, or they could choose their own topic. Either way they were encouraged to write about their own experiences and their attitudes about those experiences.

The English-dominant and the Spanish-dominant sixth-grade teachers used the journal entries in different ways which reflected their primary goals for the students. The English-dominant teacher was very concerned with academic writing skills development. She would therefore have each student select one journal entry each week (which meant every other week because Spanish and English alternated), and the student could develop the journal entry into an academic essay. (Part of my job in the sixth grade was to help the students make the transition from informal journal writing to more formal academic writing.) In Cummins' (1992) terms, the journal entry provides an example of highly contextualized, relatively cognitively unde-manding use of language, because the content is part of the child's own experience, and the structure of the journal is very informal. The academic essay, on the other hand, has less contextualization and is more cognitively demanding. Using the less demanding writing task to build a bridge to the more demanding writing task facilitates the students' development of academic competence in English.

The Spanish-dominant teacher, on the other hand, was more concerned with fluency in writing, creativity, and the development of strong opinions which were well supported, consistent with the goal of agency development. The students would hand their Spanish language journal entries in and Señor Xoci's comments would focus primarily on the content of the entries. In this sense, the Spanish journal entries provided a kind of a dialog journal for the students with the teacher.

Consistent with his emphasis on strong, well-supported opinions in the dialog journals, Señor Xoci stressed questioning and critical thinking. For example, I repeatedly heard him say to the students after he had told them something, '**me entiendes**?' (do you understand me?), and then, '**y me lo crees**?' (and do you believe me?). It seemed he was trying to get the students used to questioning what they heard rather than simply believing what the authority told them.

Since there were innumerable examples of cooperative learning activities in all of the Spanish and English content-areas that I observed which encouraged students to take responsibility for their own and the other students' learning as the students simultaneously develop academic skills, understand content, and acquire the second-language, I will describe just a few here to illustrate the norms of interaction and the assumptions on which they rely.

In kindergarten one day the students were studying the letter 'P' in Spanish. The goal of the class was for the students to make a poster which had pictures of things that began with the letter 'P' in Spanish which they would add to the alphabet posters they were making for the class. The teacher divided the students into groups, and gave each group magazines which they were to look through and find pictures of things that began with the letter 'P' in Spanish. In each group, there was at least one native Spanish-speaking child, whose role was very important to the completion of the task. The native Spanish-speaking students helped the native English-speaking students determine which pictures represented words that began with the letter 'P' by encouraging them to sound out the words in Spanish. Each small group negotiated among themselves in their selection of pictures.

The class later came back together as a large group to check the work that the small groups had done, which additionally served to reinforce the skills they were learning. Each small group of students then contributed their pictures of things that began with the letter 'P' in Spanish in order to make a group poster of things that began with the letter 'P'. The Spanish-dominant teacher's role at this stage was to take instructions from all of the students in designing the poster. When the group poster of things that began with the letter 'P' was finished, it was put up on the wall with the other alphabet posters they had made. Through this activity, students learn to use resources (magazines), work together in groups and help each other, share their work with the class, and contribute to the materials development of their class, making the job more meaningful to them, and easier on the teacher who then does not have to take responsibility for all of the materials design. The students were simultaneously acquiring literacy skills, social skills, and either acquiring Spanish as a second-language or maintaining and developing Spanish as the first language.

The next two activities that I describe from one of the sixth-grade social studies units in English also required the students to use outside resources to complete a task, and to share their findings with the rest of the class. Both of the activities were topically related; the students were encouraged to choose a country that they would like to learn more about. Each activity, however, required different uses of language and developed different academic skills.

For the first activity, the students were asked to write travel brochures about the country they had chosen. The completed product would require a relatively informal register, and was an example of a relatively cognitively undemanding task which was relatively contextualized. To get information for their travel brochure, the students were encouraged to write to the local embassy requesting information, use the library, and if they knew anything about the country, their own background knowledge. The completed brochures were displayed on the social studies bulletin board for the class to share.

Another activity revolving around the same topic, i.e. the country they had chosen, was to write and present a formal research report to the class including maps, charts, etc. Although the activity was more cognitively demanding than the travel brochure, it had been made simpler because the students had already acquired a considerable amount of background knowledge through their completion of the travel brochure activity. In this way, the students were developing academic competence, and using language to perform a variety of tasks. To encourage the students' learning from each other, the teacher included some of the information from each report on the unit test. In this way, the students were also each other's teacher.

This next example illustrates how the Spanish-dominant sixth-grade teacher gave the students considerable responsibility in their evaluation of each others' learning. One day in the Spanish language arts class, after the class discussion of a book that they had all been reading, Señor Xoci said that they would be tested on the material. Pam, one of the students, suggested that instead of Señor Xoci making up the questions for the test, that the students could make up the questions. She explained that they had done this successfully in her fifth-grade class. Señor Xoci asked her for more details, and she explained that each student would make up a question or two, all of the questions would be collected, and Señor Xoci could use those questions for the test. The student who had written a question would be responsible for helping the teacher evaluate the response. Señor Xoci agreed that this was a fine method; he granted the students the right to write and evaluate the questions, and relinquished a considerable amount of his power to the students in the process. This example illustrates the active role the students expect to take in their learning, because it was obviously appropriate for Pam to recommend a different format.

The following activity reflects an organization that was very common; the teachers often divided the students into groups who would cooperate in solving a problem, completing a task etc., and then the groups would compete with each other. This kind of structure ties members of the group to each other as they attempt to solve the problem which always revolves around some kind of skills development and uses language, either Spanish or English, in its completion. One day I observed the fifth-grade science class in English working on the National Geographic 'Jason Project'. 'Jason' is an actual robot and National Geographic provides the curriculum to schools that are interested in participating in the project. The goal of the activity that I observed was for the students to write computer programs for Jason, the robot, to walk from a position in the class to a table, pick up a particular article off of the table, and place it in another position in the room. Consistent with the school's goal of skills acquisition, the emphasis was on the students' learning how to write a computer program, in this case without actually using the computer.

To do this activity the students were divided into groups of four to write their computer program together. The next day, the teacher performed the part of the robot Jason, and followed the directions that each small group gave her in front of the entire class. For example, when group 1 was giving directions to Jason (the teacher), and the other students recognized an error, they would shout 'ERROR', and Group 1 would have to collaborate in effort to correct the error. Each group was allowed two errors before having to go back and rewrite the program. There was a competition among the groups, and the group that got the fewest errors in their computer program won.

This same organization, dividing into small groups, and then competing among the groups in front of the entire class was used in many classes; for example in a sixth-grade English social studies class, the small groups of students competed in a women's history trivia game. In a first grade Spanish-language arts class, the small groups of students competed in identifying the greatest quantity of words beginning with the letter 'b' in the text they were reading. What was common in the classes was (1) the emphasis on skills development and problem-solving abilities, and (2) the variety of activities in which the children worked together as groups, (3) in many cases competition across groups, and (4) the use of language to perform many different functions. The students were at times quite loud, but generally actively involved in their joint negotiation of the solutions to the activities.

In all of these activities, the students were simultaneously using language to acquire skills and using content to acquire language. I want to provide more description of how the actual language acquisition process naturally occurs in the lower grades. For this I turn to the two Spanish-dominant kindergarten teachers' descriptions. Señora Rodriguez explained her philosophy of language acquisition as follows:

> they are never pushed ... when they ask may I go to the bathroom ... I respond ... **Sí puedes ir al bano** [yes you can go to the bathroom] ... at first they just nodded ... then they started to repeat ... and now they just ask me in Spanish

Señora Rodriguez's codeswitch to me illustrates how she implements the plan. When the children ask a question in English, *May I go to the bathroom*, the child has raised the topic and clearly understands what the content is. The students can assume that Señora Rodriguez's response, *Sí puedes ir al bano*, is relevant to their question, and by her non-verbal contextualization cues they can see the answer is affirmative. The children thus learn the Spanish language words for the question through Señora Rodriguez's response. Señora Rodriguez emphasizes the time element involved, *at first, then, now,* which suggests her repetition of this process. The children come to associate Spanish with Señora Rodriguez and accomodate her language usage. In this way, they are to naturally and painlessly acquire the language.

My observations support Señora Rodriguez's description of the language acquisition process as occurring naturally. For example, one day on the playground I was talking with one of the Spanish-dominant pre-k teachers when a pre-k student from Morocco (who spoke French and Arabic as her native languages and was acquiring Spanish and English simultaneously) said:

S:	He's my friend [and shows the pre-k teacher a teddy bear]
T:	**Él es tu amigo, verdad?** [He is your friend, true]
S:	[Nods head and smiles]

The same philosophy of the natural approach to language acquisition partially accounts for their extensive use of songs in both English and Spanish. As Chapter 9 illustrates, the songs can function as discourse markers of speech situations and the code choice in the song can signal which language is to be used for the speech situation 'Opening' that day.

Songs are also used to teach content-areas, and to provide students from diverse backgrounds exposure to experiences they may not have had in their home life. For example, the other Spanish-dominant kindergarten teacher, Señora Gonzalez, explains her use of music in the classroom as follows:

Gonzalez:	we have some English speakers who have been in pre school ... we have some that have not had any exposure ... and what I do is ... I read to them and sing a lot of ... I use a lot of literature ... and I use a lot songs and poems and stories and riddles ... all of the oral ... I take most of my time on the language skills ... to the oral language skills
Rebecca:	with the goal of
Gonzalez:	with the goal of learning the language ... and those that are already fluent in Spanish ... they can get exposed ... so they both can get the same kind of ... some get enrichment ... and the others get the language ... and get to hear it more [lots of noise] for example today ... I in the class ... I asked them ... today we were going to use the oral language ... and I was going to talk about the foods [interruption] um ... so we do provide them ... we make sure that they use the language ... and then with song ... with a song that I taught them we talked about fruits and vegetables and other kinds of foods ... and then with a song I introduced it to them ... and then they sing the song back to me and say the names of the fruits ... and then after that ... they

> went to the housekeeping corner to play with the fruits and vegetables that we had

This excerpt reveals the teacher's philosophy to include teaching language in context, in a fun way through songs that get them involved, and then to make connections between the words of the songs that seem to be easy for the children to learn and what the words in the song (e.g. foods and vegetables) mean in the real world (e.g. simulated in the housekeeping corner). For some of the students this provides exposure to experiences they have not had before, and for others this provides enrichment in the language skills.

It is neither possible nor necessary to give an exhaustive account of the variety of methods that the teachers employ to implement the language plan and social identities project. The underlying principles in the activities that I observed are: language in context, language through content, content and skills through language, code choice by participant, student-centered cooperation, agency development, and fun. The norms that structured both the curriculum content and the classroom discourse provided students ongoing opportunities to work toward the goals of the Oyster dual-language program, that is, to (1) achieve academically, (2) develop high levels of bilingualism and biliteracy, and (3) see minority and majority students as equally capable and legitimate participants in the educational discourse.

DISCREPANCIES BETWEEN IDEAL PLAN AND ACTUAL IMPLEMENTATION/OUTCOMES: A SOCIOPOLITICAL EXPLANATION

Oyster Bilingual School does not exist in a sociopolitical vacuum and all of the individuals interact with mainstream US society with its distinct structuring norms on a daily basis. Leakage between ideal plan and actual implementation is therefore to be expected. The ethnographic/discourse analytic approach that I took to understand how Oyster's dual-language plan was interpreted and implemented in situated practice enabled me to relate the micro-level situational context of the classroom interaction to macro-level Oyster Bilingual School assumptions about how to provide educational opportunities to a linguisitically and culturally diverse student population on the one hand, and to mainstream US societal assumptions about equal educational opportunities for diverse populations on the other. This approach allowed me to describe, interpret, and explain systematic discrepancies between ideal plan and actual implementation, which yielded an understanding of how the dual-language program functions in its particular sociopolitical context.

Because the Oyster educators consider teachers integral to their success, I begin my discussion with the teachers. As mentioned, the ideal policy requires one Spanish-dominant and one English-dominant teacher in every class. Diversity is considered a resource at Oyster, and its teachers represent a wide range of languages and cultures. Representation seems to be equated with legitimization and omission with illegitimacy. It is therefore noteworthy that at the time of my study, all of the Spanish-dominant teachers could speak English but not all of the English-dominant teachers could speak Spanish. The implicit message was that Spanish speakers must speak English to participate in the educational discourse, but English speakers do not necessarily have to speak Spanish. While bilingualism is clearly the norm and considered an asset for the English-dominant teachers, it is not a necessity. In this respect, both languages are not distributed and evaluated equally throughout Oyster. In addition, at the time of my study, there were no Salvadoran teachers. This is striking when one considers that the largest Latino student population in Oyster, as in Washington, DC, is from El Salvador.

When I returned to Oyster in 1994 to ask the principal, Señora Mendoza, about these discrepancies, she said that all new Spanish-dominant and English-dominant teachers must be bilingual, preferably in Spanish and English. At that time, she said, only three of the English-dominant teachers were not bilingual. In addition, the school at that point had a full-time Salvadoran aide and a Salvadoran student teacher as part of its effort to better represent and serve the large Salvadoran population.

The ideal policy also requires that 50% of the content-area instruction be in Spanish and 50% in English. It is important to emphasize that the team-teachers have considerable autonomy in how they allocate this instruction as long as they adhere to the general guidelines of providing instruction in language arts in Spanish and English to all of the students everyday, and approximately 50% of the instruction in Spanish and English per week. In some cases, the Spanish-dominant teacher would teach a subject area one week in Spanish and the English-dominant teacher would teach that same subject the next week in English; in other cases the teachers switched subjects/languages by the month or by the semester. Some teams worked very closely together, and others worked much more independently. Regardless of this surface variation, all of the teachers organized their classes so that native Spanish-speaking students and native English-speaking students worked together in many different ways to acquire Spanish and English through content, develop academic skills in both languages, and learn to see each other as resources in their learning.

The ideal plan is for the English-dominant teacher to speak and be spoken to only in English and for the Spanish-dominant teacher to speak and be spoken to only in Spanish. Consistent with the ideal, I observed that there is little to no code-switching from English to Spanish by the English-dominant teachers, but considerable code-switching to English by the Spanish-dominant teachers. Part of this discrepancy can be explained by the fact that in both the kindergarten class and the sixth-grade class that I observed for the longest periods of time, neither of the English-dominant teachers were able to speak Spanish, making teacher code-switching impossible. There is, however, more to the explanation than individual teachers' language proficiencies. Because the language of wider communication outside of Oyster Bilingual School is English, which naturally has a very strong influence on students' language choice, leakage is to be expected within the school. I return to this point later.

Another discrepancy between the ideal of equal distribution and evaluation of Spanish and English throughout the school was apparent in Oyster's assessment practices. Although the students received grades for their classes in Spanish and English, the grades did not carry equal weight. If, for example, a student failed the third-grade reading class in Spanish, that student could be promoted to fourth grade. If the same student, however, failed the reading class in English, that student could not be promoted. This is because the DCPS (District of Columbia Public Schools) only evaluates English. I repeatedly heard concern expressed by the English-dominant teachers that the different evaluation standards made the English-dominant teachers more accountable for skills development than the Spanish-dominant teachers were. For example, one teacher wrote that one disadvantage of the team-teaching approach is that the English-dominant teachers have to do more of the work:

> A common complaint at Oyster is that the English teachers get stuck with all the paper work, and have to carry the curriculum load, while the Spanish teachers pretty much don't have to answer to anyone.

One English-dominant teacher suggested that the dual-language program could be improved by 'making Spanish instruction count as much as English'.

My observations of skills requirements in Spanish and English support these teachers' observations. For example, as I mentioned previously, the way that the English-dominant and Spanish-dominant sixth-grade teachers used the students' journals illustrated this skills discrepancy. Mrs Washington's goal was to use the journals as a bridge to academic writing, and her emphasis was on, for example, well-developed and organized paragraphs and essays with correct punctuation and capitalization. Señor Xoci's goal, on the other hand, was to use the journals to develop fluency in Spanish, and creative writing. Similarly, as my comparative analysis of the 'same event' in Spanish and English in kindergarten illustrates (see Chapter 9), there is a discrepancy between the skills required in the English and Spanish activities.

Although I also observed an unequal emphasis on skills in Spanish and English content classes, I think this teacher's solution of 'making Spanish instruction count as much as English' is difficult in practice given Oyster's sociopolitical location. Oyster cannot control mainstream US society's evaluation of Spanish and English relative to each another. As long as Oyster is a US public school, and English is the language of instruction in public schools in the United States, Oyster can do little to 'make Spanish count as much'. It can, however, make Spanish count more than it does now within the Oyster community through such internal measures as, for example, equal evaluation and equal promotion criteria. Addressing this discrepancy, however, assumes that equal skills development really is a goal within Oyster. When I mentioned this discrepancy to Señora Mendoza, she informed me that all students, native Spanish-speaking and native English-speaking alike, are currently required to take a basic skills test in Spanish (Aprenda). How they incorporate the results of this test into the educational program is an area for further research.

The ideal plan is for all students to become bilingual and biliterate in Spanish and English. Because Oyster is considered a successful school by a variety of groups that use distinct criteria, including the DCPS standardized tests in English, we can assume that LEP students become academically competent in English. This result demonstrates that the Oyster program meets the explicit goals of the Bilingual Education Act of 1988, because it 'enable[s] students to achieve full competence in English and to meet school grade promotion and graduation requirements' (PL 100–297, Sec. 7002).

Oyster's goals, however, go beyond the goals of the Bilingual Education Act to include the goal of additive bilingualism for all students. Although I do not have specific measures to support the following claims, my impressionistic observations are that while native Spanish-speaking students do maintain their Spanish, at least until the sixth grade, English tends to be their stronger language at that point in their lives. Similarly, whereas native English-speaking students understand and express their ideas well in spoken and written Spanish, their fluency and grammatical accuracy, generally speaking, is not at the same level as that of their native Spanish-speaking counterparts in spoken and written English.

This outcome can also be explained by Oyster's sociopolitical context. First, the native Spanish speakers and the native English speakers bring different second-language bases with them to Oyster and have different opportunities and expectations for using the second-language outside of the official classroom discourse. At the time of this study, it was generally assumed that the majority of the Spanish-dominant students had some foundation in the English language whereas the majority of the English-dominant students did not have the same in Spanish. Because native Spanish speakers have many more opportunities to use English outside of the official classroom than native English speakers have to use Spanish, it is unlikely that their levels of bilingualism would be the same.

This difference in English and Spanish language base and support has implications for the implementation of the language plan. With respect to the dual-language acquisition plan, the concern at the Pre-k and kindergarten level is on listening comprehension. According to the fifth-grade English-dominant teacher:

> Pre-k and kindergarten are where uh ... the system is most regimented ... because it's at those lower levels that the students need to really learn what they'll be expected to do for the next few years ... it's important there for the student to speak Spanish to the Spanish-dominant teacher and vice versa ... later it can become more flexible

Since the students all have a stronger English base, there can be more of an emphasis on skills acquisition at this stage.

The social stratification of languages in the United States also has considerable explanatory power. English is 'naturally' the language of choice for Oyster students because languages and varieties of languages other than Standard English tend to be stigmatized in mainstream US society and because English is what the Oyster students hear on the television and in the popular music that they listen to. Although the school goes to great lengths to create an environment in which English and Spanish are valued equally, the same conditions simply do not exist outside of the school. According to Señor Xoci:

Xoci: if you're talking about the white kids … the white kids already know the value of what another language is going to do for them … they know it … they really do … to a certain extent … otherwise why would their parents have put them in a school

Rebecca: so they must have that at home … because um … that's not general in this culture

Xoci: no no … so they know the value of a second-language … you know … even though they may not realize what it really means … they sort of feel a difference … they go into a restaurant and they speak Spanish … woooow … a Latino goes in there … nothing … they speak English … it's expected … so they they they … they're you know … they're getting a completely different type of reinforcement … completely differnt sorts of reinforcement

Clearly in this teacher's view, society provides distinct expectations with respect to language usage for the Anglo and Latino populations. Conversations with the other teachers support Señor Xoci's representation of societal pressures on the Latino students.

With respect to Oyster's goal of cultural pluralism, the students seem to negotiate very well in their small groups, and they seem to expect and be able to accommodate diversity as they jointly construct meaning with each other through Spanish and English within the classroom interaction. Based on their class discussions and samples of their work, the students appear to recognize discriminatory practices both in the school and outside, for example, when a teacher treats individual students or groups more or less fairly, when the contributions of women are not represented in the curriculum, or when students consider local police and media treatment of groups in the racial riots that occurred in their neighborhood in 1991. Moreover, the students articulate creative solutions to the problems they identify. For example, they may speak out to the teacher in class, or circulate petitions and protest letters, or write stories in which they describe an alternative construction of reality with, for instance, women as heroes (see Chapter 10 for further discussion).

The sixth-grade lunch table, however, was particularly telling with respect to the goal of diverse social groupings. Because there were only a few boys in the class, who all tended to socialize together, ethnic division was not apparent. Among the girls, on the other hand, the African American English-speaking girls tended to form one group, and the white English-speaking girls tended to form another. Within the Spanish-speaking female population, the white Spanish-speaking girls generally stayed together, while the darker Latinas (who happened to come from the lowest income bracket) tended to form a separate group. Although there were exceptions, and although the students all seemed to get along together in class, these patterns prevailed in their social interaction at school.

When I mentioned these groupings to the Spanish-dominant kindergarten teacher, Señora Rodriguez (who had been teaching in Oyster since the bilingual program began) she responded:

> In Kinder eh … they come with their home experiences … but they don't uh … they don't realize their backgrounds are different … by third grade they tend to be equalized … by sixth grade they are separate again..but eh … that's the teachers' job … to make the students aware of when they're separating … they should start tracking that here … these stereotypes should be broken here … it's the fault of the teacher for not watching

Señora Rodriguez reveals her assumption that the school has the obligation and the potential for breaking such stereotypes, and that the emergence of separation by social groups is *the fault of the teacher for not watching*.

Although it may be difficult to do what Señora Rodriguez suggested, I think the interaction of the Oyster educational discourse with mainstream US societal discourse accounts for the discrepancies between the school's ideal policy and the actual outcomes with respect to the students' social interaction. Oyster's students are all exposed to the norms of interaction in Washington, DC, and as represented in the mass media, where opportunities to see integrated social groupings are relatively infrequent and often negatively evaluated. The students are socialized into acquiring the norms of interaction of both the larger society and the Oyster institutional discourse. Because the norms are distinct in the two discourse worlds, leakage between the ideal plan and actual outcomes is to be expected. And, as noted in Chapter 7, Oyster is actively searching for ways to combat aggression and violence and to promote conflict resolution through peer mediation.

In sum, the implementation and immediate outcomes of Oyster's program with respect to its goals of bilingualism, biliteracy, and cultural pluralism illustrate the interaction of the Oyster educational discourse and mainstream US societal discourse. With respect to bilingualism and biliteracy, the explicit goal is for all of the students to master skills in both Spanish and English through equal representation and evaluation of Spanish and English. Close analysis of the implementation of the dual-language plan on the classroom level, however, reveals that skills in English are emphasized more than skills in Spanish, that only English is evaluated by the DCPS on standardized tests, and that not all of the teachers can speak Spanish. The outcome seems to be that all of the native Spanish speakers become competent in English, including academic English, and maintain their Spanish. The native English speakers also develop academic skills, but their Spanish, although quite good, is less fluent and less grammatically accurate than the English of their native Spanish-speaking peers. With respect to cultural pluralism, the students appear to develop good intercultural communication skills and work well in diverse groupings in their classes. They also talk about discrimination and about solutions to problems of discrimination that they identify both in and outside of school. There are divisions in their social interaction at school, however, that seem to correspond to racial, ethnic, or class lines in society. The teachers and administrators are aware of these discrepancies, and as my conversations with the principal in 1994 illustrate, many of these discrepancies are being addressed through policy changes. There remains the need for further study to see how policy changes impact on the actual implementation and outcomes.

CONCLUSION

This chapter has described, interpreted, and explained the norms that structure Oyster Bilingual School's educational discourse system, and argued that these norms be understood as in opposition to and struggling against the norms that structure mainstream US educational and societal discourses. I began by describing Oyster's multicultural curriculum content to illustrate its focus on inclusion. Rather than excluding, marginalizing, or negatively evaluating minority contributions as the Eurocentric mainstream US curriculum content does, the histories, perspectives, and contributions of the student and teacher populations at the school are central to the curriculum (i.e. Latino, Carribean, African American, and African). Students are encouraged to relate their own lives to the curriculum content, and to think critically about how social groups are represented and evaluated relative to each other.

Then I discussed the norms that structure the classroom interaction, and provided a detailed description of a wide range of typical activities that I observed throughout the school to demonstrate how the Oyster educators translate their goals into actual classroom practices. The equal distribution and evaluation of Spanish and English throughout the students' day, week and elementary school experience, and the student-centered, cooperative learning organization of the classroom interaction and assessment practices, together provide language minority and language majority students the opportunities to become bilingual and biliterate, develop academic competence through two languages, and improve their intercultural communication skills. These structuring norms also give language minority students experiences seeing themselves as having the right to participate equally in the classroom discourse, and language majority students the experience respecting that right. The Oyster school students' ongoing positioning as equal participants socializes the minority and majority students into seeing themselves as having more or less equal access to the same speaking positions and social roles at school and in society. Together, the first two parts of this chapter provided a detailed discussion of how the Oyster Bilingual School social identities project is interpreted and implemented on the classroom level.

The last section of this chapter described discrepancies between Oyster Bilingual School's ideal bilingual plan and the actual implementation that I observed throughout the course of my ethnographic/discourse analytic study. I drew on teachers' interpretations of these discrepancies and my interpretation of the larger societal discourses surrounding Oyster Bilingual School to explain these discrepancies, and I argue that the competing assumptions that structure the Oyster educational discourse, on the one hand, and mainstream US educational and societal discourse, on the other, make it impossible for the goals of the Oyster dual-language plan and social identities project to be completely realized.

So, for example, the ideal plan is for all students to master skills in both Spanish and English through the equal representation and evaluation of the two languages. Close analysis of the classroom interaction, however, reveals that English is attributed more prestige throughout the school in a variety of ways. The outcome is that all students do master skills in both languages, but the native Spanish speakers and native English speakers do not become equally bilingual and biliterate. While both groups develop academic skills in both languages, the native English speakers' Spanish is less grammatically accurate than the English of their native Spanish-speaking peers. With respect to Oyster's goal of cultural pluralism, the students appear to develop good intercultural communication skills, they work well in diverse groupings in their classes, and they seem to recognize discriminatory practices and talk about ways to address the disrimination that they identify. Within their social interaction, however, there are divisions that reflect racial, ethnic, and class tensions in mainstream US society. The teachers and administrators are aware of these discrepancies, and are looking for ways to address them. It is important to emphasize that because all of the participants at Oyster interact with mainstream US societal discourses on a regular basis, the leakage that I observed between ideal plan and actual implementation is to be expected.

As I have stressed throughout this book, the particulars of the Oyster Bilingual School discourse system are not intended to be uncritically replicated to another context. I do, however, encourage educational researchers and reflective practitioners to look closely at the norms that structure the curriculum content and classroom interaction in another educational context to understand how minority social identities are jointly constructed through local definitions of teaching and learning. The notion of positioning is key to the analysis. This study assumes that students are socialized through their participation in language-mediated activities to develop an understanding of their participation rights and obligations in the macro-level social order at school and in society through their ongoing positioning in the micro-level face-to-face interaction (see Chapter 3). In the remainder of this conclusion, I provide a series of guiding questions that researchers and practitioners can use to begin their investigations of social identity construction in another educational context.

I begin with the curriculum content, and suggest the following kinds of questions to analyse minority positioning. For example, how do the perspectives, histories, and contributions represented in the curriculum relate to the linguistic and cultural backgrounds of the students in the class? Are they central to the curriculum? Are they marginalized? Or omitted? How are minorities and their contributions evaluated in the curriculum content? Are they negatively evaluated and stereotypically limiting? Or are minority populations represented in a wide range of activities with a wide range of options available to them? Who chooses the curriculum content? The school district? The teachers? The community? The students? This list of questions is not meant to be exhaustive. Rather, it is intended to stimulate ideas about how to look critically at minority representation and evaluation in the curriculum content.

Because we cannot assume that all teachers and students interact with the same curricular materials in the same ways, it is important not to look at the curriculum content in isolation. I encourage reseachers and practitioners to look closely at the norms that structure the classroom interaction to understood how minority students are positioned relative to majority students and to their teachers. Questions like the following can guide this level of inquiry: What is the range of typical and atypical activities in the classroom? Is there a wide range of activities that make a variety of speaking positions and roles available to students? Or are there relatively few participation frameworks that repeatedly position students in the same roles relative to each other and to the teacher? How are languages used and evaluated within and across these activities? How are minority students positioned in the classroom interaction relative to majority students and to their teachers? Are they forced to assimilate to dominant ways of speaking and interacting? Or are they positioned as agents with choices who take responsibility for their thoughts, feelings, and actions? How are students assessed? Who is responsible for this assessment? The school district? The teachers? The students? Their peers? Do the norms that structure the classroom interaction position minority and majority students more or less equally? If not, do the students and their teachers understand how to recognize which practices are discriminatory? If they recognize discriminatory practices, do they have strategies to refuse those discursive practices, and to construct alternative discourses in which they are positioned more favorably? Again, this series of questions is not intended to be exhaustive, but is intended to direct researchers' and practitioners' understanding of how minority and majority students are positioned relative to each other at schools, and to understand what schools can do in response to discriminatory practices.

Together, Chapters 5–8 were intended to provided an emic understanding of how the Oyster dual-language plan can be understood as part of an underlying social identities project that aims to socialize children differently. One of my primary goals has been to describe, interpret, and explain how the Oyster dual-language program functions in its sociopolitical context. I have argued that the Oyster educational discourse can be understood as in opposition to and struggling against mainstream US educational and societal discourses about linguistic and cultural diversity. Relationships between the Oyster educational discourse, mainstream US educational discourse, and mainstream US societal discourse are reflected in the micro-level classroom interaction. Chapters 9 and 10 provide micro-level discourse analyses of the classroom interaction. These interactions, I argue, reflect and shape the macro-level social struggle that I have described throughout the book.

CHAPTER 9

Micro-level Classroom Interaction: A Reflection of the Macro-level Struggle

Chapters 9 and 10 provide a micro-level analysis of how the Oyster Bilingual School dual-language program is implemented at the classroom level. This part of the study demonstrates that an analysis of Oyster classroom practices requires an understanding of the macro-level sociopolitical struggle between the Oyster educational discourse and mainstream US educational and societal discourses. The analyses presented in these chapters illustrate first, how the Oyster educators translate their understanding of the goals of the dual-language program into practice, and second, how discrepancies between the ideal plan and actual implementation can be explained by the interaction of the Oyster educational discourse and mainstream US discourses. The following micro-level discourse analyses thus provide concrete evidence of the sociopolitical struggle that I described throughout Chapters 5–8, and increase the validity and the reliablity of the study.

Given the theoretical assumption that underlies the Oyster Bilingual School study, namely that language minority and language majority students learn what roles are available to them in the macro-level social order through their ongoing positioning as certain kinds of social beings in the micro-level classroom interaction, these classroom practices not only reflect the larger sociopolitical struggle, they contribute directly to it. By providing a wider range of opportunities to language minority and language majority students than are traditionally available in mainstream US schools, the ways in which the Oyster educators organize their program and practices ideally prepare students for a wider range of opportunities in mainstream US sociey.

This chapter illustrates how the Oyster educators translate their notion of equal educational opportunity into actual classroom practices through a comparative discourse analysis of the 'same' kindergarten speech situation in English and Spanish. My analysis describes how students are to develop communicative competence, including academic competence, in their first and second-languages through the equal distribution and evaluation of Spanish and English languages and speakers, and reveals systematic discrepancies between ideal plan and actual implementation. It also illustrates how the teachers work with students' diverse backgrounds in a variety of ways so that they can meet the equally high expectations that the Oyster educators hold for all students.

EQUAL DISTRIBUTION AND EVALUATION OF ENGLISH AND SPANISH: IDEAL AND ACTUAL

This section illustrates how the kindergarten team-teachers work together to distribute and evaluate Spanish and English equally so that students acquire their second-language, develop academic skills in both languages, and use each other as resources in their learning. Based on my observations and supported by the teachers' interpretations, the speech situation 'Opening' is the most formal language and skills lesson in kindergarten, and provides students the most structured opportunity to understand what it means to be in school. Otherwise kindergarten focuses on social skills and language acquisition in a more playful, less structured format.

Opening is the second speech situation of the day, occurring immediately after Storywriting. Opening lasts approximately 20–30 minutes, and tends to get longer as the year progresses with the teachers integrating more skills into the Opening format. To fulfill the goal of equal distribution and evaluation of English and Spanish languages and speakers, the language used in Opening alternates weekly. One week the English-dominant teacher, Mrs Davis, leads Opening in English and the next week the Spanish-dominant teacher, Señora Rodriguez, leads Opening in Spanish. I refer to the teacher who leads Opening as the official teacher, and I refer to the teacher who generally observes and/or circulates to helps certain students as the unofficial teacher. When the Spanish-dominant teacher is the official teacher, I refer to Spanish as the official language of the classroom, and when the English-dominant teacher is the official teacher, I refer to English as the official language.

The following excerpts from the 'same' kindergarten speech situation in English (on March 8, 1991) and Spanish (on March 15, 1991) clearly illustrate patterns that I observed throughout the school. There is considerable similarity between Opening in English and in Spanish on these two consecutive Fridays, reflecting the close coordination of the team-teachers in this kindergarten class. For example, the same six speech activities constitute both Openings, and they occur in the same order. These speech activities can be distinguished from one another primarily by their different ends or goals. Reflecting those different goals, I named the speech activities: (1) Opening song, (2) Today is, (3) Framework, (4) Counting girls, (5)

Counting boys, and (6) Total. The English Opening ends with an additional speech event, (7) Reading the story, which does not appear in the Spanish Opening.

Both the English and the Spanish Openings begin with a song, which signals to the children that it is time to stop writing their stories and to prepare for Opening. This use of songs is prevalent in kindergarten in Spanish and English throughout the day. Songs are very involving for the children, and seem to aid their acquisition of native-like accent and fluency in the second-language. In addition, because the children enjoy singing, the regular use of songs seems to enhance even the few reluctant students' willingness to participate in learning the second-language, and to learn content through that language.

Given that kindergarten Opening is supposed to be the same in Spanish and English, analysis of the differences between Opening activities reveals how the Oyster educators work with the very different backgrounds that students bring with them in their efforts to help all students meet equally high expectations. My emphasis will therefore be on describing, interpreting, and explaining discrepancies between the ideal plan of equal distribution and evaluation of Spanish and English in light of Oyster's sociolinguistic context. My focus on discrepancies between ideal plan and actual implementation is therefore not intended to suggest that the Oyster educators are not doing their job the way that they should. Rather, this discussion is intended to illustrate their ongoing efforts to challenge and transform dominant discourse practices.

First, Opening song is the only speech activity that is longer in the Spanish Opening than in the English Opening. This difference in length can be explained by the fact that Spanish Opening is regularly initiated by two songs, the first in English and the second in Spanish, while English Opening is initiated by only one song in English. Every morning before the more formal Opening, the students sit at their tables and write and illustrate their stories together. There is a lot of activity and their attention is on each other and on their stories and pictures. The majority of the talk during this time is in English, which is consistent with the majority of the unofficial talk at Oyster. The first song, always in English, functions as a discourse marker that it is time for the students to get ready for the Opening. Since the teachers assume that all of the native Spanish speakers have some base in English but that not all of the native English speakers have a base in Spanish, the use of English in the first Opening is more inclusive because it is comprehensible to all of the students. Señora Rodriguez's switch to a Spanish song, which the students immediately follow, signals that Opening that day is to be in Spanish. The language choice is never stated explicitly to the children, but is indicated through the song and the teacher who sings it.

Students ideally use the official language of the class in all of their interactions. Analysis of code-switching behavior, however, illustrates how students are encouraged to negotiate meaning with each other in whatever language in order to participate in the class activity and achieve academically. For example, at the end of the Total activity in Spanish, an English-dominant student switches from Spanish to English apparently to request confirmation of his comprehension from a Spanish-dominant student[1]:

192	**T and Ss:**	doce ... trece ... catorce ... quince (twelve ... thirteen ... fourteen ... fifteen) [counting students together]
193		diez y seis ... diez y siete ... diez y ocho ... diez y nueve
194		veinte ... vientiuno (sixteen ... seventeen ... eighteen ... nineteen ... twenty ... twenty-one)
195	**Rodriguez:**	hay veintiuno [there are twenty one]
196	**S:**	**me me** [raising hand and calling out]
197	**Rodriguez:**	que pasa a tí [what's the matter with you]
198	**Ss:**	[unintelligible]
199	**S:**	**is it twenty-one?** [to another (Spanish-dominant) student]
200	**S:**	**yeah twenty-one**

This brief example illustrates how knowledge of Spanish functions as cultural capital in the dual-language model. The students who are proficient in Spanish are positioned by the Limited Spanish Proficient (LSP) students, as well as by the teachers, as resources in the LSP students' learning. The students' switch to the unofficial language is not problematic in this kindergarten class or in other classes that I observed throughout the school. The primary goal of Oyster Bilingual School, like any US public school, is comprehension of content and academic skills development. However students helping each other achieve these goals is acceptable.

Analysis of code-switching behavior in this kindergarten class and throughout the school also provides evidence of the leakage from mainstream US discourse (in which English is the language of wider communication and therefore attributed more prestige than Spanish) into the Oyster educational discourse (in which Spanish and English are to be distributed and evaluated equally). Consistent with the ideal plan that the English-dominant teacher speak and be spoken to only in English and the Spanish-dominant teacher speak and be spoken to only in Spanish, there are very few examples of code-switching to the unofficial language in either the Spanish or English Opening. Because the English-dominant teacher does not speak Spanish, there are no examples of code-switching by the official teacher to the unofficial language in the English Opening. There are, however, two examples of the official teacher switching to the unofficial language in the Spanish Opening. In both cases, Señora Rodriguez's utterance in English, *excuse me,* was the same, and functioned to discipline the children (one instance of this code-switching behavior appears later in this chapter). The abruptness of Señora Rodriguez's switch to English to discipline the students may function to call attention to the force of her words. Or her switch could be unwittingly signaling to the students that English is the more serious language. This second interpretation gains support from studies of speech communities around the world in which a speaker switches to the High language in order to impress a child with the seriousness of a command (see Fasold, 1984: 203–5, for discussion of this code-switching pattern in three separate communities).

Observation of the students talking informally among themselves, for example at lunch or at recess or during Storywriting time in kindergarten, also suggests that the students attribute more prestige to English than Spanish, despite the ideal that these languages be distributed and evaluated equally throughout the school. While some students do choose to speak Spanish among themselves outside of the official classroom interaction, it is much more common to hear English than Spanish in these situations, especially among the older students. Given Oyster's sociolinguistic context, in which students are regularly exposed to English outside of school in the music that they listen to and on the television programs that they watch, such language choice is not surprising.

Although the ideal of equal distribution and evaluation of Spanish and English is not achieved throughout the school, it does seem that the status of the Spanish language and Spanish speakers is raised considerably. All of the students, regardless of linguistic background, can and do speak Spanish, and interviews with the students suggest that they value this skill and want to continue to develop and use their Spanish in the future (see Chapter 11 for further discussion).

Code-switching behavior is not the only place that one can observe discrepancies between ideal plan and actual implementation. There are also discrepancies in the skills required in the English and Spanish content-areas in this kindergarten class and throughout the school. For example, immediately following the Opening song, the official teacher begins to write on the board in exactly the same format every day. Below is a representation of what the English-dominant teacher writes when Opening is in English and of what the Spanish-dominant teacher writes when Opening is in Spanish. I have provided the English translation of the Spanish in parentheses — this information is not provided to the students on the board.

English	Spanish
Today is _____	Hoy es _____
	(today is)
We have _____ girls	las niñas _____
	(the girls)
We have _____ boys	los niños _____
	(the boys)
We have _____ students	los estudiantes _____
	(the students)

The written format is almost identical in English and Spanish, and provides the organizational framework for the remainder of the Opening activities. Consistency in content across languages here and throughout the Opening activities assists the students in developing academic skills through their first and second-languages, and helps them acquire their second-language through content. Notice, however, that in the English activity, the format includes full sentences on each line. In the Spanish activity, only the first line is a complete sentence; the other lines include only nouns and articles. We see here a first example of skills discrepancies between English and Spanish with more skills required in English.

There is a very smooth transition between the Opening song and Today is activities in English and in Spanish, and the pattern is identical across languages. In each case, as the teacher writes the first sentence on the board, the teacher and students read aloud in unison using very formulaic intonation: in English, *toda:y? … i:s? …* , and in Spanish, *ho:y? … e:s? …* In both cases, the vowels are lengthened (marked with a colon), each of the words ends in rising intonation (marked with a question mark), and the pause between words is (approximately) the same length (marked with three periods). A similar pattern can be found later in the English and Spanish Framework activities:

Framework activity in English

114	[teacher starts to write on the board. Students begin to read aloud]	
115	**Ss:**	We: …. ha:ve …
116	**S:**	Wasn't that a w …
117	**Davis:**	We
118	**Ss:**	have
119	**S:**	stomachs [laughs and a few others laugh]
120	**Ss:**	gi:rls? …
121	[pausing where she draws the line to fill in the quantity]	
122		bo:ys? …
123	**Davis:**	Oh I have another?
124		another cloud person
125	[quiet as Mrs Davis writes and they immediately go back to the task]	
126	**Ss:**	We ha:ve … gi:rls?
127		We ha:ve … bo:ys?
128		We ha:ve … students
129	**Davis:**	I'll put my number right there [points to blank space]

Framework activity in Spanish

74	**Rodriguez:**	OK
75		vamos a contar ahora? [let's count now?]
		[she begins to write on board]
76	**T and Ss:**	la:s? ni:ña:s? [the? girls?]
77		lo:s? ni:ño:s? [the? boys?] [she writes]
78		lo:s? e:stu:dia:nte:s [the? students]
79	**Rodriguez:**	hay que largo [it's so long]
80		verdad esto? [isn't this true]
81	**Ss:**	sí [yes]
82	**Rodriguez:**	que largo [how long]
83	**Rodriguez:**	OK

In both of these activities, when the teacher and students read the lines about the girls and about the boys, they use rising intonation; when they read the lines about the students, they use falling intonation. These intonation patterns provide unity within and across Opening activities in both languages. In addition, it seems that this formulaicity helps students memorize these chunks in the second-language, which seems to facilitate their development of academic skills using these chunks as the content base.

After the teacher and students read the first sentence of the Today is activity out loud, the teacher encourages the students to jointly negotiate the name of the day, the date, the month, and the year. In this activity, however, as in the written framework discussed above, there are more skills required when Opening is in English than when it is in Spanish. For example, as the beginning of the Today is activity below in English illustrates, students are also expected to provide spelling information:

Today is activity in English

20	**Ss:**	toda:y? … i:s? … [In rehearsed unison]
21	**Davis:**	if you tell me
22		if you tell me the day
23		you have to tell me what letter it starts with
24	**S1:**	⌠ F
25	**S2:**	⌡ Friday
26	**Davis:**	Juanito?
27	**Juanito:**	⌠ F [quietly]
28	**Ss:**	⎰ F
29	**Ss:**	⌡ Friday
30	**Davis:**	Juanito says it's Friday with aa:n? [rising
31		intonation-elongated to signal for them to finish]
32	**Ss and T:**	F

In this example, in response to the teacher's request for spelling information, students begin to provide the name of the day and the letter it begins with (I provide a discussion of the teacher/student interaction in the next section). Later in the Today is activity in English, the teacher also requests punctuation information.

As we see later, however, the Spanish Today is activity requires neither spelling nor punctuation information. Note also that although the Spanish Today is activity begins in the same way as the English Today is activity, the transition from the formulaic *ho:y? e:s?* to the students' providing the name of the day is marked by a song:

Today is activity in Spanish

29	**Ss:**	ho:y? … e:s? [toda:y? … i:s?]
30		domingo lunes? [in song: Sunday Monday?]
31	**Rodriguez:**	no..espérate [no..wait]

[Señora Rodriguez interrupted the activity to make a comment about a student to Mrs

Davis. When she resumes the activity in line 41, the students' rhythm is off a bit.]

41	**Rodriguez:**	Ho:y?..
42	**Ss:**	⎰ e:s?
43	**Rodriguez:**	⎱ e:s?
44	**S:**	domingo lunes? [in song: Sunday Monday?]
45	**Rodriguez:**	⎰ domingo [Sunday]
46	**T and Ss:**	⎱ mingo lunes? martes y miercoles [Sun. Mon.? Tues. and Wed.]
47		jueves y viernes y sabado? [Thurs. and Fri. and Sat.?]
48		son los días [they are the days]
49		de la semana [of the week]
50		vamos a ver [let's see]
51		que día es hoy [what day is today: end of song]
52	**Rodriguez:**	qué día es hoy? [what day is today]
53		Silvia
54	**Silvia:**	viernes [Friday]

In the English Today is activity, students are expected to know the days of the week on their own, and to provide that information in response to the teacher's request for that information. In contrast, in the Spanish Today is activity, the use of the Spanish song reinforces the names of all of the days. In this way, if the students do not know exactly what day it is in Spanish, they can simply pick the name of the day out of the song.

Analysis of each of the other Opening activities in English and Spanish reveals similar patterns; very close coordination of basic skills across languages, and more skills required in each of the English activities. At least part of this discrepancy can be explained by the sociolinguistic context in which Oyster is situated. Recall from Chapter 8 the teachers' assumptions that the majority of the native Spanish speakers have some English language base while the majority of the native English speakers have no Spanish base. In addition, there are many more opportunities for the native Spanish speakers to use English outside of the official classroom than there are for the native English speakers to use Spanish. This difference has implications for the implementation of the dual-language plan. With respect to the Spanish language acquisition plan for the native English speakers, the concern at the kindergarten level is on listening comprehension. The students need to understand Spanish in context, and understand the relationship between the Spanish and English components that they will be exposed to for the next few years. Since the students all have a stronger English base, there can be more of an emphasis on skills acquisition at this stage in English.

Recall also from Chapter 8 the teachers' concern for skill level discrepancies between English and Spanish throughout the school, not only in the early years when the primary focus is the dual language acquisition plan. Because of the distinct evaluation standards for Spanish and English, both at Oyster as well as throughout mainstream US society, the English-dominant teachers suggested that the Spanish-dominant teachers were not held as accountable for skills development as the English-dominant teachers were. The discrepancy between what skills were expected in the Spanish and English Openings in kindergarten may also reflect this general skills discrepancy throughout the school.

PROVIDING EQUAL OPPORTUNITIES TO STUDENTS FROM UNEQUAL BACKGROUNDS

Equal educational opportunity at Oyster means more than the equal distribution and evaluation of Spanish and English. Perhaps more importantly, equal educational opportunity means recognizing the very unequal backgrounds that students bring with them to school, which requires the teachers to work differently with their students so that all students can meet the equally high expectations that the teachers have for them. This section illustrates how the kindergarten English-dominant and Spanish-dominant teachers work together to include the students that they are the most concerned about in the kindergarten 'Opening' in English and Spanish. The team-teachers' marked behavior with the same low-income native Spanish-speaking Salvadoran students provides specific examples of the Oyster educators' more general concern for how to provide equal educational opportunities to this segment of their student population.

I begin my discussion with Silvia, a student who had been very quiet and seemingly uninvolved in this and other activities throughout the year. In the following excerpt from the English Opening, the unofficial teacher, Señora Rodriguez, non-verbally requests that the official teacher, Mrs Davis, call on Silvia to answer a question. Because she is standing at the back of the class, the students cannot see Señora Rodriguez's gesture:

78		[Rodriguez motions for Davis to ask Silvia from behind the class]
79	**Davis:**	and …
80		Silvia
81		Can you tell me what..
82		year it is?
83	**S1:**	nineteen …
84	**S2:**	nineteen ninety one
85	**Davis:**	[whispers] Silvia …
86		Silvia [motions for her to come to Davis]
87		[Silvia whispers to Mrs Davis]
88		[other students are talking a little while Silvia whispers to Mrs Davis]
89	**Davis:**	OK this is what she told me
90	**S1:**	I know
91		[students read aloud in unison as Mrs Davis writes on board]
92	**S1:**	nineteen [begins]
93	**Ss:**	ninety one [follow with her]

In line 78, Señora Rodriguez motions to Mrs Davis from the side of the classroom for Mrs Davis to call on Silvia. Mrs Davis' utterance in line 79, *and ...* with a relatively long pause, provides her the opportunity to attend to what Señora Rodriguez is saying without interrupting the official floor at all. With lines 80–82, *Silvia can you tell me what ... year it is?,* Mrs Davis takes up Señora Rodriguez's suggestion and explicitly invites Silvia into the interaction. Silvia sits quietly at the desk without really responding while several of the other students begin to provide the answer. Rather than incorporate the other students' correct responses into the official floor, which would have been the easiest move, Mrs Davis whispers, *Silvia* (line 85 and 86), and invites her to come and whisper the answer to her. After a bit of hesitation, Silvia approaches Mrs Davis, who leans down as Silvia whispers into her ear. Mrs Davis responds to the class in line 89, *OK this is what she told me,* and writes the correct response on the board which the other students repeat in lines 92 and 93, *nineteen ninety one.*

Whether Silvia did in fact whisper the correct answer cannot be determined by anyone but Mrs Davis and Silvia. What is important is that Señora Rodriguez's and Mrs Davis' interactional work integrated Silvia into the official classroom discourse, which all of the students witnessed. The students' repetition of Silvia's (presumed) contribution in lines 92 and 93, *nineteen ninety one,* which Mrs Davis writes on the board, functions to position Silvia as a student who knows the answer and who contributes to the students' joint construction of the answer to the larger question, *What day is today?* that structures the beginning of the Opening activity. Continued positioning of Silvia as a legitimate participant in the classroom interaction (as opposed to a student who rarely responds to the teacher's questions, or who rarely volunteers an answer) contributes to Silvia's understanding of herself, and to the other students' understanding of Silvia, as having the right to be a legitimate participant in the classroom interaction.

Such differential positioning of students could, however, have quite negative outcomes. In this case, for example, calling attention to Silvia could somehow mark her as different from the other students, and possibly encourage her to withdraw further from the class. Furthermore, teachers' assumptions about students' relative abilities can limit the educational opportunities of those students that the teachers assume have lower abilities (see Oakes, 1985, for further discussion). However, my observations of Señora Rodriguez's and Mrs Davis' behavior with their students, supported by my conversations with them about their practices, suggest that these teachers' differential positioning of students is based not on their assumptions of students' different abilities, but on their assumptions of students' different background knowledge, strengths, and needs. In fact, these two teachers, like the others at Oyster, seem to hold more or less equally high expectations for all of their students' abilities. Because the Oyster teachers assume that their students have unequal backgrounds, they need to position them differently in order that all students can meet those expectations.

Also reflecting Señora Rodriguez's efforts to include Silvia in the official classroom interaction, in the following excerpt from the beginning of the Spanish Opening, Señora Rodriguez directs her question in line 52, *Qué día es hoy* (What day is today?) specifically to Silvia. Señora Rodriguez's direct nomination of Silvia is marked because she does not generally call on students; she usually encourages them to bid for the opportunity to provide the right answer by raising their hands. More often than not, the students simply shout out an enthusiastic answer to the teacher's question.

52	**Rodriguez:**	Qué día es hoy? [what day is today?] …
53		Silvia?
54	**Silvia:**	viernes [Friday]
55	**Rodriguez:**	muy bien [very good]
56		hoy es viernes [today is Friday] [writes on the board]
57	**Rodriguez:**	muy bien Silvia [very good Silvia]

Line 52, *qué día es hoy?* (what day is today?) is the first question in the Opening activity, and it occurs immediately after the Spanish days of the week song (see discussion in last section). Since Silvia is a native Spanish speaker, she presumably knows the answer to Señora Rodriguez's question. Without hesitation, Silvia provides the correct answer, *viernes* (Friday) in line 54. In line 55, Señora Rodriguez ratifies Silvia's contribution with her utterance, *muy bien* (very good), which is consistent with her strategy of acknowledging student contributions in Spanish through her repetition of that contribution. Señora Rodriguez then repeats and expands on Silvia's contribution, *hoy es viernes* (today is Friday, line 56). Such repetition provides additional comprehensible input in Spanish, which enhances the SSL students' acquisition of Spanish. Again in line 57, Señora Rodriguez praises Silvia's performance, this time including her name, *muy bien Silvian* (very good Silvia). Señora Rodriguez's repeated praise of Silvia's contribution is marked; she rarely praises students more than once.

This interaction has several functions. With respect to the education of the entire class, one of the students has provided a correct answer, demonstrating that the task is possible, and providing correct input in Spanish for the others to acquire. With respect to Silvia, the teacher has drawn on her strength, Spanish fluency, to provide her the opportunity to demonstrate her knowledge of something the others do not necessarily know. This gives Silvia as well as the other students the opportunity to see Silvia as successful. As I mentioned earlier, repeated positioning of Silvia as successful in the classroom interaction allows all of the students, including Silvia, to think of Silvia as an equal participant who has important contributions to make to the class.

These team-teachers are also concerned about Juanito's access to educational opportunities because they claim that he began school with much lower skills than the other students. In both the English and the Spanish Openings, the teachers give special attention to his contributions and progress. For example in the English

Opening, Mrs Davis' ratification strategy is different with Juanito than with all of the other students. In general, Mrs Davis ratifies the students' correct contributions by writing them on the board in the framework they fill in together to answer the organizing question, *What day is today.* Mrs Davis rarely talks at this point in the activity. The exception to her exclusive use of written ratification can be found in her interaction with Juanito:

21	**Davis:**	If you tell me
22		If you tell me the day?
23		You have to tell me what letter it starts with
24	**S1:**	⌠F
25	**S2:**	⌡Friday
26	**Davis:**	Juanito?
27	**Juanito:**	⌠F
28	**Ss:**	{ F
29	**Ss:**	⌡Friday
30	**Davis:**	Juanito says it's Friday with aa:n?
31	**Ss and T:**	F

In this case, Mrs Davis does not ratify the correct contribution that S1 made in line 24. Instead, she calls on Juanito directly in line 26, *Juanito?* to answer her question, which he does quietly in line 27 and at the same time as the other students. It is not apparent whether the other students heard Juanito's contribution or not. In line 30, Mrs Davis invites the students to repeat Juanito's correct contribution in her utterance, *Juanito says it's Friday with aa:n?* Her rising intonation and elongated vowel signal to the students that they continue with her, which they do in line 31. Mrs Davis' ratification strategy functions to define Juanito as a legitimate participant who can and does achieve in class.

Señora Rodriguez's behavior is also marked with Juanito in the Spanish Opening. As the following excerpt illustrates, Señora Rodriguez interrupted the official class and invited me in from my position as observer to comment on Juanito's progress:

105		Juanito ven acá [Juanito come here]
106		y escribir el ocho [and write the eight]
107		[students talk among themselves as Juanito writes]
108	**Rodriguez:**	[after Juanito finishes writing] muy bien [very good]
109		[students talking]
110	**Rodriguez:**	[to me about Juanito] cuando él vino [when he came]
111		a la escuela por primera vez [to school for the first time]
112		en septiembre [in September]
113		no sabía ni el uno [he didn't know even the one]
114		nada [nothing]
115		no sabía [he didn't know]
116		[lots of Ss talking]
117		que le ponía? [what did he put?]

118	**Rodriguez:**	[to students] **excuse me**
119		[students quiet down]
120	**Rodriguez:**	[to me] este..[this]
121		yo le ponía por ejemplo [I put for example]
122		si yo le decía a Juanito [if I said to Juanito]
123		qué es esto [what is this]
124		cuántos yo tengo en la mano [how many do I have in my hand]
125		cuántos borradores [how many erasers]
126		Juanito no me podía decir [Juanito couldn't tell me]
127		que tenía un borrador [that I had one eraser]
128		y y él [and and he]
129		aprendió a contar [learned to count]
130		y después le ponía por ejemplo el uno [and later I put for example]
131		y le decía [and I said to him]
132		uno y esto aquí [one and this here]
133		cuántos hay aquí [how many are there here]
134		él no podía decirme [he couldn't tell me]
135		que esto era uno y que esto era uno [that this was one and that this was one]
136		el concepto de de de [the concept of of of]
137		del símbolo con [of the symbol with]
138		y Juanito ahora *cuenta* hasta el veinte [and Juanito now counts until twenty]
139		*reconoce* hasta el doce [he recognizes until twelve]
140	**Rebecca:**	[to Juanito who is listening and smiling proudly]
141		muy bien [very good]
142		has aprendido bastante no? [you've learned alot, haven't you]
143	**Rodriguez:**	Sí [yes]
144		este año Juanito ha aprendido mucho mucho mucho [this year Juanito has learned much much much]
145		y yo estoy muy contenta con él [and I am very happy with him]
146	**Rodriguez:**	OK

As the above excerpt makes clear, Señora Rodriguez's interruption of the official class activity was relatively lengthy as she positively evaluated Juanito's academic progress. When it appeared to me that Señora Rodriguez had finished her story, I addressed Juanito directly in lines 141–2, *muy bien .... has aprendido bastante no?* (very good ... you've learned a lot haven't you). Note that Señora Rodriguez, and not Juanito, responded to the question that I had directed to Juanito. Her utterance in line 143, *sí* (yes), provides an example of the teacher talking for the student. Rather than allow Juanito to speak for himself, Señora Rodriguez continued in lines 144–5 to summarize his progress and her evaluation of that progress. Señora Rodriguez's comments make her stance toward Juanito, and toward the kind of progress he is making, clear to me, to Juanito, and to the rest of the class.

Also note Señora Rodriguez's emphasis on how much Juanito had learned, and on her strategy of encouraging him to participate in the official class activities even though his skills were lower than those of the other students. This reflects Señora Rodriguez's assumption that Juanito has different background knowledge based on his experiences outside of Oyster, not that he has different abilities than the rest of the students. Señora Rodriguez's task, like that of the other teachers, is to observe what the individual student's strengths and weaknesses are to determine how to best help that student build on his/her strengths. Of course, Señora Rodriguez's public evaluation of Juanito's progress could backfire, for example, leading Juanito to see himself as different from and inferior to the other students in the class. Juanito's active participation and continued progress, however, suggest that Señora Rodriguez's efforts were at least not damaging and at best effective.

Another example of how the team-teachers work together to bring students they are concerned about into the interaction can be found in the English Counting boys activity, when the unofficial teacher, Señora Rodriguez, speaks Spanish to Mario during the English Opening to question his lack of participation. (Davis is the official teacher and the students' and her utterances on the transcript are the official floor.) In this excerpt, Señora Rodriguez, after questioning Mario, approaches me and quietly explains to me Mario's situation. In the transcript below, I underline the utterances that Señora Rodriguez addresses to me as part of the unofficial floor.

196	**Rodriguez:**	Mario?
197		**porqué tú no lo contaste** [why didn't you count]
198	**Mario:**	**porque él lo hizo** [because he did it]
199	**Rodriguez:**	**eso no vale** [that doesn't matter]
200	**S:**	sixteen
201	**Davis:**	uuuh
202		William told me a secret
203		He's going to write a number
204		and you're going to see if you
205		if he wrote the same number that you have in your head
206		then we'll do our math sentence
207	**Rodriguez:**	[to me] *Did you see that*
208	**Davis:**	then we'll do our math sentence
209		and see how many students we have
210	**Rodriguez:**	[to me] *He doesn't even try*
211		*He is already defeated*
212	**Davis:**	[to William] here
213		you need a chair [William writes: students watch]

214	**Rodriguez:**	[to me] *uh*
215		*He is already defeated*
216		*He doesn't try*
217		*He never tries more than what he has to*
218		[Pause]
219		*The mother has a very low esteem*
220	**Davis:**	[to William] very good
221		[to class] I hope that was what was in your head
222		Now we'll do our math sentence
223	**Rodriguez:**	[to me] *and his father is an alcoholic …*
224		*you name it*
225		*everything is against him*
226	**Ss:**	[talking to each other for a second]

In this excerpt, Señora Rodriguez's codeswitching behavior to the unofficial language of the class as she addresses Mario in line 197, *porqué tú no lo contaste* (why didn't you count) is consistent with the ideal plan that the Spanish-dominant teacher speak and be spoken to only in Spanish and the English-dominant teacher speak and be spoken to only in English. Additionally, the use of Spanish functions as the in-group language for Señora Rodriguez and Mario. Mario responds to Señora Rodriguez in Spanish in line 198, *porque él lo hizo* (because he did it), which is also consistent with the ideal plan. Señora Rodriguez concludes their interaction by rejecting Mario's explanation in line 199, *eso no vale* (that doesn't matter). She turns from Mario and approaches me to offer an explanation of his behavior. It is important to note that, in contrast to the earlier example in which Señora Rodriguez publicly commented to me about Juanito's improvement, in this case Señora Rodriguez commented to me quietly on the side of the class where the students could not hear.

Now I include only Señora Rodriguez's explanation of Mario's behavior, which at first glance gives the impression that because Mario has so many points against him, she had given up on him.

207	**Rodriguez:**	[to me] Did you see that
210		He doesn't even try
211		He is already defeated
214		uh
215		He is already defeated
216		He doesn't try
217		He never tries more than what he has to
218		[Pause]
219		The mother has a very low esteem
223		and his father is an alcoholic …
224		you name it
225		everything is against him

Señora Rodriguez's interpretation of Mario's behavior suggests that she is aware of his family background and the problems it causes him in school. Rather than considering him too difficult to work with, or attributing his lack of participation to, for example laziness, Señora Rodriguez took Mario away from the class and into the bathroom to talk to him. About 10 minutes later, they emerged from the bathroom, Mario rejoined the official English class, and Mrs Davis immediately called on him to participate in the Calendar activity (the next activity in Opening).

These examples reflect the close cooperation between the teachers to include all of the students in the classroom discourse, and to position the students as equal participants regardless of their backgrounds. In this way, the students ideally gain opportunities to see themselves as more or less equal participants in the classroom interaction. Because of the diverse backgrounds, personalities, and needs of the students, achieving these goals requires the teachers to treat the students differently.

The obvious question to all of this discussion of positioning of less proficient/less skilled/less motivated students as equal participants is: Is this unique to the Oyster dual-teaching practices and social identities project, or is this just an example of good teaching with diverse student populations. I want to emphasize that I do not think this is at all unique to Oyster Bilingual School. Given the increasingly diverse student populations in public schools throughout the United States, I believe that the general teaching and learning principles are generalizable to any other setting, bilingual or not. What is important to emphasize here is that these teaching practices reflect a concern for the development of positive minority social identities and for equal educational opportunity regardless of background, the goals of the underlying social identities project. And reciprocally, these practices make possible the achievement of such goals.

CONCLUSION

Chapters 5–8 described, interpreted, and explained how the Oyster Bilingual School dual-language program can be understood as part of a larger social identities project. The explicit goals of this program are for all students to become bilingual and biliterate, achieve academically through two languages, and develop good intercultural communication skills and understanding. The Oyster educators' assumption that minority students are not provided equal educational opportunities in mainstream US schools means that part of the Oyster agenda is to position minority students as equal to majority students. Given the Oyster assumption that their students come from very different backgrounds which do not prepare them equally for academic achievement, and the Oyster expectation that all of their students can and will achieve academically, the Oyster educators work very differently with their individual students.

This chapter presented a micro-level comparative analysis of the English and Spanish kindergarten Openings to illustrate how the dual-language program is interpreted and implemented on the classroom level. I began the chapter by showing how the kindergarten team-teachers work together to distribute and evaluate Spanish and English equally so that students acquire their second-language, develop academic skills in both languages, and use each other as resources in their learning. Analysis of each of the activities in kindergarten Opening in Spanish and in English revealed similar patterns; very close coordination of basic skills across languages, and more skills required in each of the English activities. The kindergarten analysis thus provides concrete evidence of a more general pattern that I observed throughout the school. Although students are expected to develop academic skills in both Spanish and English, there are higher standards in English (see Chapter 8 for further discussion).

At least part of this discrepancy can be explained by Oyster's sociolinguistic context. Recall from Chapter 8 the teachers' assumptions that the majority of the native Spanish speakers have some English language base while the majority of the native English speakers have no Spanish language base. Therefore, the emphasis in Spanish Opening is on language development. Since the students all have a stronger base in English, there is more of an emphasis on skills development in English Opening. Recall also from Chapter 8 that some of the English-dominant teachers expressed their concern that the unequal assessment practices at the school and in the school district led the English-dominant teachers to be more accountable for skills development than their Spanish-dominant counterparts. The discrepancy between what skills were expected in the Spanish and English Openings in kindergarten reflects this general skills discrepancy throughout the school.

The second part of the chapter demonstrated how the kindergarten team-teachers work together to provide equal educational opportunities to the students they are the most concerned about. The examples that I presented reflect the close cooperation between the teachers to include all of the students in the classroom discourse. Because of the diverse backgrounds, personalities, strengths, and needs of the students, enabling all of the students to reach the teachers' equally high expectations requires the teachers to treat individual students differently. This chapter illustrated the kindergarten team-teachers' marked behavior with the same low-income native Spanish-speaking Salvadoran students, and provides concrete evidence of the Oyster educators' more general concern for how to provide equal educational opportunities to this segment of their student population (see Chapter 6 for further discussion).

The discourse analyses presented in this chapter provide evidence of patterns that I identified throughout Oyster Bilingual School, and my understanding of the larger educational and societal discourses surrounding Oyster's educational discourse enabled me to understand the micro-level classroom processes that I was observing. The analyses presented in this chapter, like those that I present in Chapter 10, are intended to increase the validity and reliability of the study, as well as to encourage educational researchers and reflective practitioners to look closely at how discourse practices are organized in another educational context. Detailed analyses of teaching and learning across contexts can help us understand how and why a bilingual education program functions the way that it does on the local level, and contribute to our efforts to understand bilingual education more generally. I return to this point in the conclusion of Chapter 10.

Note

1   My transcription conventions are as follows. The line numbers on the excerpts correspond to the line numbers on the original transcripts. Following Tannen (1989) and Chafe (1986), each line represents an intonation unit. Dots indicate a pause, and a question mark signals rising intonation (not a grammatical question). Brackets connecting words in consecutive lines signal overlap. Code-switching is indicated by bold face. I include information about who says what to whom, loudness, non-verbal cues, translations, etc. in parentheses.

CHAPTER 10

Gaining the Right to Participate: A Classroom Analysis

Chapter 9 was primarily concerned with illustrating how the Oyster dual-language plan is implemented so that the children acquire the ability to speak both English and Spanish while simultaneously acquiring academic skills through those languages. As I have argued throughout this study, there is more to equal participation opportunities than simply having the ability to speak the language. According to Harré (1984), in order for people to be able to participate equally, they must also have the right to participate in the discourse. Although the last chapter touched on this issue, this chapter will explore in greater detail how the Oyster program is organized to provide students with opportunities to see themselves as having equal rights to participate and strategies for asserting those rights.

This chapter presents three examples from the sixth grade that illustrate how students are given and take up the right to participate. The first example focuses on the teacher. A micro-level analysis of one segment of a Spanish language arts lesson illustrates how the sixth-grade Spanish-dominant teacher's assumptions about Latino/Anglo differences in questioning strategies and participation rights in mainstream US discourse underlie his classroom practices. The teacher emphasis on student–student interaction, even in the teacher-led organization when one would not expect such interaction, is consistent with what I observed throughout the school. The second example focuses on a student's in-class participation. My analysis explores a student's response to an activity that the sixth-grade English-dominant teacher assigned which encourages the students to recognize discriminatory practices in history. The third example focuses on out-of-class student behavior. This analysis relates an excerpt from a book on Chinese History that one of the sixth-graders wrote on her own (not as part of the curriculum) to Oyster's efforts to develop students' critical perspective on discriminatory practices. Because sixth grade is the last year of students' experience at Oyster, examples of their work best reflects the cumulative effect of their socialization through the Oyster educational discourse.

QUIEN SOY YO: A MICRO-LEVEL ANALYSIS

My analysis of the following segment of classroom interaction illustrates how the teacher's assumptions about Latino and Anglo differences in perceived participation rights in the educational domain guide his methodology. As discussed in Chapter 6, Señor Xoci assumes that: (1) Latino students will question their peers, (2) Latino students will not question the teacher out of respect, (3) Anglo students know how to ask in order to make it through/in the system, and (4) Latino students need to see access as a right and not a privilege. The cooperative learning environment that the teacher creates, here as exemplified by Señor Xoci and consistent with what I observed throughout the school, provides all of the students the opportunity to share their individual work with the class, and to question each other so that they can jointly construct meaning. In addition, the students are encouraged to take responsibility for their contributions, consistent with the goal of agency development. Through such interactional experience, they ideally come to see themselves and each other as having equal right to question and participate. In this way, the students gain equal right to participate, regardless of their background. This applies specifically to the Latino students that Señor Xoci explicitly expressed concern about, and to all of the students in general.

The following excerpt is taken from a Spanish Language Arts lesson. Señor Xoci and the students had been studying poetry, and for homework he asked them each to write a poem entitled 'Quien soy yo' ('Who am I') that they would share with the class the next day. Requiring the students to share their poems with the class insures that they will all get the opportunity to participate and to be heard, and as we saw in Chapter 8, is a format regularly employed throughout the school. It is also important to mention that, for whatever reasons, several students exercised their right not to speak by refusing to read their poems aloud. In all of these cases, Señor Xoci requested and received permission to read that student's individual poem in front of the class. This refusal to participate in one format, but willingness to participate in another format suggested by the teacher, illustrates student choice and teacher flexibility, qualities that I observed throughout Oyster.

The topic that Señor Xoci selected, 'Quien soy yo' ('Who am I'), reflects the school's central concern with positive social identity development. By making student's construction of identity the topic of the class discussion, Señor Xoci helps the students see the various social identities represented within the class as legitimate. This emphasis on using who the students are, and what their diverse backgrounds offer as part of the curriculum, as discussed in Chapter 8, is evidenced throughout the school.

Consistent with an ethnography of communication approach (Hymes, 1974), I divide the speech situation, Spanish Language Arts class, into two distinct speech activities that recur throughout the class. In this case, speech activity 1 can be distinguished from speech activity 2 by distinct norms of interaction ('N', for 'Norms' on the SPEAKING grid), and by distinct goals for the activity ('E', for 'Ends' on the SPEAKING grid). The goal for speech activity 1 is for an individual to read his/her poem aloud for the rest of the class. The norms of interaction in speech activity 1 include that individual's right to the uninterrupted floor and the audience's obligation to listen. Moreover, the students must be tolerant of the individual's views and respect that individual's right to participate. The goal for speech activity 2 is for the students to negotiate the meaning of the poem read in speech activity 1 with each other. The norms of interaction for speech activity 2 include the students' right to question each other directly.

The segment that I present here consists of the first volunteer, Yvonne reading her poem (speech activity 1), and the student–student questioning period that follows (speech activity 2). Because Yvonne is the first volunteer, the students do not yet know what the norms of interaction governing their participation will be. As a result, the first cycle of speech activity 1 and speech activity 2 contains a transition period that I refer to as the 'negotiating the norms of interaction frame'. In this transitional period, it is possible to see the interactional work the teacher and students do in order to accomplish the transition from speech activity 1 to speech activity 2. As the class progresses, and the students become more familiar with what is expected of them, the transition period diminishes and disappears.

Although the content of Yvonne's poem is not the focus of this analysis, a few words are in order. The topic, 'Who am I', is very personal and provides students the opportunity to express anything they choose about themselves. That Yvonne focuses on her skin color in the first line with pride may be related to the mulicultural socialization she has gotten in the school. Skin color, like other conversations about linguistic and cultural difference, is a legitimate topic of conversation at the school.

I begin my discussion with speech activity 1 to illustrate the norms that constitute that activity. I then proceed to speech activity 2 to illustrate the distinct set of norms that guide behavior in that activity. Finally, I present the negotiating the norms of interaction frame to illustrate the interactional work that Señor Xoci and the students togther do to make the transition from speech activity 1 to speech activity 2.

In speech activity 1, lines 1–24, the norms of interaction governing participation consist of Yvonne's right to the uninterrupted floor while she reads her poem aloud to the rest of the group. All of the other students and the teacher are expected to listen, to respect her right to speak, and to be tolerant of whatever it is that she has to say. They will each have the opportunity to speak about themselves in turn, and they will also have the opportunity to discuss the poem at the appropriate time. I first present the original Spanish version, and then follow with the English version. My concern in this analysis is with the interaction that follows the poem and not with the grammatical accuracy of Yvonne's Spanish. I will return to a discussion of linguistic competence later.

Yvonne's poem in Spanish

1   Mi pelo es color de chocolate
2   No
3   Mi piel es color de chocolate
4   Mi pelo es color de café sin leche
5   Mi corazón es grande como un globo
6   Mi actitud es como un tigre
7   Mis sentimientos son suaves como una nueva flor
8   Mi vida no es perfecta, ni mala
9   Mi espíritu es grande como una escuela
10   Mis movimientos son inteligentes pero confundidos
11   Mi cerebro tiene cosas adentro que yo no entiendo
12   Yo está yo está como un tigre
13   Porque tengo un grande espiritu
14   Está temprano **when** peligro está cerca
15   Parte de yo es como una flor
16   Cuando alguien está triste
17   Yo quiero quiero a ella hacer ellos feliz
18   Todas las veces no puedo comparar
19   Nosotros como a cosas
20   Porque nosotros somos diferentes
21   Pero hay una cosa que yo quiero decir
22   Para vivir en esta vida necesita gustar a ti
23   No que a que quieres hacer
24   [pause]
25 **T:** Ok muy bien Yvonne
26   [The class claps]

English translation of Yvonne's poem

1   My hair is the color of chocolate
2   No
3   My skin is the color of chocolate
4   My hair is the color of coffee without milk
5   My heart is big like a globe
6   My attitude is like a tiger
7   My feelings are soft like a new flower
8   My life isn't perfect, but [it is] not bad
9   My spirit is big like a school
10   My movements are intelligent but confused
11   My mind has things inside that I don't understand
12   I am I am like a tiger
13   Because I have a big spirit

14   That is early [quick?] **when** danger is near
15   Part of me is like a flower
16   When someone is sad
17   I want to make them happy
18   All of the times you can't compare
19   We like [similar to] things
20   Because we are different
21   But there is one thing I want to say
22   To live in this life you need to like yourself
23   And not what you want to do.
24   [pause]
25 **T:**   Ok very good Yvonne
26   [The class claps]

As demonstrated by the lack of interruption, Señor Xoci's utterance in line 25, *OK very good Yvonne*, and the class's clapping in line 26, Yvonne's right to the uninterrupted floor and the students' obligation to listen is ratified by the group. This sharing format, with these norms of interaction, was consistent throughout the rest of this class as the other students continued to read their poems, and is a common format throughout the school.

In speech activity 2, lines 56–78, the norms of interaction governing participation are distinct. Señor Xoci's role seems to be to encourage student–student interaction. The questions are not addressed to him and he doesn't answer them. In other words,the organization of the adjacency pairs in speech activity 2 are of the form: Student: Question –> Student: Answer and not Student: Question –> Teacher: Answer or Teacher: Question –> Student: Answer. Given the personal nature of the content, it seems reasonable that the person with authority would be the author of the poem, and not the teacher who traditionally has the authority in the classroom. Such an organization demonstrates that the teacher is not assumed to have the 'right' answer; maybe there is no 'right' answer. Communication of meaning, jointly, cooperatively is the goal. If there is confusion, the students are to negotiate on equal footing. Speech activity 2 is presented below, first in Spanish and then in English. While my analysis works from the original Spanish version, for ease of discussion I work from the English translation below (codeswitches from the official class language are indicated on the transcripts in boldface):

Original speech activity 2 in Spanish
56   **Claudia:**   Yvonne
57   **so you think in a school**
58   **there's a lot of love?**
59   **Yvonne:**   **no**
60   **Susan:**   **no there's a lot of sentiments**
61   **Yvonne:**   **yeah … there's like feelings**
62   **they're different**

63		hay diferentes sentimientos
64		porque alguien que
65		**like** que
66		alguien puede ser triste en un lugar
67		y alguien puede ser feliz
68		y alguien
69		alguien puede ser **um worried**
70	**T:**	Sí
71	**Yvonne:**	y cosas asi,
72		y ponlos juntos
73		**it forms** una persona
74	**T:**	sí exacto
75		perfecto.
76		todos los elementos de la personalidad de una persona
77		claro
78		alguien …
79		muy bien Yvonne gracias
80		Susan?

[And they continue with their poems and critiquing each other]

English translation of speech activity 2

56	**Claudia:**	Yvonne
57		**so you think in a school**
58		**there's a lot of love?**
59	**Yvonne:**	**no**
60	**Susan:**	**no there's a lot of sentiments**
61	**Yvonne:**	**yeah there's like feelings**
62		**they're different**
63		there are different feelings
64		because someone that
65		**like** that
66		that someone can be sad in one place
67		and someone can be happy
68		and someone
69		and someone can be **um worried**
70	**T:**	Yes
71	**Yvonne:**	and things like that
72		and put them together
73		**it forms** a person
74	**T:**	yes exactly
75		perfect
76		all the elements of the personality of a person
77		clear

78   someone
79   very good Yvonne thank you.

In lines 56–58, Claudia asks a question directly to Yvonne, *Yvonne, so you think in a school there's a lot of love?* Claudia's direct indexing of Yvonne demonstrates her understanding that the norms of interaction include her right to ask Yvonne directly to take responsibility for her speech. Claudia's question can be interpreted in a number of ways. It is possible that one, Claudia did not understand what Yvonne said, in which case the question functions as a request for clarification. Another possible interpretation is that Claudia interprets Yvonne to be saying that there is a lot of love in a school, and that Claudia disagrees with this representation of school. In this case, Claudia's utterance can be understood as functioning as a pre-disagreement. A third possibility is that Claudia does agree that there is a lot of love in school and wants the class discussion to take up this topic. In this case, Claudia's utterance can be understood as a ratification of Yvonne's contribution as well as a topic change.

It is impossible to *know* exactly what Claudia intends with her utterance from the transcript. I merely wish to emphasize that Claudia is involved in Yvonne's poem, and attempts to jointly negotiate the meaning of Yvonne's utterance. Such active involvement and joint negotiation of meaning among students is characteristic of the cooperative learning organization that I observed throughout the school.

Yvonne responds to Claudia's question in line 59 with a short *no*, which could have ended the discussion right there. It is interesting to note that another student, Susan, picks up on Yvonne's response, *no* and develops it herself in line 60, *no there's a lot of sentiments.* Susan's contribution demonstrates her active involvement in both Yvonne's poem and in Claudia's question, and also demonstrates her understanding that the norms of interaction in this speech activity include the students' direct negotiation with each other.

Vygotsky's notion of the 'zone of proximal development' (see Chapter 4 for discussion) is helpful in understanding the effect of Susan's interactional move on Yvonne's subsequent development of her answer to Claudia's question. The notion of a 'zone of proximal development' explains how a more capable peer (in this case Susan) helps a less capable peer (in this case Yvonne) to develop by providing a model of appropriate behavior in the activity. As I discuss later, Susan was the student who initiated the discussion of Yvonne's poem in the negotiating norms of interaction frame. Now that Susan understands the meaning of Yvonne's poem (or at least thinks she does), Susan is able to help explain to Claudia what Yvonne meant in her poem. In this excerpt, Susan (acting as the more capable peer) translates Yvonne's Spanish contribution, *sentimientos* to the English word *sentiments* so that Claudia can understand Yvonne's meaning. (It is noteworthy that Claudia is a native Spanish speaker and both Yvonne and Susan are native English speakers, because the explanation provided to aid the native Spanish speaker's comprehension is in her second-language.) In line 61, Yvonne ratifies Susan's contribution with her utterance, *yeah, there's like feelings.* Helped by Susan's supplement, Yvonne continues to expand her reason for stating that her heart is as big as a school.

The code-switching in this excerpt reflects a pattern that we saw in the kindergarten analysis in Chapter 9. Claudia, the native Spanish speaker, initiates the negotiation of meaning in English. After Yvonne, the native English speaker, explained what she had meant in English to Claudia in the language that Claudia had chosen, Yvonne switches back to Spanish (the official language at that time) in line 63 to continue her explanation. The fact that Señor Xoci says nothing during this exchange demonstrates that this code-switching behavior to clarify meaning is acceptable in his class.

That Señor Xoci encourages peer interaction is demonstrated by his lack of substantive verbal participation in speech activity 2, and by his supportive back channel cues, for example in line 70 *yes.* Similarly, his utterances in lines 74–75, *yes exactly / perfect,* at the end of Yvonne's turn function to ratify her contribution. In addition to his back channeling and ratification, which supports the student–student interaction, Señor Xoci also seems to appropriate Yvonne's meaning in line 76 with his utterance, *all of the elements of the personality of a person.* Given his role as teacher of the class, and the associated power that comes with that role regardless of the classroom organization, this utterance signals that Yvonne's turn is over. This utterance, and the following affirmative utterance *claro,* signal to the class that both the meaning and the participation framework the students have negotiated are appropriate.

These norms of interaction, i.e. student–student questioning and negotiation of meaning, teacher supportive backchanneling, and teacher summarizing and ratifying these norms, were consistent throughout the rest of the class. In addition, these norms of interaction were often evidenced in cooperative learning organizations that I observed throughout the school.

In order to understand the interactional work that Señor Xoci and the students did in order to understand the appropriate norms of interaction within speech activity 2, a closer look at the 'negotiating appropriate norms of interaction' frame is required, which I now repeat (first in Spanish, then in English):

Negotiating appropriate norms of interaction frame [original Spanish]

25	**T:**	Ok muy bien Yvonne
26		[The class claps]
27	**Tania:**	[to Yvonne, not to the entire class]
28		**what was the last part?**
29	**Yvonne:**	necesitas gustar a tí
30		**and not what you want to be**
31	**T:**	alguna crítica …
32		señorita?
33	**Susan:**	yo no entiendo um..

34		la parte de la escuela
35		[pause]
36	**T:**	eres
37		eres que?
38		como una escuela Yvonne?
39		[pause]
40	**Tania:**	[to Yvonne] **read the part,**
41		**the part about the school**
42	**Yvonne:**	**my heart is as big as a school**
43	**Susan:**	**oh?**
44	**T:**	porque dijiste esto Yvonne
45	**Yvonne:**	porque una escuela es grande
46	**T:**	y también dentro de la escuela hay mucho que
47	**Student:**	OH! OH!
48	**Yvonne:**	hay
49		hay muchas personas
50		y hay **like** diferentes corazones and
51	**T:**	exacto
52	**Yvonne:**	y tienen diferentes sentimientos
53		y ponen todos los sentimientos junto
54		**that's**
55		es yo

Negotiating norms of interaction frame [English translation]

25	**T:**	Ok very good Yvonne
26		[The class claps]
27	**Tania:**	[to Yvonne, not to the entire class]
28		**what was the last part?**
29	**Yvonne:**	you need to like yourself
30		**and not what you want to be**
31	**T:**	some critique ….
32		miss?
33	**Susan:**	I don't understand um..
34		the part about the school
35		[pause]
36	**T:**	you are
37		you are what?
38		like a school Yvonne?
39		[pause]
40	**Tania:**	[to Yvonne] **read the part**
41		**the part about the school**
42	**Yvonne:**	**my heart is as big as a school**
43	**Susan:**	**oh?**
44	**T:**	why did you say this Yvonne

45	**Yvonne:**	because a school is big
46	**T:**	and also inside the school there is much what
47	**Student:**	**OH! OH!**
48	**Yvonne:**	there are
49		there are many people
50		and there are **like** different hearts **and**
51	**T:**	exactly
52	**Yvonne:**	and they have different feelings
53		and put all the feelings together
54		**that's**
55		that's me

Since Yvonne is the first volunteer, the students do not yet completely understand the norms of interaction that are to structure their participation in speech activity 2. Consequently, the transition is not smooth between speech events (however, it is relatively easy to make the expectations of student–student interaction explicit, and to have a smooth transition between subsequent speech activities 1 and 2, because speech activity 2 utilizes a participation framework that is very common at Oyster). In line 25, Señor Xoci marks the transition between speech events with his utterance, *OK very good Yvonne*. The class signals that their ratification of this utterance as a closing by their clapping (line 26). But who has the next right to speak has not yet been established.

Lines 27, 28 and 29 consist of an interaction between Tania and Yvonne. This interaction demonstrates that the students are actively involved in each other's poetry because Tania questions Yvonne in line 28, *what was the last part?*, to which Yvonne responds in lines 29 and 30, *you need to like yourself/and not what you want to be*. Yvonne and Tania are both native English-speakers, so Yvonne's switch to English halfway through the utterance can be understood as possibly reflecting her interpretation that the meaning problem was related to language. Or Yvonne might have switched to English for speed's sake, perhaps because Yvonne expected to be called on to discuss her poem. Either way, Yvonne's and Tania's interaction demonstrates their involvement, both with the class and with each other.

In line 31, Señor Xoci attempts to open the floor by inviting *some critique*. This utterance is directed to any student (other than Yvonne) in the class. He pauses as he waits for a student to participate. As teacher he generally has the power to determine the participation framework; he uses that authority to encourage all of the students to directly ask each other questions about the poem, which is consistent with his assumptions about Latino participation in the educational domain. In speech activity 2, Señor Xoci will not be the one who asks and answers questions, the role of the traditional teacher. Through his conversational moves in trying to establish the norms of interaction for speech activity 2, he accomplishes his goal of facilitating the students' development of (1) questioning skills, (2) Spanish conversational competence, and (3) an interactional history in which they see themselves as equal participants in the academic institutional discourse with the right to question. They are speaking for themselves, and taking responsibility for their thoughts, speech, and actions through cooperative learning. In other words, they are developing agency.

Susan catches Señor Xoci's eye during the pause. He recognizes her desire to participate with his utterance, *señorita?* in line 32. Susan is a white, native speaker of English. In lines 33–34 she attempts to ask a question about the poem in Spanish, the language of the class: *I don't understand um/the part about the school.* It is not obvious to whom Susan is directing this lack of understanding, because she does not index anyone directly. It is not even obvious that this utterance is a question. It is obvious, however, that this utterance is not a critique, which is what Señor Xoci originally requested. We see here that joint construction of meaning is more important than following explicit directions. In other words, mutual understanding of Yvonne's poem must precede critique. That Señor Xoci allows Susan to set the norms of interaction as questioning for clarification rather than critiquing is evidenced by his following utterances to help Susan get the clarification she indirectly requests. Susan's utterance is followed by a pause, demonstrating that the norms of interaction for who asks and answers questions have not yet been established. In a traditional teacher-centered classroom, students ask teachers questions, and teachers ask students questions. Students rarely ask other students questions directly, but as we have already seen, that is the goal for speech activity 2.

In any classroom, because the teacher has more power, it is the teacher's responsibility to determine norms of interaction governing participation. Therefore, the pause after Susan's utterance can be interpreted as an invitation for the teacher to take a turn to help the students understand what he expects them to do. Señor Xoci then invites Yvonne to take responsibility for her thoughts in lines 36–38, *you are/you are what/like a school Yvonne?* There is another pause. It seems that although Señor Xoci has indexed Yvonne directly, she still is not exactly sure what is expected of her here, so Tania, her neighbor, attempts to help Yvonne understand what Tania understands to be expected now. Tania tells Yvonne in English in lines 40–41 to *read the part/the part about the school.*

In line 42, Yvonne responds, *my heart is as big as a school,* which is a direct translation of her Spanish poem into English. Yvonne looks at Susan as she translates, demonstrating that she understands that it is appropriate for her to respond to Susan, not to the entire class. The translation without explanation shows that she interpreted Susan's question to be one of language understanding. Susan ratifies her hearing Yvonne's contribution with her response, *Oh?* in line 43; her rising intonation, however, suggests that she is not fully satisfied with this response.

That Señor Xoci is also not fully satisfied with Yvonne's translation is evidenced by his subsequent interactional moves. In line 44, he asks Yvonne directly, *why did you say this,* demonstrating his understanding that Susan still does not understand exactly what Yvonne means. Yvonne responds in line 45 *because a school is big,* but Señor Xoci apparently wants her to explore the relationship between her heart and a school further. This is consistent with his emphasis on the students' taking responsibility for what they say and to be ready to explain and defend their ideas.

Vygotsky's notion of the 'zone of proximal development' helps to understand Señor Xoci's interactional work here as well. By providing the first half of the next sentence in line 46, *and also inside of the school there is a lot of what,* Señor Xoci is partially supplementing her idea in order to help her grow, but he leaves the clause unfinished, providing the opportunity for Yvonne to finish it herself, which she does. Yvonne immediately repeats his words in line 48, *there is.* Then, in line 49, *there are many people,* Yvonne has to change the form of many in order to grammatically agree with her supplement of *people* (see original Spanish text: *hay **mucho** que* (line 46) — singular masculine form for the unmarked case changed to ***muchas** personas* (line 49) — plural feminine). Yvonne continues to supplement Señor Xoci's original supplement, demonstrating her confirmation of his addition. Through Señor Xoci's guidance, Yvonne is able to continue in her own personal development of how to take responsibility for her thoughts. Señor Xoci's utterance in line 51, *exactly* could be interpreted as encouraging Yvonne to continue. At least, this seems to be Yvonne's interpretation, because that is what she proceeds to do in the next few lines. This utterance could also be interpreted as a signal to Yvonne, and to the class, that this is the kind of participation and negotiation of meaning that is the goal of speech activity 2.

This sharing and critiquing of each other's work, as I mentioned in Chapter 8, is characteristic of many of the activities in which the students participate. In this way the students ideally gain an interactional history in which they come to see themselves as having not only the ability to speak two languages, but also the right to participate in the official educational discourse.

REFUSING THE DISCOURSE

As mentioned earlier, it is necessary but not sufficient for the students to develop interactional histories in which they see themselves as equals within the educational discourse. The minority students also need to be able to recognize when they are positioned negatively in the discourse, and to develop strategies to refuse that positioning and reposition themselves more favorably. In addition, the majority students need to be sensitive to this process so that they do not contribute to the perpetuation of discriminatory practices. The multicultural curriculum content, which revolves around history as a struggle between peoples, provides students such discursive opportunities.

The next segment provides an illustration of how the curriculum is designed to provide the students with practice in potentially problematic situations. In this way, they become aware of problems they may face outside of Oyster that position them negatively, and they develop the resources to position themselves as agentive.

During Black History Month Mrs Washington, the sixth-grade English-dominant teacher, gave the students a case study to read about Yvonne Braithwaite Burke who is now a prominent black judge. In the reading, Burke describes her experience as a black student, about the same age as these students, in an all white school. Burke tells a story about her class going on a class picnic to a whites-only park, which meant that Burke was not allowed to go. Burke's story represents her feelings of exclusion as instrumental in her decision to become a judge who fights for equal rights. At the end of the reading, Mrs Washington asked the students to respond to the following question: 'How would you have felt and what would you have done if you were Yvonne Braithwaite Burke?'. The students wrote their responses for homework, and shared their thoughts in class the next day.

In the next few pages I provide an analysis of one of the Latino student's responses which demonstrates her involvement with the task, her exploration of alternatives, and most importantly her agency. I number each of Elena's sentences for ease of discussion.

> 1 I would have felt really, really angry because first of all I was part of that class, and I had as many rights as the others in the class. 2 And second of all, I would be mad because they could have had the picnic in a park where blacks WERE allowed.
>
> 3 Then I would complain to the teacher and the principal. 4 I would tell them why I was angry and that what they had done was not fair. 5 That I was part of this class too! 6 I would say I expected at least an apology. 7 If they didn't apologize, I would tell my parents and I don't know if they could do anything, but at least I would know I had done the right thing.

I begin my discussion with an overview of the structural and functional organization of Elena's two-paragraph, seven-sentence response. In the first paragraph, which consists of two sentences, Elena represents her emotional reaction of anger, supported by reasons for her response. Consistent with the whole-language, multicultural curriculum approach, emotion is an integral part of the learning process, not something external to the learning process which should be left outside of the class so as to not interfere with more 'objective' learning. The second paragraph, which consists of five sentences, outlines the steps Elena would take to right what she constructs as unjust treatment.

Before I continue the analysis, a brief observation is in order with respect to language usage and skills development. In the last segment that I discussed, the poem 'Quien soy yo' ('Who am I ') was written at home in Spanish and shared in class the next day. In this segment, the students' response to the reading is written at home in English and shared in class the next day. As I mentioned earlier, this sharing format is used very often throughout the school activities. While my goal with the last excerpt was to represent the dynamics of the student interaction in response to the poem, and my goal in this excerpt is to discuss the student's written response, I want to point out some differences between the Spanish and English content-area instruction that are representative of what I found throughout the school.

In the last excerpt, I presented an African-American native English-speaker's work in Spanish and the following discussion. Recall that there was some code-switching to English for clarification of meaning, which seemed acceptable within the classroom discourse. Although I did not mention it there, the students' Spanish grammar was often simple, and at times incorrect. It was obvious from the exchange that took place in response to the poem that grammar was not a concern that day, or in my observation, was not generally a concern in the Spanish content-area classes in the sixth grade. The emphasis was on communication of meaning.

In this excerpt, Elena is a native Spanish speaker who is working in English. There are no codeswitches to Spanish in the English class, which as I have already explained can be attributed at least in part to the fact that the English-dominant teacher does not speak Spanish. In addition, the students have no difficulty express-ing themselves in English, which as I have mentioned can be explained at least in part by the sociopolitical context surrounding the Oyster discourse. Elena's English is both grammatically correct and complex, and appropriate for her writing purpose. The discrepancy between Spanish fluency and English fluency for the native English speakers and native Spanish speakers respectively is representative of what I observed throughout the school.

I repeat paragraph 1 (sentences 1 and 2) in order to discuss Elena's representation of her emotional response to the class's exclusion of her from the field trip because she was black.

> 1 I would have felt really, really angry because first of all I was part of that class, and I had as many rights as the others in the class. 2 And second of all, I would be mad because they could have had the picnic in a park where blacks WERE allowed.

In the first and second sentences, Elena constructs her response as *really, really angry*, and *mad*. In each case, she provides a reason for her emotional response, introduced by the discourse marker *because*. Her first reason involves a sense of community, *I was part of that class*. Based on Elena's understanding of the notion of community, i.e. of being a part of something (which as we have seen is emphasized throughout the Oyster discourse), everyone within the community ideally has *as many rights as the others in the class*. The construction of all students' having equal rights within the discourse is consistent with the ideal in mainstream US society, which as we have seen is rejected as myth by the Oyster collective. The Oyster goal is to provide an educational discourse in which all students see themselves as equal participants. Elena's response suggests her belief that this is part of the student's rights. Or if this sentence does not reflect her actual belief, her response at least suggests her recognition that the 'right answer' because Mrs Washington's class involves an emphasis on equal rights.

Elena's second reason for being angry relates to choice, another goal of the Oyster social identities project. According to Elena's construction, *they could have had the picnic in a park where blacks WERE allowed.* Elena represents the class's behavior as unjust because the class did have choices; they were not obliged to go to the *whites-only* park, but could have searched for a more inclusive option. Given her reasons for the class's unjustly excluding her, i.e. denial of her right as a part of the community, and given the other choices the class had available to them, Elena presents herself as legitimate in her angry emotional response.

But an emotional response on the part of one individual who has been treated unjustly is not sufficient for action. Based on my observations, social action is part of the goal of the Oyster social identities project. Social action is also presupposed by Mrs Washington's original question: 'How would you have felt and what would you have done?' In the second paragraph, Elena outlines her action. I repeat paragraph 2 here for ease of reference.

> 3 Then I would complain to the teacher and the principal. 4 I would tell them why I was angry and that what they had done was not fair. 5 That I was part of this class too! 6 I would say I expected at least an apology. 7 If they didn't apologize, I would tell my parents and I don't know if they could do anything, but at least I would know I had done the right thing.

There is a summary of Elena's representation of the participants, processes, and circumstances involved in her action to right what she perceives as unjust behavior toward her (see Halliday, 1985, for a further discussion of functional approach to discourse analysis on which this is based).

Participant		Process	Participants/Circumstances
(3)	I	complain	to teacher
	I	complain	to principal
(4)	I	tell	them why
(5)	I	be	part of class too
(6)	I	say	
	I	expect	apology
(7)	I	tell	parents
	I	do	right thing

An agentive individual takes action, refuses an unfavorable position, and repositions herself favorably. With paragraph 2, Elena describes the steps she would take to change her position. She would complain to people in power, equipped with evidence. She would demand an apology. The receipt of an apology from the teacher and principal would demonstrate to Elena their recognition of their wrong behavior, thus positioning Elena as right.

Sentence 7 demonstrates Elena's recognition of the possibility that the teacher and principal may refuse her discourse by not apologizing. Elena has a clearly thought-out plan of action; her next step would be to tell her parents, but she understands that they too might be powerless. The important issue to Elena is expressed in sentence 7, *at least I would know I had done the right thing*. The *right thing* in Elena's construction is to recognize and confront unjust behavior with evidence, stand up for her rights, and display her agency. Elena's response was ratified by the other students and by Mrs Washington as a 'good' solution. Elena's solution was similar to the solutions offered by the other students.

In sum, this sample of a sixth-grade student's work which makes explicit the 'right' way to confront discrimination, and which was ratified as a 'good' response, helps to make explicit expectations underlying the curriculum content. Not only are skills to be developed, and content to be mastered, but students are encouraged to recognize discriminatory positioning and reposition themselves favorably. This goal of the social identities project, however, is not limited to the curriculum content. The following example demonstrates how one of the sixth-grade students, deals with a contradiction in the classroom discourse by asserting her agency.

One day in the Spanish math class, the majority of the students were screaming and jumping enthusiastically in response to Señor Xoci's questions. Yolanda, a native Spanish-speaking Panamanian girl who is generally one of the most outspoken participants in the class, was behaving in a noticeably different manner (I missed the beginning of this activity to see what had caused her reaction, but it is not important to my discussion). Yolanda was sitting in her seat with her hand in the air, staring straight at the teacher. She was not moving or calling out, markedly different from her usual style, and in contrast to the other students. After about five minutes of this, when everyone had more or less calmed down, Señor Xoci called on Yolanda in Spanish. She responded in English:

1	**Yolanda:**	how come you told me
2		I have to raise my hand
3		and they can just scream out
4		all over the place
5		I've been here with my hand up
6		just like you told me
7		and you didn't even see me
8		that's not fair (her emphasis)
9		you're not treating me right (her emphasis).
10		(she folded her arms across her chest and stared straight ahead)
11	**T:**	Yolanda all right
12		you're right
13		I'm I'm sorry
14		it's not
15		I wasn't fair to you
16		thanks for telling me
17		please come talk to me about this later

| 18 | and we'll work it out |
| 19 | **vale?** (Ok?) |

Since this segment is relatively complex, I will break it down to illustrate the speech acts and positions that Señor Xoci and Yolanda take up and/or refuse.

According to Davies and Harré (1990), it is impossible to understand positioning without considering the associated notions of speech act and storyline. Their use of speech act, however, differs from the traditional linguistic notion which concentrates on speaker intention. In contrast, Davies and Harré see conversations as a structure of indeterminate speech actions which can become determinate speech acts to the extent that they are taken up by the other conversants. It is important to understand that the speaker's utterance, i.e. speech action, can perform multiple speech acts simultaneously. What the conversants take the topics and storylines to be will influence the way they take up each other's indeterminate speech actions as determinate speech acts. With this in mind, we can proceed to a discussion of Yolanda and Señor Xoci's interaction in order to understand how this student is learning to recognize and confront contradictions.

The first storyline involved Señor Xoci as teacher and Yolanda as student with a disciplinary problem. Apparently, Señor Xoci had told Yoland to raise her hand and not to call out. He had thus positioned himself as the authority with the power to make rules and Yolanda as the subordinate who must obey. The speech action was therefore disciplining.

Yolanda apparently initially took up Señor Xoci's speech action as he had presumably intended. She was sitting still with her hand raised, exactly as he had ordered. In this sense, his indeterminate speech action had become determinate. But his failure to recognize Yolanda when she had done what she was told led to a renegotiation, that is, it set off a new chain of speech actions. Yolanda's hand was raised, not because she was answering his question, but because she was angry at Señor Xoci's unfair treatment. The same non-verbal action, Yolanda's raised hand, can therefore be newly interpreted as a different social act.

When Señor Xoci called on Yolanda, apparently unaware of his unfair treatment, he probably expected her to ask a question or answer one of his questions in Spanish as a student with raised hand normally does. But Yolanda refused this discourse, thus demonstrating one aspect of her agency. That Yolanda was refusing Señor Xoci's discourse was evidenced very strongly by her use of English instead of Spanish, the official language of the class. Now let us look closely at each of Yolanda's statements to see how she positioned herself and Señor Xoci relative to each other, and what storyline she was following.

In lines 1–4, Yolanda utters, *how come you told me/I have to raise my/hand and they can just scream out/all over the place,* which, if we look only at the surface syntactic structure, looks like a request for information. But the fact that Yolanda did not pause after this utterance suggests that Yolanda did not want an answer to this question. This utterance, one speech action, performed at least two speech acts. First, it functioned as a complaint of Señor Xoci's unfair treatment. It can also be seen as a request for (1) Señor Xoci's public recognition of of his unfair treatment, (2) an explanation, and (3) possibly an apology for such treatment. Yolanda positioned herself as the recipient of unfair treatment, and she positioned Señor Xoci as unfair. The storyline she evoked was one of injustice.

Yolanda continued in lines 5–7, *I've been here with my hand up / just like you told me / and you didn't even see me,* which demonstrates Yolanda's following one of the norms of interaction in the classroom: any opinion you have is legitimate as long as you can support it with evidence, and take responsibility for your words and actions. With this statement, Yolanda positioned herself as reasonable and as one who adheres to the established rules of conduct on two levels. Not only did she raise her hand, as Señor Xoci had told her, but she also substantiated her complaint with hard evidence. Her utterance has further positioned Señor Xoci as unjust. Yolanda continued this storyline of injustice in lines 8–9, *that's not fair/you're not treating me right.* She refused Señor Xoci's discourse by not speaking Spanish. She justified this refusal with examples, concluded with her opinion of Señor Xoci's behavior, and that was all she had to say. In this respect, Yolanda was clearly displaying her agency to Señor Xoci, the rest of the students, and to herself.

It is important to remember that justice, fairness, and equal treatment for all are some of the most valued qualities in Oyster, and form the core of the social identities project. Yolanda's utterances constructed Señor Xoci as wrong and unjust, a serious contradiction with Señor Xoci's construction of himself. Let us look closely at his response to see how he reconciled the contradiction that Yolanda brought to his attention.

Note that Señor Xoci's response to Yolanda, like Yolanda's utterance, is in English. And recall that the Spanish-dominant teacher is to speak Spanish and be spoken to only in Spanish. Although Yolanda switched to English, the explanation is not one of language comprehension, because Yolanda is a native speaker of Spanish. Perhaps Señor Xoci's use of English can be understood as symbolically reflecting his attempt to reconcile with Yolanda by using the language that she has chosen. Or perhaps it could be a subtle revelation of a hidden value 'use English, the High language for serious purposes'. Support for this interpretation can be found in Chapter 7, in which the Spanish-dominant kindergarten teacher switched to English, the High language in mainstream society, to discipline the children, as well as in other speech communities around the world (Fasold, 1984).

With lines 11–12, *Yolanda alright / you're right,* Señor Xoci accepted Yolanda's positioning of him as wrong and unfair. In order to successfully reconstruct himself as a fair, just individual, Señor Xoci had to do some repair work. In line 13, Señor Xoci apologizes, *I'm I'm sorry.* Part of being a fair person, the position he needed to reconstruct for himself, is being able to admit to your mistakes. So this speech action functioned as both an apology for his unfairness, and the beginning of his attempt to reposition himself as fair.

Señor Xoci began his next utterance with *it's not* (line 14), but changed to *I wasn't fair to you* in line 15. His shift from the impersonal *it's* to the personal *I* can be interpreted as reflecting his willingness to take full responsiblity for his earlier mistake, and emphasizing his position as fair. He continued by thanking Yolanda in line 16, *thanks for telling me.* Why would Señor Xoci thank Yolanda at this point? Perhaps he was thanking her for bringing a personal mistake to his attention, so he could remedy the problem. Or perhaps he was thanking her for displaying her agency to him and to the rest of the class. She demonstrated for all of the students that she saw injustice, challenged it, and reconciled the problem. This is exactly the kind of minority social identity that Oyster is trying to develop in order to succeed in mainstream US society.

Why didn't Señor Xoci stop there? He continued in lines 17–18, *please come talk to me about this later and we'll work it out.* What was left for them to work out? Señor Xoci publicly recognized his unjust behavior and apologized, which enabled him to reposition himself as fair. His lengthy response, taking up official class time, demonstrated to the class that this kind of injustice is a serious issue, and something that he and Yolanda may need to work out personally. It also positioned Señor Xoci as the kind of person who is willing to go out of his way to correct a wrong, further demonstrating his fairness.

In line 19, *vale?* (Ok?), Señor Xoci switched back to Spanish, the official language of the class and the language he is to always use. With this speech action, Señor Xoci demonstrated that he had finished working out the problem with Yolanda, and it was time to continue with official classroom business. His use of rising intonation invited her ratification of the problem as resolved.

It was obvious that Yolanda accepted this because she continued in the class, and spoke Spanish with the rest of the class. She had displayed her agency and had reconciled a problem in a satisfactory manner. This kind of interactional experience provided practice for interaction in mainstream US society when the individual is faced with injustice. It is the school's goal for these kinds of skills to become second nature so that the students have the ability to position themselves agentively when they leave Oyster.

CONSTRUCTING AN ALTERNATIVE DISCOURSE

I have argued throughout this study that Oyster constructed an alternative educational discourse based on their assumption that mainstream US society does not provide equal educational opportunity to minority populations. I have also argued that central to their alternative discourse is the students' development of agency, which requires recognizing and refusing discriminatory practices, and constructing alternatives which are more equitable. I have attempted to illustrate how the curriculum is organized around this principle. I provide the following example of one of the sixth-grade student's stories that reflects her recognition of a historical omission, her refusal of that representation, and her construction of an alternative. This example was not part of her schoolwork; it was a task she took on herself. I am not saying that Oyster necessarily caused this student to write this story. I am saying that the story illustrates the student's critical thinking about historical representations, questioning those representations, and constructing an alternative, which is an important goal of the Oyster social identities project.

Specifically, Beth, a white native English-speaking student showed me a book that she had written about the Shang Dynasty. When I was reading Beth's book, the first thing that struck me was that three of the five warriors that she described were women. For example, Beth writes in the introduction of the book:

> **Yoshi Orimo:** Orimo grew up in Korea, where she learned Tae Kwon Do, a form of Karate. Later she came to Chung Kuo and studied Shang at the age of 12. At 15 she was given the title of the Unicorn. Yoshi Orimo was the fastest thing on two feet, all silk and steel and lightening. Unfortunately she was poisoned at the young age of 36.
> **Seiji Sato:** Sato was trained in Shang beginning at the age of 5. Sato was one of the only people brave enough to enter the Basht Woods. Now she walks among the gods as an immortal.

In one of my conversations with Beth, I asked her where she had gotten her ideas for the book:

Rebecca:	Ok and you were telling me about um … you said that you read a book about a princess or a?
Beth:	it was a girl
Rebecca:	yeah
Beth:	and she became a knight … and they were really neat..
Rebecca:	um what do you remember about the story
Beth:	um
Rebecca:	that inspired you to write this … because what's interesting about here is that you have a whole lot of warriors that are women
Beth:	yeah because um … that's one thing … because in history they hardly ever had anyone that were women … they usually just passed them over … even if they did something … so I decided that … that the women that I made up should be more recognized

As I discussed in Chapter 4, I came to understand the Oyster social identities project as concerned with providing equal educational opportunities to any minority (in the power sense) student, rather than exclusively to Latino students as I had originally thought. The teachers that I talked to emphasized their concern with Latino, African American, and lower socioeconomic populations. Although I once saw a bulletin board with student essays about women's historical contributions, I never observed gender to be a major concern within Oyster. However, the underlying principle of the social identities project is that all groups, including those who have traditionally been marginalized, have equal right to participate. This clearly can be extended to gender relations, as Beth points out in her explanation of the need to write a history in which *the women that I made up should be more recognized.*

I include one of Beth's stories entitled 'Anj'la and Norrin' that reverses traditional gender relations in mainstream US society: the woman is positioned as wiser than the man and responsible for peaceful reconciliation of conflict.

Anj'la and Norrin

Norrin was ruler of Sarain many years ago. About 100 years after Miache, Zefram, and the Jewel disappeared, Norrin found the Jewel while hunting. He did not know what such a beautiful jewel was doing in the dirt, so he brought it back to his wife Anj'la, who was wise beyond her years. Anj'la recognized the Jewel at once. Norrin was not Gifted, and had heard only the legends of the Jewel. But Anj'la, knowing herblore and having a little of the Gift, knew the full extent of the Jewel's powers. With the Dominion Jewel, Sarain was saved from many civil wars, until one day Norrin lost the Jewel. After that there was a violent civil war that ripped Sarain apart. Norrin and Anj'la were killed, and the throne was left to their daughter Marental. She was a wise ruler, and brought Sarain back to a peaceful land again. But the Jewel was still lost. It eventually made its way to Old Chitral, who lives in Chitral's Path at the Roof of the World, waiting for someone to fight it for the Jewel. Take it for the saving of a troubled land.

Beth's story demonstrates her rejection of traditional representations of women as not as wise or as powerful as men. Her story illustrates her construction of an alternative discourse for women: the women are wise and powerful. Power is indirectly defined as the ability to stop war and bring peace to the land, which also opposes traditional definitions of power as brute force. This refusal of traditional discourse which positions the minority negatively (or omits the minority contribution entirely), and construction of an alternative in which the minority is positioned favorably is consistent with the goals of the Oyster social identities project.

CONCLUSION

My ethnographic/discourse analytic study of Oyster Bilingual School has argued that Oyster's bilingual program has two complementary agendas that together challenge the unequal distribution of rights in mainstream US schools and society. First, the dual-language program is organized so that language minority and language majority students have the opportunity to develop the ability to speak two languages and to achieve academically through both languages. Second, the social identities project is organized so that language minority students gain experience seeing themselves as having the right to participate equally in the academic discourse, and the language majority students gain experience respecting that right.

This chapter has provided micro-level analyses of excerpts of sixth-grade inter-action and student work that illustrate how the teachers socialize their language minority and language majority students into seeing themselves as having equal participation rights at school. The chapter began by providing a concrete example of the discursive construction of agency. We saw how Señor Xoci's assumptions about cross-cultural differences in Latino/Anglo participation rights inform the way that he organizes classroom practices, which are intended to position students as individuals who can make choices and take responsibility for their thoughts, feelings, and actions. Because the Oyster educators assume that students need strategies to counter discrimination outside of school, they design their program and practices to provide students the opportunity to develop strategies to challenge the negative positioning they may encounter. The second part of the chapter presented examples of how the curriculum content and classroom interaction in the sixth grade are organized to provide students with the opportunity to recognize discriminatory positioning, refuse discriminatory discourse practices, and reposition themselves more favorably in alternative discourses. The third part of the chapter presented an example of a student's recognition of an important historical omission, and her efforts to write a more inclusive history.

The micro-level interactions presented in this chapter and in Chapter 9 provide concrete evidence of the patterns that I identified throughout the school, and increase the validity and the reliability of the study. In addition, these and other interactions like them reflect and shape the larger sociopolitical context of Oyster Bilingual School. My ethnographic/discourse analytic study has demonstrated that an analysis of how a dual-language program functions on the local level would be incomplete without an understanding of classroom level processes. Likewise, my analyses of classroom level processes would be incomplete without an understanding of macro-level relationships between Oyster's alternative educational discourse and main-stream US educational and societal discourses. Integrating the levels of analysis, and continually moving from one level to another, allows for a more comprehensive understanding of what is going on at Oyster Bilingual School and why.

Because of the teachers' powerful role in socializing students into understanding their speaking positions and social roles at school and in society, classrooms and schools can be considered rich ground for social change. As I have emphasized throughout this book, the notion of positioning is key. Mainstream US schools can continue to reflect and perpetuate the subordinate role of minority students through forced assimilation to majority ways of speaking and interacting. Or they can organize their programs and practices to challenge the subordination of minority students, and help their students see themselves as agents, who can make choices and take responsibility for their thoughts, beliefs, and actions. While the particulars of how the Oyster educators are not directly translatable to another context, these underlying goals are clearly generalizable. I turn now to Chapter 11, the conclusion of the book, which takes us beyond Oyster Bilingual School.

CHAPTER 11

Beyond Oyster Bilingual School: Implications for Research and Practice

The ethnographically-oriented discourse analysis of how the Oyster educators interpret and implement their bilingual program illustrated how the Oyster educators (1) believe that mainstream US educational and societal discourse practices discriminate against minority students; (2) refuse that discourse; and (3) have constructed an alternative educational discourse that enables their linguistically and culturally diverse student population to achieve more or less equally. Analyzing Oyster's dual-language plan as an integrated part of the school's cultural communication system allowed us to see that their successful program is about much more than language in the traditional sense. Oyster Bilingual School's discourse practices reflect an ideological assumption that linguistic and cultural diversity is a resource to be developed by all students, and not a problem that minority students must overcome in order to participate and achieve at school.

Oyster's educational policies, curricular choices, classroom organizations, and assessment practices provide concrete evidence of how the educators are working together to promote social change by elevating the status of Spanish and Spanish speakers in particular and of minority languages and minority populations more generally throughout the school. Language minority and language majority students' socializing experience through this educational discourse encourages them to see linguistic and cultural diversity as a natural way of life. The school's emphasis on developing linguistic and cultural resources is intended to provide all students more options than those traditionally available to students in mainstream US schools and society.

233

This final chapter goes beyond the case study of Oyster Bilingual School to suggest directions for research and practice in other educational contexts. I have divided the chapter into two parts. The first part addresses the question: 'What happens when the students leave Oyster Bilingual School?' Intertextual analysis of stories that Oyster Bilingual School students told during the first year of their experience in the monolingual public junior high school that many attend after they graduate from Oyster provides a preliminary understanding of the kinds of tensions these students experience in a mainstream US school. In addition to suggesting ways that practitioners can alleviate similar tensions for language minority students in other contexts, this discussion further supports the argument that Oyster has constituted itself by an alternative to mainstream US educational discourse with respect to language use and intergroup relations.

Ethnographic research, however, aims to provide more than a local theory about the context under study. As Watson-Gegeo (1988: 580–1) writes,

> a carefully done emic analysis precedes and forms the basis for etic extensions that allow for cross-cultural or cross-setting comparisons ... The ethnographer first seeks to build a theory of the setting under study, then to extrapolate or generalize from that setting to others studied in a similar way. The comparison must be built on careful emic work, and it must be recognized that direct comparison of the details of two or more settings is usually not possible. Comparison is possible at a more abstract level, however.

Because no other dual-language program has been studied in a similar way to date, cross-setting comparisons are impossible at this stage in our understanding. The second part of the chapter therefore summarizes the major theoretical and methodological points of the ethnographic/discourse analytic approach that I took to understand how Oyster's dual-language program functions in its local context. This discussion is intended to assist other researchers who want to take a similar approach to understanding another dual-language education context.

WHAT HAPPENS WHEN STUDENTS LEAVE OYSTER?

After describing how Oyster's program is organized to challenge mainstream US discourse practices, I am regularly asked: 'What happens when the students leave Oyster?' This very general, open-ended question is then followed up by a series of questions like the following: Do the native Spanish-speakers maintain their Spanish language and culture as their experience in the bilingual school explicitly recommends? Or do they assimilate to monolingualism in English and to white middle-class norms as mainstream US schools generally encourage? Do the native English-speakers continue to develop their Spanish? How do these language minority and language majority students interact with students from different backgrounds? Do they value linguistic and cultural diversity and seek out integrated groups? Or do they segregate themselves according to linguistic, ethnic, and racial boundaries that generally divide groups in mainstream US schools and society?

The majority of these questions are yes/no questions, and suggest that the larger question — 'What happens when students leave Oyster?' — may have a relatively straightforward answer. I learned quite accidently, however, that the story is more complicated than this. At the beginning of my second year at Oyster, I was teaching an Introduction to Language class at Georgetown University. One of my students, Jim, a native English-speaking white male, chose to write on his speech community and his experience in a bilingual elementary school which turned out to be Oyster Bilingual School. It is important to emphasize that Jim did not know I was conducting research at Oyster nor did I know that he had graduated from Oyster at the time he wrote his essay.

In two paragraphs taken from that essay, Jim describes and evaluates the Oyster Bilingual School experience. The first paragraph is consistent with what the Oyster educators described, and is consistent with my observations. The second paragraph, however, presents what he evaluates as the most important part of his story (italicized).

> My speech community is truly a different community in many respects. The most interesting aspect of my speech community is that it is so infiltrated with people of Hispanic origin. There are so many Hispanics that twenty years ago the DC Public Schools System converted the neighborhood school to a bilingual format. It is one of the oldest bilingual schools in the country and its format is truly unique. The Hispanics and natives are mixed equally into classes and the subjects are taught half in Spanish and half in English. Its uniqueness comes in the fact that once the children learned English, their Spanish lessons were not discontinued. As a result, I learned how to speak Spanish at age five, yet I was still studying science and social studies in Spanish at age twelve.
>
> This was a great experience for me because not only did I learn a foreign language at a young age, I also learned to deal with non-native speakers, made many long-lasting friendships, learned from teachers who taught in different styles than the typical American teacher and most importantly *now see the alienation of the Hispanic student as he gets away from bilingual school and into high school and college* [my emphasis]. I recently met the top student of my elementary school class and she has no plans to go to college. Many of my elementary school classmates now have babies and are destined to live like their parents. This problem will affect America in the next few years and it was because of my educational experience that I'm aware of this problem.

Jim's story alerted me to the need to investigate what happens when students leave Oyster. I therefore decided to follow the students I had worked with for a year when they were sixth graders at Oyster to the monolingual junior high school they attended in seventh grade. Of the 21 students who had been in the sixth-grade class, 11 attended this school. I interviewed all of them about their experiences in both schools, and consistently found stories that reflected forces pulling them away from seeing Spanish and English as valuable and from seeing Spanish and English speakers as equal. These stories illustrate the pressure that the students experience not to speak Spanish and not to be identified with Spanish speakers in the monolingual junior high school.

The following story arose in response to a question I asked Gabriela, a native Spanish-speaking Salvadoran student who had gone to Oyster, about why native Spanish speakers do not associate with students they call 'ESLs' who speak Spanish at the junior high school. The transcript is marked to reflect the categories of people that Gabriela mentions: Native Spanish speakers who speak English are italicized; native English speakers, either black or white are set in bold italic; and ESLs who are native Spanish speakers that do not speak English are boldfaced.

Gabriela: well ... because ... what happens in this school is ... ok if *you're* real good friends with **somebody** ... let's say **a black person** or a **white person** ... right?

Rebecca: you mean yourself as a *Latino person*

Gabriela: yeah ... ok and *they* find *you* hanging around or talking with an **ESL person** ... then *they* start talking bad about *you* and everything .... *they* start calling *you* names and everything ... that's why *people* don't hang around with **ESLs**

Rebecca: like what kind of names

Gabriela: well ... *they* start calling *you* the names *they* call the **ESL people** ... like *they* start making fun of *you*

Rebecca: like what

Gabriela: well ... today in the hall **this ninth grader** called **this ESL person** an enchilada and everything ... all these Spanish names right? so

Rebecca: and what kind of ... who was the ninth grader ... from where

Gabriela: *she* was black ... *she* was from Washington

Rebecca: so it's um ... so it's not ... is it um ... the Latinos who speak English who were born here? ... do they treat the ESLs the same way? ... or?

Gabriela: [*you*] just stay away from **them** so *you* don't get the same treatment

Gabriela's utterance, *what happens in this school,* reflects her assumption that other things happen in other schools, for example in Oyster where she and I had worked together the year before. Her utterances, *and they find you hanging around or talking with an ESL person, then they start talking bad about you and everything,* reflects her expectation of peer pressure in the monolingual school to not speak Spanish and to not associate with Spanish speakers. The negative treatment she describes echoes the Oyster educators' description of the problem for native Spanish speakers in mainstream US discourse, which led to the construction of Oyster in effort to resolve this problem (see Chapter 5). Gabriela's resolution to the problem, *just stay away from them so you don't get the same treatment,* illustrates her movement away from her native language and culture in order to assimilate into the native English-speaking category. Her lexical choice is reminiscent of how, for example, Señora Ortega and Señor Xoci metaphorically talked about being forced to leave their native language, culture, and identity.

In the next story, Yvonne evokes and rejects the language-as-problem orientation (Ruiz, 1984) that characterizes mainstream US discourse in favor of Oyster's language-as-resource orientation (Ruiz, 1984). Yvonne is a native English-speaking African American student who learned Spanish at Oyster. In this first excerpt, the message is clear that a black native English speaker should not speak Spanish in the monolingual junior high school.

> like one day my friend Raquel ... um Raquel doesn't speak English so I was talking to her in Spanish ... and one of my friends said **stop talking like that girl** [codeswitches to AAVE intonation to construct dialog] **that's not your language**

Yvonne's statement reflects the racial tension that prevails throughout Washington, DC between the African American and Latino communities, and which is characteristic of many cities in the US. At this point in her life, at least in conversation with me, Yvonne says she views the Spanish language and her Spanish-speaking friends favorably. She explained her reason for wanting to maintain her Spanish, become a lawyer, and fight for equal rights in the District as follows (boldface indicates her emphasis):

Yvonne: because I'm bilingual for one thing ... I want to *prove* that being bilingual *does* get you somewhere
Rebecca: what do you mean ... why did you say prove
Yvonne: because nobody thinks being bilingual means anything ... I mean ... how many bilingual schools *are* there in DC

In this excerpt, Yvonne reflects her awareness and rejection of mainstream US discourse's evaluation of bilingualism, and her choice to fight to prove the legitimacy of the language-as-resource orientation that characterizes Oyster's discourse. This illustrates Yvonne's recognition of choice in how we use language to represent and evaluate each other.

The following excerpts from two of the native Spanish-speaking students' stories reflect tension between the expectation of assimilation to white middle-class ways that characterizes mainstream US discourse, and the expectation of cultural pluralism in which diversity is expected, tolerated, and respected that characterizes the Oyster discourse. This first excerpt is taken from a conversation in which Rosa, a native Spanish-speaking Mexican student who attended Oyster, and I were talking about social groupings at the junior high school. The part that is bold italic reflects the mainstream expectation of assimilation and the part that is italicized reflects the Oyster expectation of cultural pluralism:

> you know ... but if they ask me you know ... who who ... where are you from ... I would always say ... *although people confuse me ... they think I'm from here*

> *right … and I could always say … oh you know … I am … but I don't say that*
> *because I know … I'm proud of being from Mexico*

Rosa, at least in conversation with me at this point in her life seems to reject pressure
to abandon her Mexican identity. Isabel, a native Spanish speaker from Salvador
that graduated from Oyster, described similar pressures to me as follows: 'my friend
said why don't you just tell people you're white … no one would know the
difference'.

As this preliminary analysis makes clear, there is no easy answer to the question:
'What happens when the students leave Oyster?' Some of the native Spanish
speakers may continue to positively evaluate the Spanish language and Spanish-
speaking people and choose to develop their native language and that aspect of their
social identity. Others may choose to reject their native language and cultural
background in effort to alleviate the negative evaluation of themselves as speakers
of Spanish and as different. And of this group some may later in life learn to
positively evaluate their native language and culture as Señor Xoci and Señora
Ortega recount they did. While it is impossible to predict the outcomes of the
students' socialization through Oyster's alternative educational discourse, this
analysis raises several theoretical issues that suggest directions for educational
practice in other contexts.

The case study of Oyster Bilingual School builds on the theoretical assumption
of the constitutive nature of discourse. That is, people develop their understanding
of who they are and their relation to others in the social world through their
experience in language-mediated interactions. My preliminary research on students'
experiences at Oyster Bilingual School and beyond demonstrates how local ideologies about language use and social interaction structure social relations very
differently in the two schools. This work reflects the central role of local values,
meanings, and practices in the social construction of identity which I understand to
be a dynamic, negotiated, and negotiable process. How social identities are constructed and displayed shows tremendous variation across contexts, which suggests
that discourse communities have choices in how they organize themselves. The
ideological choices that schools make, whether consciously made or not, have
important implications for minority students.

The case study of Oyster Bilingual School demonstrates that schools can collectively organize and construct alternative discourses that position minority students
more favorably that mainstream US discourse does. It also suggests extending the
Oyster model or models like it that are organized to socialize minority students, by
which I mean other than white middle-class native English-speaking students, into
seeing more options than those traditionally available to them. Educational programs and practices like those at Oyster that do not require minority students to
assimilate to mainstream ways in order to participate and achieve in school, but that
provide minority students with other choices in how they define and evaluate

themselves, can help minority students find creative ways to alleviate the kinds of tensions that we saw in the Oyster graduates' stories.

Before I proceed to a discussion of how researchers can investigate how dual-language programs function in other contexts, I want to draw attention to another important theoretical point. That is, we see a contradiction between the way that the Oyster educators metaphorically represent language, culture, and identity as relatively static and as separate and separable from the individual on the one hand, and the emergent culture and social identities they are jointly constructing with the Oyster students' on the other. By recognizing and rejecting discriminatory practices against language minority students in mainstream US society, and by constructing Oyster's alternative educational discourse, Oyster Bilingual School is making it possible for language minority students to develop positively evaluated minority social identities whose differences are expected, tolerated, and respected in school; identities which, at least from the Oyster perspective, are not readily available in mainstream US discourse.

RESEARCHING DUAL-LANGUAGE PROGRAMS IN OTHER CONTEXTS: A MULTI-LEVEL ANALYSIS

The ethnographic/discourse analytic approach that I took in the Oyster Bilingual School study builds on the theoretical assumption of the constitutive nature of discourse mentioned earlier. Because I assume that the micro-level socializing classroom discourse is shaped by the macro-level institutional and societal levels of discourse, this section describes how researchers and practitioners, working either independently or in collaboration, can take a similar approach to analysing relationships between another dual-language policy and the multiple levels of context in which it is situated. This approach allows researchers and/or practitioners to see that discrepancies between ideal policy and actual implementation can be understood as macro-level power struggles between competing ideological discourses that are working themselves out in the micro-level classroom level interaction. While the particulars of the sociopolitical struggles and the explanations for those struggles are likely to vary considerably from one context to another, the discrepancies that the researcher identifies can suggest areas to target for reform.

The defining features of dual-language programs provide an excellent entry point for analysis across the levels of context that I describe in the remainder of the chapter. As discussed in Chapter 1, dual-language education programs serve balanced numbers of students from two language backgrounds who study the content-areas through two languages. While the two languages are clearly separated for instructional purposes, students from both language backgrounds are integrated for the majority of their content-area instruction. All dual-language programs have three goals in common (of course, a particular program may have additional goals): (1) all students are to become bilingual and biliterate; (2) all students are to achieve academically in both languages; and (3) all students are to develop improved intergroup understanding and relations. In order for students to develop bilingual proficiency, dual-language programs last at least four to six years. These programs are characterized by a language-as-resource orientation that draws on the native languages and cultural backgrounds of the two student populations as resources in achieving their goals. While recognizing diversity in student backgrounds, teachers have equally high expectations of academic achievement for all of their students. These defining criteria provide the grounding for an investigation of how a particular dual-language program is interpreted and implemented in any educational context.

Understanding relationships among the multiple levels of authority in the school

Conceptualizing dual-language-planning as dynamic, ideological processes that are shaped by the multiple levels of authority within the school context offers a theoretical basis for the methodological approach that I describe in this section. This assumption requires the researcher to develop an understanding of what the levels of authority are within the school, with attention to power relations within and across these decision-making levels. Because Chapter 4 provides a detailed description of how I investigated this point at Oyster Bilingual School, here I limit my discussion to areas that researchers may want to consider as they attempt to gain an insider's understanding of how a dual-language program functions in another school context.

First and foremost, it is essential to consider the dual-language program's relationship to the larger school structure. At Oyster, the dual-language plan is an integral part of the entire school structure. Analysis of how the program relates to the institutional level of context, although labor intensive, was relatively straight-forward. Perhaps because Oyster's dual-language program has been firmly established throughout the entire school for over 20 years, and/or because the Oyster educators have a genuine commitment to Oyster community members' ongoing communication about how the program functions, my analysis of how the dual-language program achieved its goals revealed considerable coherence in assumptions across the levels of institutional authority (i.e. policymaker, administrator, teacher, see Chapter 4 for further discussion). I found that all of the Oyster educators were working toward the same goals with the same ideological assumptions about language use and cultural diversity in relation to academic achievement. Linguistic and cultural diversity was consistently constructed as a resource to be developed, not as a problem to be overcome. This coherence translated into consistent implementation of the dual-language program on the classroom level throughout the school.

Not all programs, however, are implemented throughout the entire school. Some programs are implemented only in the lower grades and plan to spread through the grades over time. Other programs are located only in particular 'teams', or 'charters' or 'small-learning communities' (see Christian & Whitcher, 1995, for a survey of this program variation). In these cases, it is important to understand what the dual-language program means to the administrators, educators, and students, who work inside of the dual-language program as well as to those who work outside of the program in other parts of the school. There may be competing discourses, for example, about the value of bilingualism, or about the possibility of students studying content-areas through two languages and achieving in both languages, or about what the target populations can and should be expected to achieve. It is especially important to investigate the possibility of competing discourses in developing dual-language programs because such competition will make it more difficult for the program to meet its goals in the way the policy articulates.

Questions like the following can guide this level of analysis. Is there coherence in assumptions about how the program is to function among those who work within the dual-language program as well as those who work outside of the program in other parts of the school? Does everyone support the program goals and understand the defining criteria? For example, do the people who make decisions that affect the composition of the program (e.g. placement, curriculum design, assessment) operate under the same assumptions that define dual-language programs? Furthermore, how is this program represented and evaluated throughout the school? As a special program for the gifted and talented? As a remedial program for Limited English Proficient students? Educators' and students' beliefs about the goals of the program and about the students it serves will influence how the program is implemented on the classroom level.

Let us take the notion of 'target population' to illustrate the importance of going beyond the literature and/or beyond the official policy to investigate educators' beliefs and practices. Dual-language programs, by definition, target students from two different language backgrounds and clearly separate the two languages for purposes of instruction. This definition could suggest a program assumption of two different target populations that are defined by language background. The researcher, however, should not be limited by the categories of students that the educational policy explicitly identifies. Ongoing observations of interactions at school and open-ended interviews with program students, teachers, and administrators can help the outsider understand what categories are relevant to the participants.

For example, while language background is clearly an important organizing principle at Oyster Bilingual School, the categories *native Spanish speaker* and *native English speaker* are not the only categories that matter to the people who interact with each other there. The categories *majority* (white middle-class native English speaker) and *minority* (other than majority, e.g. African American, Salvadoran, native Spanish speaker, etc.) are very important to the teachers and administrators at Oyster who see mainstream US educational and societal discourse as discriminatory against minority groups. *Socioeconomic class* is another very important category that the teachers organize their practices around because they believe that the students from low-income backgrounds have fewer educational supports and more emotional problems at home than students from middle- or upper-income backgrounds. The teachers also believe that the categories *language background* and *socioeconomic class* often get confused because the native Spanish speakers tend to come from low-income backgrounds and the native English speakers tend to come from middle-income backgrounds. And as we saw earlier in this chapter, the category *ESL* is also relevant to the native Spanish-speaking Oyster graduates when they go to the junior high school because of the stigmatization of this social group in that school context.

The categories that are socially relevant at Oyster and the relationships across categories will more than likely not be the same in another educational context, and they may change over time at Oyster. Through open-ended interviews and ongoing observations, researchers can identify what categories are meaningul to the various participants in the context under study. The important theoretical point to keep in mind is there are multiple facets of social identity, and that any facet may be more or less relevant depending on the activity being investigated. So, for example, language background may be a very important marker of social identity in some activities, while gender and/or ethnicity and/or socioeconomic class may be more or less salient in other activities. The goal of the analysis is to develop an insider's understanding of what aspects of social identity are meaningful and how they are meaningful under what circumstances. Such an analysis will yield an understanding of how difference is socially constructed through discourse in that educational context.

The assumption that social identity is dynamic and continually negotiated through ongoing interaction in language-mediated activities means that the choices educators make in how they organize educational programs and classroom practices have powerful implications for students' understanding of themselves relative to each other and of the opportunities available to them. I will return to this point in my discussion of the classroom level of context.

The point to be emphasized to researchers who are investigating how the dual-language program is interpreted throughout the school level of context is that it is essential to listen to what the various educators and students at the school say about the dual-language program. Key to understanding Oyster's perspective on its successful program is its opposition to mainstream US school and societal treatment of language minority populations. This takes us to a discussion of the societal level of context.

Relating program goals to societal assumptions

As previously mentioned, the three policy goals, (1) bilingualism for students from both language backgrounds, (2) high expectations of academic achievement for all students, and (3) the development of a culturally pluralistic atmosphere characterized by positive intergroup understanding and relations, provide the basis for comparison across all of the levels of context. On the societal level, the researcher can ask: 'What are mainstream societal beliefs and practices relative to these policy goals historically and today for the populations that the program is intended to serve?'

Taking the United States as an example, we have seen that since World War I mainstream schools and society have generally assumed that an individual must speak Standard English and behave according to white middle-class norms in order to have access to mainstream US institutions. Standard English (the majority language) and white middle class speakers of Standard English (language majority speakers) are therefore attributed more prestige than other language varieties or speakers of other language varieties in mainstream US schools and society. This assumption has different implications for language minority and language majority speakers relative to US institutions.

I will begin with the language majority population. In order to achieve in school and get a good job in US society, the language majority speaker traditionally has not needed to become bilingual or to learn how to interact with people from other cultural backgrounds. In fact, not only has such linguistic and intercultural competence been unnecessary for language minority speakers, it has been considered exceptional.

The situation has been quite different for language minority speakers. Since the turn of the century, mainstream US societal institutions have exerted considerable pressure on language minority speakers to become monolingual in English and to assimilate to white middle-class Standard English-speaking norms. The minority language and cultural background have generally been considered problems that the language minority individual must overcome in order to participate effectively in mainstream US institutions. It is also important to mention that expectations for achievement have tended to be lower for language minority populations. Although discrimination based on background has been illegal in the United States since the Civil Rights Act of 1964 was passed, considerable research has demonstrated that language minority speakers in general, and native Spanish speakers in particular, have been systematically blocked from equal educational opportunities in mainstream US institutions. Such systematic discrimination reflects and contributes to ongoing misunderstandings and tensions between linguistically and culturally diverse social groups (see Chapters 2 and 3 for further discussions of these points).

Because the goals of a dual-language program are in opposition to the norms that structure relations in mainstream US society, we can expect that efforts to implement a dual-language program in the United States will not be met without resistance and struggle. We can also expect to see evidence of the macro-level sociopolitical struggle in the micro-level classroom interaction. Oyster Bilingual School has an established dual-language program that is considered successful by a variety of sources, and we saw gaps between the ideal policy and actual classroom implementation that were explained by understanding relationships between Oyster's norms and mainstream US societal norms. New programs should certainly anticipate some resistance, and should prepare ways to identify and counter that resistance. I will return to this point in my discussion of the situation level of context below.

It is important not to generalize from the mainstream US societal level of context to other national contexts. Researchers investigating how dual-language programs function in another national context will need to consider sociopolitical relations, both historically and currently, between the target language groups in the society in question. Questions such as the following can guide this level of analysis. Who are the target language groups? What are mainstream societal assumptions about language use, academic achievement, and intergroup relations for the target populations today? Historically? How have these assumptions shaped opportunities at school and in the workforce for the various target populations?

Any discussion of mainstream school and societal assumptions, however, is necessarily based on general tendencies. There is likely to be considerable variation in community assumptions and expectations relative to the goals of dual-language programs that will influence how the policy is interpreted and implemented in practice. The researcher will therefore need to investigate how the dual-language policy interacts with local community beliefs and practices.

Relating community beliefs and practices to program goals

Since my concern in the Oyster Bilingual School study was to understand the Oyster School educators' interpretations about what made their program successful with its target populations, I did not directly investigate the community level of context myself. The Oyster educators, however, repeatedly expressed their assumptions that the *school* must understand local beliefs and practices in order for them to know how to work with their target populations. These educators emphasized in numerous ways how they work with the various populations they identify in the community in order to ensure that everyone understands and shares the same goals about the children's education. The assumption is that if parents, for example, do not share the school's assumptions about bilingualism, academic achievement, and intergroup relations, the children will be receiving mixed messages and the policy is unlikely to succeed. According to the Oyster educators, it is therefore the school's responsibility to find ways to understood, build on, and transform if necessary, community beliefs and practices that relate to their children's education (see Chapter 6 for further discussion).

Before researchers can investigate the community beliefs and practices relate to the goals of the dual-language program, they must determine what the relevant communities are. Dual-language programs, by definition, target students from two different language backgrounds and clearly separate the two languages for purposes of instruction. This definition seems to reflect an assumption of two different speech communities that are clearly separate and separable. Consideration of actual speech communities in which dual-language programs may be situated, however, helps us see that this assumption is problematic. In Puerto Rican migrant communities and

Mexican migrant communities in the United States, for example, the 'community' may extend beyond the local neighborhood (i.e. to include the island or Mexico) and 'community' members' spoken and written language proficiencies may range from monolingual in Spanish to Spanish-dominant to bilingual to English-dominant to monolingual in English. Likewise, specific families may be made up of individuals who have a wide range of spoken and written proficiencies in both languages. Researchers therefore need to gain an insider's understanding of the nature of the relationships between the two languages and the speakers of those languages on the local level.

At Oyster, for example, there was an organized effort to define the school as a community that crossed language, class, and cultural lines. It became obvious to me that the Oyster community was a relevant unit of analysis. As discussed in the last section, within that community sometimes language was a defining feature. At other times, either class and/or socioeconomic status was a more relevant social group marker. Whatever the actual social stratification of speakers and languages in the community under study, the same theoretical point needs to be kept in mind. Like the notion of social identity discussed above, a speech community needs to be understood as something negotiated, negotiable, dynamic, and situated.

Once researchers have identified the relevant communities and target populations, they are ready to investigate how a particular dual-language program interacts with local community beliefs and practices. Again, a focus on the program goals can help guide this level of analysis, which leads to questions such as the following. What are these groups' attitudes about bilingualism and about each other? How do they use the two languages in their everyday lives? What kinds of political, economic, and face-to-face interactions occur between social groups? What are the community members' expectations for their children's academic achievement and career options? How do the community members' beliefs and practices relate to the school's assumptions about their target populations? An ethnographic/discourse analytic approach similar to the one taken in this study can help researchers address these questions in the community in which they are working.

Relating the micro-level classroom interaction to the larger levels of context

The macro-level contextual forces described in the last sections influence the micro-level of the classroom interaction through which and into which students are socialized. Because the last several chapters have provided extensive analysis of how I analysed Oyster's classroom practices, detailed discussion of the approach is not necessary here. What is important to emphasize is that all of these assumptions about language use, intergroup relations, and academic achievement can influence how the program goals are realized on the classroom level. One possibility is that the dual-language plan is interpreted and implemented more or less coherently throughout the program and there is little discrepancy between ideal plan and actual classroom implementation. In this case, the dual-language education program is well-implemented and successfully meets its goals of promoting bilingualism, academic achievement, and positive intergroup relations. Comparative studies of how well-implemented dual-language programs function in their particular sociopolitical contexts will then make it possible for us to address more general questions about whether and how dual-language programs are an effective means of educating language minority and language majority students.

When researchers do identify discrepancies between ideal plan and actual classroom level implementation, they can turn to their analysis of the larger societal, community, and institutional levels of context to understand how the macro-level power struggles are working themselves out in the micro-level classroom interaction. In this case, researchers and/or practitioners need to first identify an actual discrepancy. Taking Oyster Bilingual School as an example, the ideal plan is that the English-dominant teacher speaks and is spoken to only in English, and the Spanish-dominant teacher speaks and is spoken to only in Spanish. This ideal reflects Oyster's ideal of equal distribution of English and Spanish throughout the school. Analysis of the classroom interaction, however, revealed that there was more code-switching to English in Spanish than there was from Spanish to English in the content classes by the teachers and by the students.

The theoretical assumption that different people may have different interpretations about what is going on and why in an interaction requires the researcher to consider various participants' perspectives as potential sources of explanation for an observed behavior. Open-ended conversational interviews about observed discrepancies, combined with a developing understanding of how larger institutional, community, and societal assumptions and expectations about that particular observed behavior, can help the researcher understand the nature of the actual discrepancy and how that may relate to other disrepancies that the researcher has observed throughout the educational discourse system.

Returning to the previous example, my observation of more code-switching to English from Spanish than from Spanish to English was explained to me in a variety of ways. First, many of the English-dominant teachers did not speak Spanish, making teacher code-switching to English impossible. All of the Spanish-dominant teachers, however, spoke both languages so teacher code-switching was a possibility. Not all of the English-dominant students could speak Spanish while all of the Spanish-dominant students had at least some base in English. My ongoing ethnographic/discourse analytic research across the multiple levels of context in which Oyster Bilingual School was situated allowed me to see how the social stratification of Spanish and English in mainstream US society could explain the leakage between ideal plan and actual implementation that I was observing on the classroom level.

When we understand the nature of an observed discrepancy between ideal plan and actual implementation, it is possible to design context-specific ways to address that discrepancy. In the case described earlier, the Oyster educators argue that if they made Spanish count as much as English within the school, then they may be able to further challenge the dominance of English throughout the school. Concrete steps they have taken in recent years are to require standardized tests in both Spanish and English instead of only in English, and to require that all new hires be bilingual in Spanish and English. Whether these efforts succeed in making Spanish count as much as English at school, and thereby reduce the tendency for English to be used more often than Spanish throughout the school, is an area for further research. What needs to be emphasized is the educators' ongoing reflection on their practice, and their efforts to work together to find creative ways to reduce the gaps between ideal plan and actual implementation. The dual-language program, as part of the larger social identities project at Oyster Bilingual School, is clearly a dynamic and negotiated process.

Researchers in other dual-language contexts will undoubtedly observe other discrepancies between ideal plan and actual implementation. They may also observe similar discrepancies, but the particular nature of the relationship between the program, school, community, and societal levels of context may lead to a different explanation for those observed discrepancies. The point to be emphasized is that when practitioners understand why their program is not functioning in the way that they intend, they are in a better position to find a creative way to address the problems they identify. Research that documents how educators are designing and implementing new dual-language programs is desperately needed to further our understanding of these dynamic, negotiated, situated processes.

CONCLUSION

Dual-language programs have attracted considerable interest and funding in the United States because they are considered an effective means of providing educational opportunities to language minority and language majority students. Oyster Bilingual School, for example, has successfully organized its program and practices so that the linguistic and cultural diversity of its student population is drawn on as a resource to be developed, and not as a problem to be overcome. This example provides evidence that we have choices in the ways that we organize discourse practices, and that these choices have serious implications for language minority and language majority students.

While I consider myself an advocate for well-implemented dual-language programs because of the opportunities they make available to individual language minority and language majority students as well as to the larger society, I end this book with a note of caution. We have seen that research on dual-language programs and practices is a challenging and context-specific process. Practitioners in developing programs need to understand the complexity involved in designing and implementing a program that aims to challenge mainstream societal assumptions about how to educate a linguistically and culturally diverse student population. They need to anticipate resistance to their program goals from a variety of sources. Perhaps most importantly, they need to be prepared to reflect on their own ideological assumptions about linguistic and cultural diversity, and about how they can work together with the rest of the school and community to develop a shared understanding about what their collective goals are and how they can reach them.

As we saw in Chapter 2, the English-Only movement is becoming a powerful force in mainstream US discourse, and bilingual education is on the defensive. Just as we have seen with other models of bilingual education in the past, researchers are now being asked whether dual-language education is effective. Before we can have any meaningful conversation about this very general question, I urge policy-makers, researchers, and practitioners to look closely at how well-implemented programs function on the local level.

References

Adamson, H.D. (1993) *Academic Competence*. New York: Longman.

Austin, J. L. (1975) *How to Do Things with Words*. Cambridge, MA: Harvard University Press.

Baker, C. (1993) *Foundations of Bilingual Education and Bilingualism*. Clevedon: Multilingual Matters.

Baker, K.A. and de Kanter, A.A. (1981) *Effectiveness of Bilingual Education: A Review of the Literature*. Washington, DC: Office of Planning and Budget, US Department of Education.

Bamgbose, A. (1989) Issues for a model of language-planning. *Language Problems and Language-planning* 13 (2), 24–34.

Bialystok, E. (ed.) (1994) *Language Processing in Bilingual Children*. New York: Cambridge University Press.

Bourdieu, P. (1977) *Outline of a Theory of Practice*. Cambridge: Cambridge University Press.

Bourdieu, P. (1993) *Sociology in Question*. London: Sage.

Brinton, D.M., Snow, M.A. and Bingham Wesche, M. (1989) *Content-Based Second-language Instruction*. Boston, MA: Heinle & Heinle.

Butler, J. (1990) *Gender Trouble: Feminism and the Subversion of Identity*. New York: Routledge.

Cameron, D. (1990) *The Feminist Critique of Language: A Reader*. New York: Routledge.

Canale, M. and Swain M. (1980) Theoretical bases of communicative approaches to second-language teaching and testing. *Applied Linguistics* 1 (1), 1–47.

Carbaugh, D. (ed.) (1990) *Cultural Communication and Intercultural Contact*. Hillsdale, NJ: Lawrence Erlbaum.

Casanova, U. (1995) Bilingual education: Politics or pedagogy? In O. García and C. Baker (eds) *Policy and Practice in Bilingual Education: Extending the Foundations* (pp. 15–24). Clevedon: Multilingual Matters.

Cazden, C.B. (1988) *Classroom Discourse: The Language of Teaching and Learning*. Portsmouth, NH: Heinemann.

Chafe, W.L. (1986) How we know things about language: A plea for catholicism. In D. Tannen (ed.) *Languages and Linguistics: The Interdependence of Theory, Data, and Application. Georgetown University Round Table on Languages and Linguistics* 1985 (pp. 214–25). Washington, DC: Georgetown University Press.

Chaudron, C. (1988) *Second-language Classrooms: Research on Teaching and Learning*. Cambridge: Cambridge University Press.

Chick, J.K. (1990) The interactional accomplishment of discrimination in South Africa. In D. Carbaugh (ed.) *Cultural Communication and Intercultural Contact* (pp. 225–52). Hillsdale, NJ: Lawrence Erlbaum.

Christian, D. (1994) Two-way bilingual education: Students learning through two languages. In *The National Center for Research on Cultural Diversity and Second-language Learning: Educational Practice Report 12*. Washington, DC: Center for Applied Linguistics.

Christian, D. (1996) Language development in two-way immersion: Trends and prospects. In J. Alatis, C.A. Straehle, M.Ronkin, and B. Gallenberger (eds) *Linguistics, Language Acquisition, and Language Variation: Current Trends and Future Prospects* (pp. 30–42). Washington DC: Georgetown University Press.

Christian, D. and Whitcher, A. (1995) *Directory of Two-way Bilingual Programs*. The National Center for Research on Cultural Diversity and Second-language Learning. Washington, DC: Center for Applied Linguistics.

Clifford, J. (1988) *The Predicament of Culture: Twentieth-Century Ethnography, Literature and Art*. Cambridge, MA: Harvard University Press.

Clifford, J. and G. E. Marcus. (1986) *Writing Culture: The Poetics and Politics of Ethnography*. Berkeley: University of California Press.

Coates, J. (1986) *Women, Men, and Language: A Sociolinguistic Account of Sex Differences in Language*. New York: Longman.

Cooper, R.L. (1989) *Language-planning and Social Change*. Cambridge: Cambridge University Press.

Crawford, J. (1991) *Bilingual Education: History, Politics, Theory and Practice*. Los Angeles: Bilingual Education Services.

Crawford, J. (1992) *Hold Your Tongue: Bilingualism and the Politics of English Only*. New York: Addison Wesley.

Crawford, J. (1997) *Best Evidence: Research Foundations of the Bilingual Education Act*. Washington, DC: National Clearinghouse for Bilingual Education.

Cummins, J. (1987) Bilingualism, language proficiency, and metalinguistic development. In P. Homel, M. Palij and D. Aaronson (eds) *Childhood Bilingualism: Aspects of Linguistic, Cognitive and Social Development* (pp. 57–73). Hillsdale, NJ: Lawrence Erlbaum.

Cummins, J. (1989) The sanitized curriculum: Educational disempowerment in a nation at risk. In D.M. Johnson and D.H. Roen (eds) *Richness in Writing: Empowering ESL Students* (pp. 19–38). New York: Longman.

Cummins, J. (1992) Language proficiency, bilingualism, and academic achievement. In P.A. Richard-Amato and M.A. Snow (eds) *The Multicultural Classroom: Readings for Content-area Teachers* (pp. 16–26). New York: Longman.

Cummins, J. (1995) Heritage language teaching in Canadian schools. In O. García and C. Baker (eds) *Policy and Practice in Bilingual Education: Extending the Foundations* (pp. 134–138). Clevedon: Multilingual Matters.

Davies, B. (1990) Agency as a form of discursive practice: A classroom scene observed. *British Journal of Sociology of Education,* 11 (3), 341–61.

Davies, B. and Harre, R. (1990) Positioning: The discursive production of selves. *Journal for the Theory of Social Behavior* 20 (1), 43–63.

Dulay, H., Burt, M. and Krashen, S. (1982) *Language Two.* New York: Oxford University Press.

Duranti, A. (1988) Ethnography of speaking: Toward a linguistics of the praxis. In F. Newmeyer (ed.) *Linguistics: The Cambridge Survey* Vol. 4 (pp. 210–28). Cambridge: Cambridge University Press.

Eckert, P. and McConnell-Ginet, S. (1992) Think practically and look locally: Language and gender as community-based practice. *Annual Review of Anthropology* 21, 461–90.

Edelsky, C. (1981) Who's got the floor? *Language in Society* 10, 383–421.

Erickson, F. and Shultz, J. (1982) *The Counselor as Gatekeeper.* New York: Academic Press.

Fairclough, N. (1989) *Language and Power.* New York: Longman.

Fairclough, N. (ed.) (1992) *Critical Language Awareness.* New York: Longman.

Fairclough, N. (1993). *Discourse and Social Change.* Cambridge: Polity Press.

Fasold, R. (1984) *The Sociolinguistics of Society.* Oxford: Basil Blackwell.

Ferguson, C. A. (1959) Diglossia. *Word* 15, 325–40.

Fetterman, D. M. (1989) *Ethnography Step by Step.* Newbury Park, CA: Sage.

Fishman, J. (1973) Language modernization and planning in comparison with other types of national modernization and planning. *Language in Society* 2 (1), 23–42.

Freeman, R. (1986) A sociolinguistic anaylis of a sixth grade transitional bilingual classroom. Unpublished.

Freeman, R. (1993) Language-planning and identity planning for social change: Gaining the ability and the right to participate. PhD thesis, Georgetown University.

Freeman, R. and McElhinny, B. (1996) Language and gender. In S.L. McKay and N.H. Hornberger (eds) *Sociolinguistics and Language Teaching* (pp. 218–80). New York: Cambridge University Press.

Gal, S. (1989) Language and political economy. *Annual Review of Anthropology* 18, 345–67.

Gal, S. (1995) Language, gender, and power: An anthropological review. In K. Hall and M. Bucholtz (eds) *Gender Articulated: Language and the Socially Constructed Self* (pp.169–82). New York: Routledge.

García, O. and Otheguy, R. (1995) The bilingual education of Cuban-American children in Dade County's ethnic schools. In O. García and C. Baker (eds)

Policy and Practice in Bilingual Education: Extending the Foundations (pp. 93–102). Clevedon: Multilingual Matters.

Gee, J.P. (1990) *Social Linguistics and Literacies: Ideology in Discourses.* Bristol, PA: Taylor & Francis.

Gee, J.P. (1991) What is applied linguistics? Paper delivered to Second-language Research Forum, University of Southern California, Los Angeles.

Genesee, F. (1987) *Learning Through Two Languages: Studies of Immersion and Bilingual Education.* Boston, MA: Heinle & Heinle.

Goffman, E. (1981) *Forms of Talk.* Philadelphia: University of Pennsylvania Press.

Goode, J. and Schneider, J. (1994) *Reshaping Ethnic and Racial Relations in Philadelphia: Immigrants in a Divided City.* Philadelphia: Temple University Press.

Grice, H.P. (1975) Logic and conversation. In P. Cole and J.L. Morgan (eds) *Syntax and Semantics* Vol.3 (pp. 41–58). New York: Academic Press.

Gumperz, J. (1981) Conversational inference and classroom learning. Ethnography and language in educational settings. In J. Green and C. Wallet (eds) *Advances in Discourse Processes V* (pp. 3–24). Norwood, NJ: Ablex.

Gumperz, J. (1982) *Discourse Strategies.* Cambridge: Cambridge University Press.

Hakuta, K. (1990) Language and cognition in bilingual children. In A.M. Padilla, H.H. Fairchild and C.M. Valdez (eds) *Bilingual Education: Issues and Strategies* (pp. 47–59). Newbury Park, CA: Corwin Press Inc.

Hall, K. and Bucholtz, M. (eds) (1995) *Gender Articulated: Language and the Socially Constructed Self.* New York: Routledge.

Halliday, M.A.K. (1985) *An Introduction to Functional Grammar.* London: Edward Arnold.

Hammersley, M. and Atkinson, P. (1995) *Ethnography: Principles in Practice.* New York: Routledge.

Harré, R. (1984) *Personal Being.* Cambridge, MA: Harvard University Press.

Harré, R. (1990) *Georgetown University Lecture Series.* Washington, DC: Georgetown University Press.

Haugen, E. (1983) The implementation of corpus planning: Theory and practice. In J. Cobarrubias and J. Fishman (eds) *Progress in Language-planning: International Perspectives* (pp. 269–89). The Hague: Mouton.

Heath, S.B. (1981) English in our language heritage. In C.A. Ferguson and S.B. Heath (eds) *Language in the USA* (pp. 6–20). Cambridge: Cambridge University Press.

Heath, S.B. (1983) *Ways with Words: Language, Life, and Work in Communities and Classrooms.* Cambridge: Cambridge University Press.

Heller, M. (1994) *Crosswords: Language, Education and Ethnicity in French Ontario.* Berlin: Mouton de Gruyter.

Heyck, D. (1994) *Barrios and Borderlands: Cultures of Latinos and Latinas in the United States.* New York: Routledge.

Holmes, J. (1978) Sociolinguistic competence in the classroom. In J.C. Richards (ed.) *Understanding Second and Foreign Language Learning* (pp. 134–62). Rowley, MA: Newbury House.

Hornberger, N. (1988) *Bilingual Education and Language Maintenance: A Southern Peruvian Quechua Case.* Dordrecht: Foris.

Hornberger, N. (1991) Extending enrichment bilingual education: Revisiting typologies and redirecting policy. In O. García (ed.) *Bilingual Education Focusschrift in Honor of Joshua A. Fishman* Vol. 1 (pp. 215–34). Philadelphia: John Benjamins.

Hornberger, N. (1997) *Indigenous Literacies in the Americas: Language-planning from the Bottom Up.* New York: Mouton de Gruyter.

Hymes, D. (1974) *Foundations in Sociolinguistics: An Ethnographic Approach.* Philadelphia: University of Pennsylvania Press.

Hymes, D. (1990) Epilogue to 'The things we do with words'. In D. Carbaugh (ed.) *Cultural Communication and Intercultural Contact*. Hilldale, NJ: Lawrence Erlbaum.

Johnson, D.W., Maruyama, G., Johnson, R., Anderson, D. and Skon, L. (1981) Effects of cooperative, competitive, and individualistic goal structures on achievement: A meta-analysis. *Psychological Bulletin* 89, 47–62.

Kessler, C. (ed.) (1992) *Cooperative Language Learning: A Teacher's Resource Book.* Englewood Cliffs, NJ: Prentice Hall Regents.

Kramsch, C. (1991) The challenge of the learner: Learning language in context or language as context? Plenary address delivered at the Annual Meeting of the American Association of Applied Linguistics, New York.

Labov, W. (1972) The transformation of experience in narrative syntax. In W. Labov (ed.) *Language in the Inner City* (pp. 354–96). Philadelphia: University of Pennsylvania Press.

Lakoff, G. and Johnson, M. (1980) *Metaphors We Live By.* Chicago: The University of Chicago Press.

Lambert, W.E. (1987) The effects of bilingual and bicultural experiences on children's attitudes and social perspectives. In P. Homel, M. Palij and D. Aaronson (eds) *Childhood Bilingualism: Aspets of Linguistic, Cognitive, and Social Development* (pp. 197–221). Hillsdale, NJ: Lawrence Erlbaum.

Lefcowitz, E. (1990) *The United States History Timeline.* New York: Terra Firma Press.

Lemke, J.L. (1989) Semantics and social values. *Word* 40 (1), 37–50.

Lemke, J.L. (1993) *Talking Science: Language, Learning, and Values.* Norwood, NJ: Ablex.

Lindholm, K. (1990) Bilingual immersion education: Criteria for program development. In A. Padilla, H.H. Fairchild and C.M. Valdez (eds) *Bilingual Education: Issues and Strategies* (pp. 91–105). Newbury Park, CA: Corwin Press.

Malakoff, M. and Hakuta, K. (1990) History of language minority education in the United States. In A. Padilla, H.H. Fairchild, and C.M. Valdez (eds.) *Bilingual*

Education: Issues and Strategies (pp. 27–44). Newbury Park, CA: Corwin Press.

Martin-Jones, M. and Heller M. (1996) Introduction to the special issues on education in multilingual settings: Discourse, identities, and power. *Linguistics and Education* 8, 3–16.

Master Teacher (1990) Volume 21, No. 20.

McGroarty, M. (1992) The societal context of bilingual education. *Educational Researcher,* 21 (2), 7–9.

Mertz, E. (1982) Language and mind: A 'Whorfian' folk theory in United States language law. *Sociolinguistic Working Paper,* 93, 1–21.

Michaels, S. (1986) Narrative presentations: An oral preparation for literacy with first graders. In J. Cook-Gumperz (ed.) *The Social Construction of Literacy* (pp. 94–116). New York: Cambridge University Press.

Mishler, E.G. (1986) *Research Interviewing: Context and Narrative.* Cambridge, MA: Harvard University Press.

Mohan, B.A. (1992) What are we really testing? In P.A. Richard-Amato and M.A. Snow (eds) *The Multicultural Classroom: Readings for Content-area Teachers* (pp. 258–70). New York: Longman.

Mohatt, G. and Erickson, F. (1981) Cultural differences in teaching styles in an Odawa school: A sociolinguistic approach. In H. Trueba, P. Guthrie, and K. Au (eds) *Culture and the Bilingual Classroom: Studies in Classroom Ethnography* (pp. 105–19) New York: Newbury House.

Moll, L. (1995) Bilingual classroom studies and community analysis. In O. García and C. Baker (eds) *Policy and Practice in Bilingual Education* (pp. 273–80). Clevedon: Multilingual Matters.

Morison, S.H. (1990) A Spanish–English dual-language program in New York City. In C. Cazden and C.E. Snow (eds) *The Annals of the American Academy of Political and Social Science* (pp. 160–9). Newbury Park: Sage.

Neustupny, J.V. (1983) Toward a paradigm for language-planning. *Language-planning Newsletter* 9 (4), 1–4.

Nieto, S. (1992) *Affirming Diversity: The Sociopolitical Context of Multicultural Education.* New York: Longman.

Ochs, E. (1988) *Culture and Language Development: Language Acquisition and Language Socialization in a Samoan Village.* New York: Cambridge University Press.

Oakes, J. (1985) *Keeping Track: How Schools Structure Inequality.* New Haven: Yale University Press.

Ovando, C.J. and Collier, V.P. (1985) *Bilingual and ESL Classrooms.* New York: McGraw Hill.

Oyster Bilingual School (1980) *The History and Politics of Oyster Bilingual School.* Washington, DC: Author.

Oyster Bilingual School (1988) *Oyster Bilingual School Teachers' Handbook.* Washington, DC: Author.

Oyster Bilingual School (1993) *Oyster Bilingual School Fact Sheet, March.* Washington, DC: Author.

Oyster Escribe staff (1991) *Oyster Bilingual School: Escuela Bilingüe* (pp. 6–12). Miami, FL: DDL Books & Silver Spring, MD: Intac.

Peal, E. and Lambert, W.E. (1962) The relationship of bilingualism to intelligence. *Psychological Monographs* 76, 546.

Pedraza-Bailey, S. and Sullivan. T.A. (1979) Bilingual education in the reception of political immigrants: The case of Cubans in Miami, Florida. In R.V. Padilla (ed.) *Bilingual Education and Public Policy in the United States* (pp. 376–94). Eastern Michigan University: Bilingual Bicultural Education Programs.

Philips, S. U. (1983) *The Invisible Culture: Communication in the Classroom and Community on the Warm Springs Indian Reservation.* New York: Longman.

Pica, T. (1988) Interlanguage adjustments as an outcome of NS-NNS negotiated interaction. *Language Learning* 38 (1), 45–73.

Pica, T. (1991) Input as a theoretical and research construct: From Corder's original definition to current views. *International Review of Applied Linguistics* 29 (3), 189–94.

Pica, T. Young, R., and Doughty, C. (1987) The impact of interaction on comprehension. *TESOL Quarterly* 21 (4), 737–58.

Pike, K. (1954) *Language in Relation to a Unified Theory of the Structure of Human Behavior.* California: Summer Institute of Linguistics.

Ramirez, J.D., Yuen, S.D. and Ramey, D.R. (1991) *Executive Summary Final Report: Longitudinal Study of Structured English Immersion Strategy, Early-exit and Late-exit Transitional Bilingual Education Programs for Language Minority Children.* San Mateo, CA: Aguirre International.

Reddy, M. (1979) The conduit metaphor. In A. Ortony (ed.) *Metaphor and Thought* (pp. 284–324). Cambridge: Cambridge University Press.

Ricento, Thomas (1995) A brief history of language restrictionism in the United States. In *Official English? No! TESOL's Recommendations for Countering the Official English Movement in the US.* TESOL Sociopolitical Concerns Committee. http://www.ncbe.gwu.edu/miscpubs/tesol/official/restrictionism

Richard-Amato, P.A. and Snow, M.A. (1992) *The Multicultural Classroom: Readings for Content-area Teachers.* New York: Longman.

Ruiz, R. (1984) Orientations in language-planning. *Journal of the National Association for Bilingual Education* 2 (8), 15–34.

Ruiz, R. (1994) Language policy and planning in the United States. *Annual Review of Applied Linguistics* 14, 111–25.

Saville-Troike, M. (1989) *The Ethnography of Communication: An Introduction.* Oxford: Basil Blackwell.

Schegloff, E. (1988) Discourse as an interactional achievement II: An exercise in conversation analysis. In D. Tannen (ed.) *Linguistics in Context: Connecting Observation and Understanding* (pp. 135–58). Norwood, NJ: Ablex.

Schieffelin, B. and Ochs, E. (eds) (1990) *Language Socialization Across Cultures.* Cambridge: Cambridge University Press

Schiffman, H.F. (1996) *Linguistic Culture and Language Policy*. New York: Routledge.

Scollon, R. and Scollon, S.B.K. (1981) *Narrative, Literacy, and Face in Interethnic Communication*. Norwood, NJ: Ablex.

Scollon, R. and Scollon, S.B.K. (1995) *Intercultural Communication*. Cambridge, MA: Basil Blackwell.

Scott, J.W. (1992) Multiculturism and the politics of identity. *October* 61, 12–19.

Searle, J. (1969) *Speech Acts: An Essay in the Philosophy of Language*. New York: Cambridge University Press.

Searle, J. (1975) Indirect speech acts. In P. Cole and J.L. Morgan (eds) *Syntax and Semantics* Vol.3 (pp. 59–82). New York: Academic Press.

Secada, W. (1990) Research, politics, and bilingual education. In C. Cazden and C. Snow (eds) *English Plus: Issues in Bilingual Education. The Annals of the American Academy of Political and Social Science* (pp. 81–106). Newbury Park, CA: Sage.

Skutnabb-Kangas, T. (1984) Children of guest workers and immigrants: Linguistic and educational issues. In J. Edwards (ed.) *Linguistic Minorities, Policies and Pluralism* (pp. 17–48). London: Academic Press.

Sleeter, C.E. and Grant, C.A. (1991) Race, class, gender and disability in current textbooks. In M.W. Apple and L.K. Christian-Smith (eds) *The Politics of the Textbook*. New York: Routledge and Chapman & Hall.

Street, B.V. (1995) *Social Literacies: Critical Approaches to Literacy in Development, Ethnography, and Education*. New York: Longman.

Tannen, D. (1986) *Conversational Style: Analyzing Talk Among Friends*. Norwood, NJ: Ablex.

Tannen, D. (1989) *Talking Voices: Repetition, Dialogue, and Imagery in Conversational Discourse*. Cambridge: Cambridge University Press.

Tannen, D. (1992) Interactional sociolinguistics. In W. Bright (ed.) *International Encyclopedia of Linguistics*. New York: Oxford University Press.

Tannen, D. (1993) What's in a frame: Surface evidence for underlying expectations. In D. Tannen (ed.) *Framing in Discourse* (pp.14–56). New York: Oxford University Press.

Tannen, D. and Wallat, C. (1993) Interactive frames and knowledge schemas in interaction: Examples from a medical examination/interview. In D. Tannen (ed.) *Framing in Discourse* (pp.57–76). New York: Oxford University Press.

Troike, R. (1978) Research evidence for the effectiveness of bilingual education. *NABE Journal* 3, 13–24.

Urciuoli, B. (1996). *Exposing Prejudice: Puerto Rican Experiences of Language, Race and Class*. Boulder, CO: Westview Press.

Vygotsky, L.S. (1978) *Mind in Society: The Development of Higher Psychological Processes*. (Edited by M. Cole, V. John-Steiner, S. Scribner, and E. Souberman). Cambridge, MA: Harvard University Press.

Watson-Gegeo, K. (1988) Ethnography in ESL: Defining the essentials. *TESOL Quarterly* 22 (4), 575–91.

Wertsch, J.V. (1985) *Vygotsky and the Social Formation of Mind.* Cambridge: Harvard University Press.

Willig, A.C. (1985) A meta-analysis of selected studies on the effectiveness of bilingual education. *Review of Educational Research* 55, 269–317.

Woolard, K. (1985). Language variation and cultural hegemony: Towards an integration of sociolinguistics and social theory. *American Ethnologist* 12 (4), 738–48.

Zentella, A.C. (1981) Language varieties among Puerto Ricans. In C. Ferguson and S. Heath (eds) *Language in the USA* (pp. 215–38). Cambridge: Cambridge University Press.

Index

Author Index

258

Subject Index